# The Anatomy
## of Buzz

# The Anatomy of

# Buzz

**Creating Word-of-Mouth Marketing**

Emanuel Rosen

HarperCollins*Business*

HarperCollinsBusiness
an imprint of HarperCollins*Publishers*
77–85 Fulham Palace Road,
Hammersmith, London W6 8JB

www.fireandwater.com/business

Published by HarperCollins*Publishers* 2000
1 3 5 7 9 8 6 4 2

Published in the USA by Currency/Doubleday 2000

A catalogue record for this book
is available from the British Library

ISBN 0 00 257104 8

Set in Iowan Old Style

Printed and bound in Great Britain by
Clays Ltd, St Ives plc

To Daria,

Noam, Yonatan,

Maya, and Mika

# Contents

# Foreword

**New products and services spread** among the consumer public through interpersonal communication networks. These networks are for the most part invisible. They often operate in mysterious ways. Thus we are largely blind to this very powerful marketing process. No wonder that we fail so often in our efforts to diffuse innovations.

Emanuel Rosen here illuminates the reality of how "buzz" can be launched and managed so as to more rapidly reach a critical mass of adopters for one's innovation. Buzz can boost a new idea in the marketplace, or it can destroy one. Both outcomes have occurred, as Rosen shows us, for understandable reasons.

A rich profusion of both positive and negative experiences involving buzz is exposed in this book. My favorite example is the launch of EndNote, a software product for scholars that Emanuel Rosen and his colleagues introduced with a demonstration at the UC Berkeley Faculty Club one afternoon several years ago. Word-of-mouth communication took it from there.

Ever had to redo your references from APA style to *JAMA* style? I have. When I used EndNote, I had my first contact with Emanuel Rosen. My next intersection occurred in spring 1998, when Emanuel contacted me by e-mail about the role of buzz in the diffusion of innovations. The next day he flew to Albuquerque and met with my class on diffusion.

This field began sixty years ago with a study of the spread of hybrid seed corn among Iowa farmers. The research found that the innovation spread slowly, over about twelve years, even though hybrid seed increased farmers' yields by 20 percent. At first a very few venturesome farmers adopted, they talked with their neighbors and friends, and these in turn told others about the new idea. The cumulative rate of adoption formed an S curve over the dozen years of the innovation's diffusion, driven by people talking to other people. Today, some five thousand studies later, we know a great deal more about the diffusion model.

The present book advances these understandings by focusing on the person-to-person process by which information moves through networks. The role of buzz is analyzed as it helped make the PalmPilot diffuse rapidly, how it made a particular new book become an overnight sensation, and how other consumer products sank like lead balloons, despite expensive marketing campaigns.

Rosen draws strategies for creating buzz, such as seeding an innovation with key members of the audience for the new idea. Giving away free samples is wasteful unless they go to the right people, as Rosen explains. The author here uncovers vital details of how a wide range of companies, programs, and organizations have used buzz—and in certain cases been used *by* buzz.

I find this book to offer a fascinating look at the nature of interpersonal networks and how they can be activated. I cannot remember being so influenced by a book in the past several years. The world now is somewhat easier for me to understand.

I commend it to you. If you like it, too, tell others.

EVERETT M. ROGERS
University of New Mexico
March 2000

# Acknowledgments

**There isn't much formal research** on buzz, so in writing this book I relied heavily on the experience of people who have observed the phenomenon and were willing to share their thoughts about it. My own experience with buzz has been mostly in the software industry, so I am especially grateful to people who told me about the phenomenon in other lines of business. People such as Jim McDowell (automotive), Ed Colligan (hardware), Brian Maxwell (consumer products), Reid Rosefelt (independent movies), Alan and Joyce Amaral (toys), Morgan Entrekin and Elisabeth Schmitz (book publishing), Ava DeMarco (fashion accessories), and Margot Fraser (footwear).

These people were willing to stop for a moment and share their observations and insights about word of mouth. I learned a great deal from every one of them. Thanks to Keith Fox, Marleen McDaniel, Cynthia Typaldos, Montrese Etienne, George McMillan, Jim Callahan, Rob Bennet, Charlotte Stuyvenberg, John Rizzo, Helen Rockey, Andrew Beebe, Carl Lennertz, Barry Berkov, Patricia Kelly, Jeff Salmon, Jennifer Gilbert, Kevin Conroy, Dave Kapell, Kim Wylie, John Hawks, Pini Gamzo, Mark Ouimet, Stephen Hollander, Leigh Feldman, Rochelle Newman, Steve Douty, Susan Taylor, Josh Sommer, Darwin Schmidt, Ted Sartoian, Gordon Paddison, Karen Edwards, Kimbal Musk, Maureen Blanc, Arlene Henry, Ed Niehaus, Heidi Roizen, Kamran Elahian, Lois Paul, David Ellington, Kevin Custer, Steve Rubin, Bill McKiernan, Joe Gillespie, Ron Ricci, Len Short, Stacy Horn, George Paolini, Chris Moore, Fred Rogers, John Yost, Tom Daley, Ramanathan Guha, Nirav Tolia, Tom Hall, Alyssa Berman, William New, Jr., Edward Burlingame, Jeff McElnea, David Arctur, Paul Huber, Bob Stevens, Bill Schjelderup, Dana Siebert, Dan Whaley, Jim Desrosier, Chris Scott, Scott Karren, Chad Kinzelberg, Ray Anderson, Steve Cony, Arthur Hughes, Tanya Roberts, Jaleh Bisharat, Jane Howes, and Dean Kephart.

I would like to pay special tribute to one person—the late Linda Pezzano, whom I interviewed a year before she died. Highly creative and energetic, she was a pioneer in word-of-mouth marketing and played a major role in the success of products such as Trivial Pursuit and Pictionary.

Resellers are often in a special position to observe how word spreads in the marketplace. I greatly appreciate the insights I got from several of them: Karen Pennington, David Unowsky, Gary Gray, Beth Reynolds, Mark Benno, Barry Schwartz, and Mike Barnard. I also want to thank the customers I interviewed. They include early owners of the BMW Z3, readers of the book *Cold Mountain*, and users of the Palm. I wish I could list them all here, but I'd like to send special thanks to Mike Jordan, Lynne Jenkins, Glenn Kowalsky, Jim

Thompson, Margaret Van Siclen, Lyn Palme, Janice Shank, Jody Denison, Michael Ford, and Jo Alice Canterbury.

Many writers, analysts, and researchers helped with this project. First, I am deeply indebted to Everett Rogers, who's been studying Diffusion of Innovations for several decades. His enthusiasm and support from the very beginning of this project have been invaluable! I am also grateful to Tom Robertson, Elihu Katz, Gabriel Weimann, Mark Granovetter, Jonathan Lomas, John Myers, Susan Fournier, Bernd Heinrich, Michael Gale, Lucky J. Meisenheimer, David Sheff, Josh Karliner, Colin Campbell, Seymour Merrin, Patricia Seybold, Ronni Marshak, Stewart Alsop, Mike McGuire, Joseph Byrne, Felipe Korzenny, Sandra Wong, Jeff Tarter, Andy Reinhardt, Rafe Needleman, and David Hogan.

Several members of the International Network for Social Network Analysis were especially open and supportive: Barry Wellman, David Krackhardt, Tom Valente, Ron Rice, Valdis Krebs, and others. Several marketing research firms provided reports that helped me better understand the word-of-mouth phenomenon. Special thanks to Phil Wiseman at Maritz Marketing Research, Diane Crispell at Roper Starch Worldwide, and John Goodman at e-Satisfy.

Haim Zaltzman and Kerry Shaw were instrumental in research and fact checking. I wish I could have included everything that they found—there's just *so* much of it. Thanks also to the many people who helped in providing information, locating photographs, and arranging interviews. Special thanks to Mrs. Jenny Bell Whyte, to Sarah Sherman, and to Michael Sherbon for searching for that picture from an article by the late William H. Whyte, Jr. To Reut Dimand I am grateful for fixing some of the photographs in the book.

A number of people were kind enough to read the manuscript or parts of it at various stages and offer valuable suggestions and encouragement. They include Everett Rogers, Erik Steiner, Tom Valente, Bill Barnes, Mel Kopmar, Barak Libai, Steve Jurvetson, Mark Granovetter, Don Norman, Konrad App, Patrick Corman, Adrienne

Gordon, Roberta Saxon, Rich Niles, Martin Fong, Ken McDonnell, Martin Mendel, Itamar Simonson, Betsy Kopmar, Kimberly Mattingly, Alison Hamilton, Greg Tananbaum, and Arie Ruttenberg.

My agent, Daniel Greenberg, of James Levine Communications, Inc. has been instrumental in getting this book published, and thanks, Patricia Seybold, for introducing me to Daniel! Helen Rietz and Meredith Alexander did a superb job in editing the book at different stages. Roger Scholl at Doubleday was enormously helpful in tightening the manuscript and turning it into a book. Many thanks go to the wonderful teams at Doubleday in the United States and at HarperCollins in the United Kingdom who have shown so much enthusiasm (and patience).

I learned a great deal about word-of-mouth from my experience with EndNote, and for that I have to thank the team that has developed such a superb product and has created the special user experience that comes with it: Rand, Bill, Sid, Talia, Martin, Jeff, Noah, John, Eric, Rich, Larry, Sam, Darragh, Randy, Peter, Greg, Ezra, Gary, Jeff, Pamela, Anne, Dave, and William. And, of course, thanks to Rich and Lenore Niles for years of productive partnership! Many more people have been involved both in the United States and internationally, but there's simply not enough room to list them all. There are three people, however, that I want to thank especially: Kimberly, Alison, and Greg, who have been instrumental in making sure that word about EndNote spread as it has.

Finally, I would like to thank the five people to whom I've dedicated this book: Daria, Noam, Yonatan, Maya, and Mika, who all served simultaneously as my editors, research assistants, coaches, and family. Thank you.

# How

# Buzz

# Spreads

Part

One

# What

# Is Buzz?

**1.** **I first witnessed how buzz** travels years ago. In 1988 I was working at a typical start-up software company in California: five people, four Macs, one PC, and a lot of hope. We had a single product, EndNote, a reference tool for researchers, and it was still a few months away from release. We hadn't advertised it. In fact, only a handful of people in California knew it existed. Yet we had just received our first order in the mail—and that order came from Princeton, New Jersey. All five of us stood around that purchase order, staring at it and trying to figure out how someone a continent away had learned of us.

Several months earlier I had joined the company's founder, Rich Niles, to help him market the software. EndNote is designed to help researchers keep track of their references and compile bibliographies at the end of their research papers. Not a very sexy product, I admit, but a very useful tool when you need to organize your research and follow the nitty-gritty requirements of different journals. Rich came up with the idea after he saw how much time his wife, who's a scientist, was spending compiling bibliographies. Every academic journal has its own protocol for the way they want bibliographic information organized. One journal would want a reference to look like this:

Rogers, Everett M. <u>Diffusion of Innovations</u>. 4th ed.
New York: Free Press, 1995.

While another journal would want it to look this way:

Rogers, E. M. (1995). *Diffusion of Innovations*. (4th ed.). New York: Free Press.

Even with a word processor, you can imagine how tedious this task is when you have to go through and make these changes hundreds of times every year. EndNote stores references in a database format and can display them in any bibliographic style.

When the purchase order we got from New Jersey came in, we called the customer who had placed the order. How had he heard of EndNote? Apparently one of the few people who'd attended a sneak preview of our product in Berkeley, California, several days earlier had been so excited about EndNote that he posted an enthusiastic message on an electronic bulletin board used by academics. One of those academics had just become our first customer.

Before I joined that start-up, I was a copywriter in an advertising agency, and in my mind marketing worked like this: Companies advertise, customers see the clever advertisements that copywriters like me worked to create, and then—and *only* then—customers buy the products. But this obviously was not what was happening with that EndNote purchase order, and in the following nine years I was reminded thousands of times that in the real world things operate very differently. Since that first order more than two hundred thousand copies of EndNote have been sold, and most customers have told us that they heard about the product not from advertising, not from dealers, not from magazines—but rather from friends and colleagues.

That's how I became interested in buzz.

After this experience I started to pay more attention to word of mouth. But I was still not sure how important it was in other markets. Maybe, I thought, word of mouth played a significant role only in the academic market or only for software? Once I started researching the topic, however, it became clear that this is not the case. Buzz plays a major role in the purchasing process of many products:

■ Sixty-five percent of customers who bought a Palm organizer told the makers of this device that they had heard about it from another person.

■ Forty-seven percent of the readers of *Surfing* magazine say that the biggest influences on their decisions about where to surf and what to purchase come from a friend.

■ Friends and relatives are the number-one source for information about places to visit or about flights, hotels or rental cars, according to the Travel Industry Association. Of people they surveyed, forty-three percent cited friends and family as a source for information.

■ Fifty-seven percent of customers of one car dealership in California learned about the dealership by word of mouth. "This is not unusual," says Jim Callahan of the Dohring Company, which conducts surveys for about five hundred car dealerships around the country every year.

■ Every year we hear about movies such as *The Blair Witch Project* or *There's Something About Mary* that are driven by word of mouth. Fifty-three percent of moviegoers rely to some extent on a recommendation from someone they know, according to a study by Maritz Marketing Research. No matter how much money Hollywood pours into advertising, people frequently consult with each other about what movie to see.

■   Seventy percent of Americans rely on the advice of others when selecting a new doctor, according to the same study. Sixty-three percent of women surveyed for *Self* magazine cited "friend, family or co-worker referral" as one of the factors influencing over-the-counter drug purchases.

And yet most of today's marketing still focuses on how to use advertising and other tools to influence *each customer individually*, ignoring the fact that purchasing many types of products is part of a *social process*. It involves not only a one-to-one interaction between the company and the customer but also many exchanges of information and influence among the people who surround that customer. Len Short, executive vice president of advertising and brand management at Charles Schwab, summed it up this way: "The idea that a critical part of marketing is word of mouth and validation from important personal relationships is absolutely key, and most marketers ignore it."

## What Exactly Is Buzz?

A kid stands outside a school leaning against the fence. He's about thirteen, wearing jeans and a baseball cap, and playing with a yo-yo. He's good. A younger kid walks by, carrying a backpack that may weigh as much as he does. He stops. His eyes follow the yo-yo that now spins in the air in ways that would make Newton go back and check his gravity theories.

"Where'd ya get it?" the young kid asks softly.

The older kid keeps working.

"What kind is it?" the younger kid asks a little louder this time.

"Yomega," says the older boy. "The Brain."

"Brain?"

"They call it 'The Brain.' It knows when to come back to your hand. It's cool."

This type of exchange is the basic building block of buzz. I call it a "comment." When you add up all the comments made at a certain point in time about this yo-yo, you get the buzz about Yomega. In the end, buzz is the sum of all comments about a certain product that are exchanged among people at any given time.

Now, my definition of buzz is broader than others. *Newsweek*, for example, defined buzz in a 1998 article as "infectious chatter; genuine, street-level excitement about a hot new person, place or thing." This is a journalist's definition of the new: what's hot, what's attracting people's attention not just today but this very hour. Marketers and entrepreneurs, however, have a lot to gain from exploring what customers are saying about their products, not only when they are ultra new but also when these products are established. For this reason I've chosen to discuss buzz in a more general sense. Buzz is all the word of mouth about a brand. It's the aggregate of all person-to-person communication about a particular product, service, or company at any point in time.

People all around the world constantly exchange comments about everything, from golf to the meaning of life. Comments use many vehicles, but whether they move over phone lines, in e-mail messages, on paper, or over the dinner table, comments always start in one brain and end up in another. "*Tootsie* is my favorite movie of all time." This "comment" came from my brain and has just landed in yours. Billions of comments move between people in this way every day. Comments about relationships, movies, food, money. Comments in Japanese, English, Swedish. Comments that convey excitement, puzzlement, indifference, surprise. In this book I focus on those comments that are exchanged about products and services.

# How Does Buzz Travel?

**Buzz travels in** invisible networks. To better understand what a network is, it's useful to think of a rough parallel: the airline system. Imagine that you're sitting in a control room where you can see all the flight routes in the world. On the large screen in front of you, all the airports are represented by dots (these are called "nodes"), and all the routes among them are represented by lines (these are called "links"). The first thing you'll probably notice are hub airports, which are the transfer points for numerous flights. You'll also notice some clusters in certain areas. All the airports in France are somehow connected to each other, and the airports in Japan are closely connected among themselves in a similar way. Of course, Tokyo and Paris are also connected to each other, so ultimately every airport in Japan can be said to connect with every airport in France.

Now imagine that you're in a different control room, but from *this* control room you see not the connections between airports but those made between *people*. All 6 billion people on our planet. On a huge screen (say, the size of a screen at an Imax theater) there are 6 billion little blue dots, connected by thin glowing lines. The huge diagram represents an information network that consists of established connections between people. These are the invisible networks. Here, too, there are hubs, people who are especially well positioned to transmit information. Here, too, there are clusters, areas where people are more densely connected to each other. And here, too, these clusters are connected among themselves, so ultimately everyone is somehow linked to everyone else.

As you look at this huge screen, you notice a constant flow of green sparks between certain nodes. These are comments. This is buzz. When the boy who talked about Yomega said, "It's cool," a green spark went from the node that represents him to the node that represents the little boy. Sometimes there is an exchange of sparks back and forth between two or more nodes, representing a conversation. Sometimes sparks move from one node to thousands or millions of other nodes, such as when Oprah recommends a book to viewers of her show or Walt Mossberg of *The Wall Street Journal* writes about the latest thing in the computer industry.

This image is the foundation of this book: 6 billion glowing blue dots—the people on this planet—some of whom are linked by established connections. Green sparks—comments—constantly travel over these established connections. As new friendships are formed, new blue lines or connections appear. Some connections gradually disappear as people lose touch.

If you could put a filter in front of this huge picture that would weed out all the comments relating to other subjects, you'd be able to see the buzz about *your* company or product. The people at Yomega would perhaps see only those green sparks going on about their yo-yos. A maker of a medical device would see all the comments being made among physicians about a new product. A book publisher would see how many comments are transmitted about a new title, where in the networks there's more buzz and where there's less, where the buzz starts, where it is blocked, and so on . . .

To illustrate this concept I decided to take a snapshot of the buzz surrounding the movie *Shakespeare in Love* among some students at a West Coast university shortly after its release. My assistant, Haim Zaltzman, asked students to name individuals with whom they had discussed the movie. We weren't conducting a scientific study—it was just a way to translate to a real-life example the image of how networks work. Based on our results we were able to draw the following illustration, depicting just a minuscule fraction of the buzz about the movie. Each figure represents a student. The gray lines represent social ties. On top of some of these gray lines, the thin black lines indicate the path of comments exchanged about the movie between two students.

This again is merely an encapsulation of the buzz at a given

**A snapshot of the buzz about *Shakespeare in Love* among eight students.**

point in time among these eight students. A month later the pattern of buzz may have been totally different. It also reflects only the buzz about that particular product—just one movie.

Although it's not very likely that you'll ever sit in front of such a screen and be able to watch how the buzz about your product spreads in the invisible networks, there is value in visualizing it. In this first part of *The Anatomy of Buzz* I'll begin to explore the workings of the invisible networks and the buzz that spreads through them. In the second part I'll identify success factors associated with good buzz. Finally, in the third part I will look at specific techniques that stimulate the flow of these comments in the invisible networks.

# The Invisible

# Networks

**2.**

**Kamran Elahian is still proud** of Momenta, a sleek-looking computer that made the cover of *Byte* magazine in November 1991. The machine was built in a shape of a pyramid, slightly larger than a sheet of paper. You'd handwrite your notes on the screen, although you could also attach a keyboard to the computer. "You could even unfold it and put it on top of an overhead projector," he says enthusiastically, as if he still had some units in stock for sale.

Elahian founded Momenta in 1989. A Silicon Valley entrepreneur with a couple of business-to-business success stories behind him, he wanted to create the first pen-based computer to go beyond niche markets, one that would be used by executives on the road. At first the prospects looked rosy. Elahian hired a team of executives from big Silicon Valley companies. They started development and began getting the market excited. At the 1991 Comdex, the preeminent annual computer-industry trade show, everybody was talking about Momenta. The fifteen-foot model of the pen-based computer Elahian created could not be ignored even at this glitzy show.

The ads the company created were elegant. A two-page ad in *PC Magazine* showed a businessman lying on his stomach using Momenta. The caption read, "Please do not attempt this on just any computer." The text that followed described a computer that "has finally caught up with the way you work," equipped with a wide range of unique, pen-specific software. "You can write directly on the screen," it read. "Or use the keyboard."

The PR campaign was well orchestrated and got the media's attention. "It sounded like a great concept," says Rafe Needleman, who wrote for *Infoworld* at the time. Andy Reinhardt, who worked for *Byte* magazine, also remembers the anticipation. He was intrigued by the interesting approach, the good funding, and the impressive management team. As a result of these PR efforts, the Momenta computer was featured on the covers of eight magazines.

Everything was so right, and yet, in the three years between 1989 and its bankruptcy in 1992, Momenta lost more than $40 million and left dozens of people without jobs.

I tell this story to make a point. Buzz is not about elegant advertising or glitzy trade shows. It's about what happens in the invisible networks—the interpersonal information networks that connect customers to each other. It's about what customers—the people who pay money for products—tell each other about these products. And the word on the street about Momenta wasn't great.

Why wasn't the buzz great? Because the product wasn't great. Buzz starts with a superior user experience, and nothing in this book will help if your product doesn't deliver such an experience. Moreover, the Momenta team broke one of the basic rules in managing buzz: Never set expectations that you cannot exceed or at least meet. Users I talked to remember the first time they put their hands on a Momenta computer as a very disappointing experience. "The technology didn't live up to the hype," explains Needleman. Momenta was slow, and the screen was hard to read. Poor handwriting recognition. Not enough software. A short battery life. All of these things sparked disappointment rather than excitement.

The fact is that marketing budgets are not the key to good buzz. "We didn't [realize] that this is not something that you can push on people," says Elahian, who now is chairman of several (much more successful) high-tech companies. "Humble marketing" may sound like an oxymoron, but it's not. When you look at the early days of a product like the Palm, which got tremendous word-of-mouth support, you see just that. "Our mantra was 'Underpromise and overdeliver,'" says Ed Colligan, former vice president of marketing at Palm Computing. Of course, variables such as timing, technology, and pricing all played a role in the PalmPilot's success and in Momenta's failure, but one cannot ignore the different styles of marketing. The Momenta team tried to push its computer on customers, while the Palm team let the product spread almost by itself through the invisible networks, allowing people to discover the product, get excited about it, and tell their friends. They didn't push. This was right for the mid-1990s, and it is even more right in today's climate.

## Why Have Networks Become So Important?

Invisible networks have always been important in the diffusion of certain products. Today they are critical and can no longer be ignored. In order to compete, companies must understand that they are selling not to individual customers but rather to *networks* of customers. There are three reasons for the increased importance of buzz: noise, skepticism, and connectivity.

**1. Customers can hardly hear you.** There's too much noise. A lot has been written about information overload, so I'll be brief. In his book *Information Anxiety,* Richard Saul Wurman argues that "a weekday edition of the *New York Times* contains more information than the average person was likely to come across in a lifetime in seventeenth-century England." In addition to editorial information, each customer is exposed to an avalanche of commercial messages. Advertising experts estimate that each customer may be exposed to more than fifteen hundred ads every day. To protect themselves, consumers filter out most of the messages they are exposed to from the mass media. They *do,* however, listen to their friends.

**2. Customers are skeptical.** I remember once standing at our booth at a trade show. We were about four weeks away from releasing a new version of our software. A young scientist stopped by the booth, and I showed him how the new software worked. He was impressed, but when I told him that this version was going to be released in a month, he turned around before I could say anything, muttered "Vaporware," and walked away. It didn't matter to him that I'd just showed him a working version (which had been under development for more than a year). As far as he was concerned, this software didn't exist, and he obviously didn't believe that it was going to be released in four weeks. Research shows that most customers share a similar sense of skepticism. According to a survey by the public relations firm Porter Novelli, only 37 percent of the public considers information that comes from a software or computer company "very or somewhat believable." If you're with a pharmaceutical company, the number is 28 percent. Car manufacturers rate 18 percent, insurance companies 16 percent. And can we blame people for being so skeptical? Think of your own experience as a customer. How many times did you feel misled or disappointed?

**3. Customers are connected.** The third and the most dramatic reason for the rise in the importance of invisible networks is that customers have found new tools for sharing information. Customers have always talked to each other, but now, on the Internet, giving and asking for advice is just easier. It's as simple as typing a sentence and sending it off into cyberspace. "What camera should I buy?" one customer asks and provokes a heated discussion on one newsgroup. "Should I get DVD?" another customer asks on a different forum. In a discussion group for pregnant women, an emotional debate over Similac versus breast-feeding is taking place. On a forum for Jeep owners, a new owner asks what to say to his friends who tease him about the reliability of his new car ("They bought transportation appliances, you bought a piece of history," one veteran Jeeper tells him).

These new tools allow customers to communicate not only with people they know but with total strangers. They essentially allow each customer to *broadcast* information to the rest of the world. And it's not limited to discussion groups. Look at the software Third Voice, for example. It lets customers add their own notes to companies' Web sites. "We're glad you're here," one Web site for a car company greets you. "Whatever," one user comments. Next to the "What's New" link, another person posts a note about his experience with their car: "I was spending so much on repairs from 16,000 miles on that I could not afford to keep it. I bought [another brand] three years ago . . . problem solved!!"

Information and influence are no longer held by a few top journalists. These media people can still be very influential, but so can the thousands of customers who use Web sites and newsgroups to express their opinions. Instead of just *Car & Driver*, a leading magazine for car enthusiasts, we see thousands of Web sites for car owners managed by car owners. There are hundreds of customers' Web sites related to Jeep and more than a thousand Mustang-related Web sites. Message boards on different on-line forums have discussions about almost every model. The writers of *Car & Driver* still have an impact, because every message they generate is printed in 1.2 million copies, but the many connected customers are emerging as good sources for information as well—providing a second tier that cumulatively can be as important as media reviewers.

Ed Niehaus, president of NRW, a PR firm in Silicon Valley, uses a rock concert metaphor to describe the shift. In the old days it was clear that the stars—the press and analysts—were up onstage and "regular customers" were in the audience. "The Internet suddenly puts a next ring of people, the people in the first twenty rows, onstage," says Niehaus. Perhaps the best-known case of a company that experienced the power of "the people in the first twenty rows" is Intel. In 1994 a college professor noticed a division error in Intel's Pentium chip. In a way that professor was suddenly onstage, and he grabbed hold of the microphone. The news about the minor error spread quickly on the Internet and even more quickly when Intel tried to belittle the problem. Customers flooded Intel with e-mails and phone calls. At one point the company was getting 25,000 calls a day requesting a no-questions-asked return policy on the microprocessor. Intel refused at first. But the chipmaker was bombarded with bad press, and its stock dropped sharply—stocks are very responsive to buzz. Eventually Intel had to change its policy. The company ended up taking a write-off to the tune of $475 million. The lesson to Intel? "Pay attention to the people who are onstage, and there are a lot more of them than there ever were before," says Niehaus. Intel has since adopted a much more proactive approach, monitoring the Internet for possible complaints and publishing extensive documentation of bugs.

The power shift is seen across industries. Hollywood has tried for years to control and manage word of mouth, by releasing information selectively and covering any problems behind a wall of secrecy. Now, on the Internet, customers can spread rumors (true or false) that are fueled by industry insiders who serve as "spies." "A guy living in his basement can bring the studios to their knees," says Reid Rosefelt, president of Magic Lantern, a PR firm in the film industry.

Customers are very aware of the power shift. Here's a comment one car owner sent me about the company that sold him his car: ". . . for years they have been able to pull the wool over our eyes. Well, that has ended." Ten years ago this customer could have told his family and friends about his experience with the car company. Now look at all the options that he has to share his frustration (or his joys) with thousands, even millions, of other people:

- He can e-mail his thoughts to all of his friends.

- He can participate in chats or newsgroups to voice his opinion.

- He can annotate the Web site of the car company with his own comments about their claims.

- He can rate the car on a consumer Web site such as Deja.com or Epinions.com.

- He can publish the information on his own Web site.

- He can start a Web site dedicated to that car company (a fan site or a protest site).

"If [the car company] had their way," he wrote, "owners would be forbidden to speak to each other. We know too much." But customers *can* talk to each other now, thanks to the Internet, and they do. And, of course, to the thousands of conversations that we see in public newsgroups and on-line forums we should add countless private conversations, comments and exchanges of information.

## The Rise of Aggregated Buzz

New tools that are emerging on the Net can make electronic word of mouth even more powerful tomorrow. I call them "Aggregated Buzz Tools." They are essentially databases that store people's experience with products and services. Perhaps the best-known example of such a tool in the off-line world is the Zagat Report. Nina and Tim Zagat, two lawyers from New York City, started this as an informal restaurant poll they shared with friends. In 1979 they published their first *Zagat New York City Restaurant Survey.* The idea was simple: Instead of relying on the opinion of a few restaurant critics, why not hear what *many* people think about a particular restaurant? Restaurantgoers volunteer to submit their ratings on special forms. The people at Zagat summarize these ratings and publish them in their familiar burgundy guides. The democratic approach to ratings seems to be attractive to many people. In 1998 more than six hundred thousand copies of the New York guide of Zagat were sold according to the company. Since May 1999 the report has been accessible on-line.

Several Internet start-ups are developing new tools that hope to become the Zagats of all other product categories—cameras, cars, appliances, and so on. For these tools to succeed, their creators need to address three issues: attracting enough people to participate, preventing ballot-stuffing, and making the information relevant to customers. One company that has an interesting way of addressing these issues is Epinions.com. First, they do it by asking readers of the reviews to rate the reviews themselves, so biased reviews will go to the bottom of the list and reviews that most people find useful will rise to the top. They also keep track of how many times a review is being read. "If you write a review and no one reads it, then it's going to fall off to the bottom," says Bill Gurley of Benchmark Capital, one of the venture capital firms backing the company.

They also try to mimic word of mouth as it happens off-line. "In the real world you don't walk out on the street, flag down the first guy, and say, 'Hey, what's your opinion on this?'" says Nirav Tolia, CEO of the company. You also don't conduct a survey of a random hundred people. "You go to a person you trust," says Tolia. So on Epinions.com you don't simply see three hundred reviews of a popular book. You see reviews by people whose opinion *you* respect. How does the system know who they are? It learns over time whom you trust by the ratings you give other people's reviews. You can also tell the system explicitly who your trusted friends are, and this will guarantee you'll see their reviews first.

Further down the road, if enough people submit ratings of products, such tools can cause a real consumer revolution, giving customers accurate information on failure rates of products and customer satisfaction levels. The answer to a question like "Which microwave oven breaks the least amount of times?" exists out there in the world. The problem is that it is currently scattered over several million brains. Aggregated buzz tools could summarize it in one place.

## What Does It Mean in Terms of Marketing?

If these aggregated buzz tools take off, the importance of quality will increase even more. If your company makes a CD player that breaks five times a year, this information will suddenly become public knowledge. As a result, the best marketing advice here would be advise the R&D department to make a better CD player.

It will also mean higher standards in customer service. Irate customers don't have to wait for these tools to post horror stories on-line—they complain on-line today. But if service ratings become standard, they will become a competitive tool for companies that get high ratings. For example, before you open a new checking account at a bank, you may take a peek at one of these sites to see how customers rate your bank on service. The level of detail these tools will allow goes far beyond what any magazine could ever achieve. Once they're ubiquitous, you'll even be able to compare levels of service in different branches in your neighborhood, or chart how consistent service has been over a period of time.

Keep in mind that the editors of such sites will also be very influential, because they will be setting the agenda. Part of the outcome of any rating is determined by selecting which features the public is asked to rate. Suppose dishwashers are rated on how clean the dishes get, on loading capacity, and on their design. If the strongest features of the dishwasher your company makes are its energy-saving aspects and low noise level, it won't necessarily fare well. You would want to educate the editors about the importance of these features. This is especially true for new or evolving product categories, where features are still changing.

Overall, aggregated buzz tools are good news to companies with high-quality products and excellent service and bad news to companies that try to get away with less than the highest standards. This doesn't mean, unfortunately, that bad companies will disappear. But the rise of democratic measuring tools is likely, over time, to improve the quality of products and services we use.

And this is just the beginning of a major power shift. Although Baby Boomers are a big part of the current revolution, many Boomers still don't rely on others as much. But for Generation Y—the 60 million born between 1979 and 1994—asking for advice on-line is second nature. Word of mouth is how they shop. As this generation gains buying power in the next ten years, expect buzz to become even more important. As more customers will spend more time on the Internet. As an explosion of wireless communication devices will increase customer connectivity even further. As these mobile devices will tap in to the Internet, customers will get even more connected to this vast depository of opinions, often right at the point of purchase.

## "Word of Mouth on Steroids"

**The fact that** customers are connected can work for or against companies. Both good and bad buzz spreads much faster. "It's word of mouth on steroids," says Steve Douty, former vice president of marketing at Hotmail, a company that may have experienced the fastest adoption rate of a new product ever—from 0 to 12 million subscribers in just eighteen months. The Internet accelerates buzz in ways that were hard to imagine just a few years ago. Granted, Hotmail didn't generate much revenue during its life as a start-up. But to learn about buzz on the Net, we need to look at those companies that have been successful in creating it.

The Hotmail story started in 1995, when two young men from Silicon Valley, Sabeer Bhatia and Jack Smith, decided to start a company that would develop Java programming tools to help publish databases on the Internet. Both of them worked for a different company at the time and didn't want to use the company's e-mail account for their start-up. This gave them an idea that sounded much more interesting than the Java tools—a free e-mail service that could be accessed through the Web.

Bhatia and Smith started making the routine rounds among venture capitalists, trying to raise money. After about twenty rejections they came to the venture capital firm of Draper Fisher Jurvetson (DFJ). Venture capitalists are used to hearing inflated numbers, but Steve Jurvetson remembers Bhatia's as being "the most hallucinogenically optimistic forecasts that you could imagine." Still, DFJ liked the idea and gave the young men $300,000 in seed money. In the course of their meetings, Tim Draper of DFJ suggested that they add a line at the bottom of each e-mail message sent by a subscriber of the service: "Get your free e-mail at Hotmail.com." This, he thought, would help spread the word as people used the service. Bhatia and Smith were concerned initially that this might turn people off. "It took a meeting or two before they agreed," Jurvetson recalls.

The service was launched on July 4, 1996, Independence Day. The day was symbolic of the fact that their e-mail service was independent of your computer, of any software or portal. As people found out about the free service, they would tell their friends. The word started to spread, both electronically and as the result of face-to-face conversations. It was good old word-of-mouth marketing, at Internet speed. One person would adopt the service, and others would follow in just days. "We would notice the first user from a university town or from India, and then the number of subscribers from the region would rapidly proliferate," Jurvetson and Draper later wrote. Students were one early group to adopt the service. Before Hotmail was available, they juggled e-mail addresses between school, home, and summer jobs. Now they had one e-mail address that was accessible from any computer with Web access.

Within two months of its launch, Hotmail had more than 100,000 registered users. Bhatia and Smith went around Silicon Valley with beepers, hooked to the server, that buzzed whenever they reached a certain benchmark. This (real) buzz was very helpful, as they were going through their second round of financing. On November 11 the company announced that it had more than half a million subscribers. Eighteen months after its launch, Hotmail had 12 million subscribers. Looking back at Bhatia's "hallucinogenically optimistic" forecasts of subscriber growth, Jurvetson comments, "He more or less hit them, or beat them."

Buzz travels faster on the Internet in part because it combines local and nonlocal communication. The students who adopted Hotmail talked about it locally at the dorms and classrooms, but they also spread the word, by using Hotmail, to their friends and family back home and to their buddies at other schools. Moreover, when John sent a message to Mary, he didn't even have to say anything about Hotmail. She would see that the message came from john@hotmail.com, and then she would notice the little line at the bottom of the message: "Get your free e-mail at Hotmail.com." The speed was enhanced by the fact that the young company reduced the friction that usually prevents people from buying things: noise, cost, and physical delivery. Noise may prevent people from hearing about a brand, cost may prevent them from buying it, and complex or expensive delivery may prevent them from ordering it. Hotmail removed two of these barriers: cost and physical delivery. The service was free, and you could get it without leaving your desk. And it used word of mouth to get around the noise barrier.

Hotmail did almost no advertising. It was a vivid demonstration of the impact of Internet buzz. "Money can help, but word of mouth rooted in a great user experience wins!" says Montrese Etienne, who did the PR for Hotmail. "Just look at the growth of ICQ, GeoCities, Hotmail, eBay, etc. All are babies of word of mouth."

## Think Networks

Traditionally, marketers have focused on categories. They would identify a category—people who own a dog and two cars—and target it. In their 1993 book, *The One to One Future*, Don Peppers and

Martha Rogers shifted the focus to the interaction between a firm and each individual customer. A network perspective doesn't contradict either of these points of view. It just approaches the issue from a different angle by emphasizing that there is a lot of interaction *among* customers—between people *within* each category and *across* categories.

There are studies on diffusion of innovations—on how new concepts and ideas spread through social systems. A classic model in this field divides people into five categories: innovators, early adopters, early majority, late majority, and laggards. The distribution of these adopters follows a bell-shaped curve. At first only a few daring people adopt an innovation, such as a DVD player; then it starts to take off until it reaches a peak. As it becomes more and more difficult to find potential adopters who don't already own a DVD player, the number of new adopters goes down.

This is a useful perspective to analyze the market as a whole. But to get a better understanding of how word of mouth spreads, we need to look at the *micro* level—at networks. For example, a person buying a Palm organizer in Silicon Valley in 1999 would be categorized as an "early adopter" by using a market perspective, because he or she is buying it earlier than most other potential adopters in the United States. "But in reality, if this person is working in the high-tech industry and they're just getting a PalmPilot now, they've demonstrated a certain amount of resistance and hesitancy to innovate," says Dr. Thomas Valente of the University of Southern California, who studies the diffusion process. The PalmPilot was introduced in 1996; it has achieved high penetration among employees in the high-tech industry. A network perspective allows us to see that even though a person adopts "early" in terms of the overall market, he or she may be late in his or her own network.

For individual companies, a network perspective is often more useful than the aggregated one. Looking at networks helps in creating tactics that a company can execute to accelerate adoption. As an entrepreneur or a marketing manager, thinking only in terms of categories or types of adopters can point you in the wrong direction. If instead you think about networks, understanding that early adopters are sprinkled throughout society, you might think of ways to bring your product to them. In the case of the Palm organizer, instead of marketing to engineers in Silicon Valley, you might pursue early adopters in pharmaceutical firms in the Midwest who have the potential of spreading the word to a different group of people.

Imagine that you're in that control room I described in the beginning of the chapter. On the huge screen in front of you are 6 billion blue dots—each representing an individual on this planet. Each connected by thin blue glowing lines. That's where we must start. For these are the invisible networks.

# How Important Is Buzz to Your Business?

Buzz doesn't affect all businesses in the same way. The role it plays in your business depends on four factors: the nature of your product, the people you're trying to reach, your customer connectivity, and the strategies used in your industry. Since these factors can change over time, the importance of buzz to your business and industry can fluctuate.

## It Depends on the Nature of Your Products

We all know that some products do not tend to produce discussion. Paper clips, for example, will not generate much buzz whatever you do. They're cheap, they're simple, and there's nothing new about them. This last point is key. When paper clips were new, during the second half of the nineteenth century, people probably talked about them more than they do now, much in the same way that people talked about Post-it notes when they came out. How much new information is attached to a product, or to a whole product category, is key to predicting how much buzz it will get. The excitement is higher in the early days of a category, and so are prices, risks, and uncertainties. Over the years, as the novelty wears off, as the product becomes simpler and the monetary risk lower, people still talk about it—just not as much. This is a natural process that accompanies the life cycle of each product.

So what types of products *do* people buzz about? Products that somehow create high involvement among customers:

- *Exciting products,* such as books, records, and movies. Customers I interviewed said things like "I fell in love with it" or "it grabbed me" to describe their first encounter with certain products they later talked about.

- *Innovative products.* People talk about them both because these products may provide new benefits and because people are impressed by the ingenuity of the creators. The early Web browsers—Mosaic and later Netscape— generated incredible buzz because people saw the usefulness of these tools and admired the creativity of the people who invented them.

- *Personal experience products.* When personal experience is needed to assess the product or the service, buzz can be expected. Hotels, airlines, cars, books—all fall under this category.

- *Complex products* like software or medical devices. Here the motivation derives from the need to reduce risk. When people don't understand products, they have to talk in order to make sense of them.

- *Expensive products,* such as computers or consumer electronics. Risk is the major motivation here, too.

- *Observable products,* such as clothes, cars, and cellular phones. People tend to talk about what they see. If your product is invisible to them, they are less likely to discuss it.

Let us call these high-involvement products "conversation products." Obviously I suggest this not as a definition but rather as a name or label for the products that people tend to talk about.

## It Depends on the People You're Trying to Reach

The second factor in determining the importance of buzz to your business is your audience. Different audiences have a different propensity to talk about products. It's part of the culture. Many Hispanics, for example, tend to rely more on their peers for advice on everything from beer to banking, according to Felipe Korzenny, principal and co-founder of Cheskin Research. "If you observe the behavior of people, say, in Mexico City," he says, "they don't take a map out to find an address. They ask." One study found that Japanese companies use more referral sources than American firms in searching for services such as advertising, banking, and accounting.

Age can play a role here, too. Young people, who tend to socialize more and be more influenced by their peers than their elders, seem to talk more about products. A study by Roper Starch found that twentysomething women who liked a clothing item recommended it twice as many times as did Baby Boomers who liked the item. Another study from Maritz Marketing Research shows that 58 percent of people between 18 and 24 rely on others to some extent when selecting a new car, while only 30 percent of people 55 or older do.

Even scientists rely heavily on word of mouth in purchasing products. Scientists broadcast information they gather through journals, conferences, lectures, and informal conversations. The exchange of information is a way for them to enhance their research, and they often apply this idea to their purchasing behavior as well.

The same is true of immigrants. When my wife and I came to this country from Israel, we were like two walking question marks: "Is a Toyota a good car?" "What type of instant coffee should we get?" "What are English muffins?" Word of mouth exists among all people. Only the *level* of buzz varies from community to community.

## How Connected Are Your Customers?

The more connected your customers are to each other, the more you depend on their buzz for future business. To see the full impact of this, look at a company like Cisco that has always served a tightly connected customer base. Cisco sells the hardware devices that glue the Internet together; almost by definition, all of its customers (network administrators and information technology managers) are heavy users of the Internet. "Our company started by word of mouth. There was no advertising," says Keith Fox, vice president of corporate marketing at Cisco. Since 1984, buzz about Cisco has been spreading relentlessly on the Net. Several Internet newsgroups are dedicated to Cisco's products.

What this connectivity means to Cisco is that they have to be very open and direct with their customers. If they screw up, their customers will find out about it within minutes. The importance of high-quality products and top service increases, and the cumulative satisfaction of customers becomes critical. That's why Cisco ties its executive compensation to an index of customer satisfaction that is measured every year by an independent company. At Cisco, being close to the customer—an idea to which many pay lip service—becomes a reality. John Chambers, president and CEO of the multibillion-dollar company, spends much of his time visiting customers. "Religiously, John comes to visit me here in New York once a quarter," one corporate customer told the *New York Times.* "Other companies say, 'We listen to the customer,' but you don't often get the chief executive sitting down with you like that. The guy really is listening to the market."

## The Need for Buzz Varies According to Your Marketing Strategy

Your marketing strategy—as well as those of your competitors—may affect the degree to which you rely on buzz. Central purchases, for example, can somewhat reduce your dependency on word of mouth. Pepsi reduces the need for buzz when it cuts a deal with a high school to have only Pepsi vending machines on campus.

In the early 1990s, Dr. Bill New was trying to promote a medical device that detects hearing problems in children. Early detection can make a tremendous difference in the development of children, yet only eleven hospitals in the United States were routinely screening newborns for hearing disorders in 1993. How do you create buzz about this innovation to accelerate the adoption of this useful device? Dr. New had a choice: spread the word among physicians or promote the idea higher up to make screening mandatory. New did both, but the *focus* of his marketing has been on the latter. In recent years several states have passed laws to mandate the test, which now takes place in more than four hundred hospitals. Using this strategy, Dr. New bypassed the need to convince each physician separately to conduct the test. It's the law.

Of course, in most cases you can reduce your reliance on buzz only to a limited extent. If you market a conversation product, people will talk about it, even if the purchasing was done centrally. Kids still talk about what the best soft drink is, even when all the vending machines in their school are loaded with Pepsi. Physicians still talk about how useful a medical device is, and this may influence a centralized purchasing decision.

# Why We
# Talk

**3.**  **Buzz is powerful because it** is in our genes.

Just look out the window and consider the communication patterns of a simpler life form—in this case, birds. To understand why birds communicate, I talked to Dr. Bernd Heinrich of the University of Vermont. He studies, among other things, ravens. And ravens, as it turns out, have their own buzz. Heinrich and his colleagues wanted to know how ravens find out about food in the cold winter of Maine, and therefore they ran some experiments to study the issue. They obtained the carcass of a cow from a farmer, then went into the forest and put the carcass out in the snow. They waited in a nearby cabin or behind a snow-covered spruce-fir blind. After a few days a common raven appeared up in the sky and discovered the carcass.

This bonanza of food could feed a single bird for the entire winter. But, to the surprise of Dr. Heinrich and his colleagues, the raven flew away without taking a bite. A few days later the raven was back—this time with dozens of other ravens. The scientists repeated this experiment twenty-five times, and the results were always the same: When one or two ravens detected food, they came back several days later with family and friends in tow.

But isn't a raven better off keeping the secret to itself? Apparently not. "Having more pairs of looking eyes increases the likelihood that all birds will be fed, and on a continuous basis," the scientists explained. We're all familiar with similar behavior among ants and bees: Bees (who really should get the credit for inventing buzz) communicate through dancing. A honeybee that finds a patch of flowers goes back to its hive and performs a dance that tells the other bees where to go. A black carpenter ant that finds food sprays a secretion that excites the other ants to follow it to the food source.

All these examples illustrate that talking is not an incidental activity we engage in when we don't have anything better to do. It is rooted in some basic needs we share with other living creatures. Understanding the motivation behind word of mouth is the first step in stimulating people to talk about your product. So let's step back for a moment to examine the reasons we talk.

## 1. We Talk Because We Are Programmed to Talk

The most fundamental reason we talk is no different from the reason ravens communicate about food. Sharing information is an effective survival mechanism for ravens, bees, ants, and . . . people. We may no longer *need* to trade knowledge about bison hunting, but

we're still programmed to do so. And when it comes to certain survival issues, like hunting for a job, we *do* count on tips from others—
studies have shown that most people find out about their jobs
through other people. This reliance on others as sources of information becomes most obvious in crisis situations. In 1980, when usage
of Rely tampons was linked to cases of fatal toxic shock syndrome,
women all over the country started warning each other about the
brand. The same thing happened in the case of the Tylenol poisoning
in the early eighties—my mother-in-law even called us from Israel to
make sure that we didn't use Tylenol capsules.

Sharing information is vital also when it comes to surviving
on the job. Consider, for example, an engineer who's designing a new
piece of hardware. The engineer must make sure that he chooses
components not only that are suitable but also that will be available
in the market in the same configuration when his product goes into
production. This type of information can be obtained only from other
people, not from company literature. "Hardware engineers tend to
hang out together, in fear of missing the one critical word-of-mouth
factoid that might save them their jobs," Jerry Kaplan, who ran a
hardware company in Silicon Valley, wrote in his book *Startup*.

## 2. We Talk to Connect

**Another explanation for** talking is our need to establish alliances. As I'm writing this paragraph, I hear a soft and constant chatter from the other room. My teenage daughter is on the phone again.
This is part of her daily routine. Back from school, she gets on the
phone with friends until I ask about homework. Although perhaps it's
more apparent with teenagers, we all are constantly occupied with
communicating with each other. What we're really doing, according to
Robin Dunbar, author of *Grooming, Gossip, and the Evolution of Language*,
is very similar to what apes and monkeys do when they groom each

other: establish and maintain alliances and social ties. In small groups of primates, members of a network can manage alliances through grooming. Dunbar theorizes that as groups became larger, grooming every other member became impractical; language, he suggests, evolved as a much more efficient tool for managing alliances. Whether one agrees with Dunbar's evolutionary theory or not, the end result is pretty clear: We constantly groom each other with words.

Moreover, we don't use highbrow concepts like "quantum mechanics" to accomplish this "grooming" but simple phrases like "So he said" or "She told her boss" or "Did you see John's new car?" In fact, we are "fascinated beyond measure," as Dunbar puts it, with the minutiae of everyday social life. Dunbar and his colleagues have found that about two-thirds of people's conversations revolve around social issues: "Who is doing what with whom, and whether it's a good or a bad thing; who is in and who is out, and why." I'm re-minded of this constantly when I see my daughter on the phone.

Products are caught in the middle of this "grooming" process. Consumption is such a major part of our lives that products and services are always good conversation pieces. "What aftershave are you wearing?" the assistant at the dentist's office asked me the other day. "So what did you use for the stuffing?" someone asked over Thanksgiving dinner. It's easy to incorporate products into small talk. When you're at a hotel and you want to start a conversation with someone, asking about a good local restaurant or about the laptop the person is using makes more sense than asking about the meaning of life. "I went to New York," you tell your friend. "Where did you stay?" she may ask, or "Did you see any good plays?" or "What airline did you fly?"—all questions that can lead to discussion of products and services.

I took a coffee break after writing the last paragraph, and on my way back from the kitchen I noticed that my daughter (still on the phone) was flipping through the dELia*s catalog. I assume that the girl on the other end of the line was doing the same thing. Apparently there was some neat stuff on page forty-eight. "You see what the girl on the right is wearing? No, not her skirt, the sweater!" For readers who don't have teenage daughters, dELia*s is a catalog started by two Yale graduates in 1994. The company's sales in 1998 were $158.4 million. When you hear the constant chatter about dELia*s among my daughter's friends, you start to understand why the company gets between three thousand and five thousand unsolicited catalog requests a day, and why Stephen Kahn, the young CEO of the company, calls it "a gorgeous, gorgeous business."

My daughter could have chosen her clothing by herself as easily, but that would have not been the same. When shopping with friends, she's buying *and* connecting at the same time. Understanding that this is sometimes the motivation behind buzz can help companies be realistic about the word-of-mouth activities behind their products. dELia*s certainly did many things right to turn their catalog into a conversation piece in my daughter's life (good selection, frequent mailings, good service, cool Web site), but for my daughter and for many of her friends it's the *conversation* that matters most. Today it's about dELia*s. Tomorrow it's about something else.

In other cases we use products to send messages to the people around us. By announcing to the world what book we read, where we ate last night, or what electronic gadget we bought, we tell others about our wealth, sophistication, and smarts. Look at soft drinks: "Everyone knows I drink regular Coke," one woman told Susan Fournier of the Harvard Business School, who has studied people's relationships with brands. "If they were to see me with a Diet Coke, they would be . . . surprised. Because I sort of make a statement when I don't drink Diet that I don't do what everybody else does, that I don't really care about the extra calories that much . . ." By drinking regular Coke this woman is telling her networks that she doesn't need to pay attention to calories. Words are often the currency we exchange to manage an important asset: our reputation. And products help us do that.

Often the need to connect is associated with creating impressions of oneself. We tend to recommend books or movies that convey messages that *we ourselves* want to send to the world. "We're always trying to convince other people of our own views, and a good book can be a wonderful way to do that," one customer said to me in explaining why he posted a review of the book *Cold Mountain* on Amazon.com.

This sense of mission helps explain why people give books as gifts. It's a way to connect that reaffirms the values and taste that both gift giver and recipient share. Janice Shank from California, for example, sent copies of *Cold Mountain* to her brother, her sister, and two friends in Switzerland. She sent copies of two other books she loved, *The Perfect Storm* by Sebastian Junger and *The Fisherman's Son* by Michael Koepf, to five other people. "Books for me are a vehicle for connection," she explains.

## 3. We Talk to Make Sense of the World

**A friend of** mine who used to live in the Sinai desert told me how every afternoon the men of a Bedouin tribe would gather in the *magaa'd,* a central tent used for social gatherings. They would sit all afternoon and into the night around a small fire and talk. What would they talk about? "Everything: life, food, where to buy what, what's the best price for gas and cigarettes, where to go next." Bedouins are nomads who are in constant search for good grazing sites for their herds of sheep, goats, and camels. The *magaa'd* became their "newsgroup" hundreds of years before computers were invented. A guest from another part of the Sinai Peninsula would stop by to report some rainfall around where he lived. The men would discuss that, as it meant that in two to three weeks they could expect good grass around that area, and it might be time to move on. Word of mouth has always served two functions: to spread information

("There's rain not far from here") and to analyze it ("Maybe we should go there").

A few years ago a ship that was on its way to Saudi Arabia sank not too far from the coast of the Sinai desert. Entrepreneurial Bedouins got some boats and started to make trips to the sinking ship to bring merchandise to the shore. Buzz in the *magaa'ds* around Sinai became intense. For weeks the shipwreck was the main topic of conversation: what you could get from that ship, who would give you the best price, and so on. Suddenly the Bedouins—who usually eat pita bread, olives, and rice—had to figure out the difference between La Vache Qui Rit and other brands of French cheese. There was a lot to talk about.

In a way, living in Western society is like having hundreds of such sunken ships loaded with merchandise all around us. We are constantly bombarded with new products that we need to make sense of. Once again, there's a lot to talk about.

## 4. We Talk to Reduce Risk, Cost, and Uncertainty

Asking information of others often can save us time. If a customer is looking for the best mutual funds and he knows that a reliable friend has spent three days researching this topic, why not ask for the friend's advice? Most people have better ways to spend their time than reading about tax-exempt income funds. Do you need a security system for your house? The fastest way to get information is to ask what your neighbors use.

Asking for advice can also reduce risk. When I moved to Menlo Park, I had to leave my previous physician behind and find a new doctor. By asking around I reduced the risk of getting a second-rate doctor or getting stuck with a physician I didn't like. A study by Maritz Marketing Research shows that I'm not alone: Seventy percent of Americans rely to some extent on the advice of others when selecting a new doctor. Such "risk" can be psychological or monetary.

Customers are scared (and rightly so) of being ripped off, buying something they won't be able to use, or simply paying too much. Checking with friends before they invest their hard-earned dollars (especially in big-ticket items) is a good way to reduce this risk.

Customers who are less experienced have a higher perceived risk, and therefore they tend to rely on others more often. But that is not to say that experienced customers don't ask around. They do, for two reasons: First, they're concerned about risks, too, and second, they often enjoy talking about the topic much more than a novice would. "I wanted to know what kinds of things were not working and why," one experienced bicycle racer said. When he decided to buy a new mountain bike, he didn't simply drive to the nearest store. He knew that makers of mountain bikes were experimenting with different double-suspension designs, and he wanted to make sure he got one that worked well, so he began his research by consulting with three friends—two mountain bike racers and one mechanic.

## 5. We Talk Because It Makes Economic Sense

**Often we can** benefit directly from talking about products. Sometimes this is true because of what economists call "network externalities"—the fact that certain products become more valuable as more people use them. These network effects are easy to see in interactive technologies. If you're the only person in the world who owns a fax machine, its value to you is zero. To increase that value, you are likely to encourage others to get their own fax machines. The same effect took place in the diffusion of e-mail. "If you use it every day, you want your doctor to be connected up so you can send a question to him, or your accountant so you can schedule something with him or share ideas," Bill Gates explains. Gates's Microsoft has benefited greatly from another incarnation of the same phenomenon. By encouraging others to use Microsoft Word, a customer is making it easier for *him-*

*self* or *herself* to share word-processing files with them. Customers understand that they can benefit from having their colleagues use the same operating system: More software will be developed for it, and it will be supported locally.

Talking about products makes economic sense in other cases as well. A CEO of a company may recommend a business book to employees if he or she believes that by reading the book they will become more effective in pursuing the organization's goals. An investor who has put a lot of money into a certain stock is potentially increasing its value by telling everyone about the great returns he's been getting. A customer who buys a new car and tells his friends about its superior performance is indirectly contributing to its popularity and thus to the higher resale value typically associated with popular models.

Competitors often benefit from spreading *negative* buzz. When the gas industry was threatened by Edison's electric lighting, it belittled the significance of the innovation and exaggerated its dangers. When Federal Express was losing money in its early years, some competitors sent customers copies of news articles that mentioned the losses. Negative comments often come from those who are already invested (financially or psychologically) in a different technology. When George Eastman introduced paper negatives that were supposed to replace the bulky and fragile glass negative, he encountered a lot of, well . . . negative buzz from the current user base at the time. An article from *The American Journal of Photography* from spring 1886 describes the reaction users had to the innovation. They complained, among other things, that the paper would rot in time and that the odor of the castor oil used was "disagreeable." But when they were asked by the author of the article if they had actually tried the new negative, "the answer has generally been: 'Nope; but so-and-so has, and he don't appear to think much of them'—or something to that effect." In all these scenarios people talk to benefit from the outcome financially (sometimes in indirect ways).

## 6. We Talk to Relieve Tension

"**It all started** in one of those little clothing factories in Taiwan. A box of newly made coats ready to be shipped to the United States was left open accidentally. A poisonous Asian snake thought it would be a good place to lay its eggs. Somewhere on their way to a Kmart store in Detroit, Michigan, the eggs hatched. Several weeks later a shopper at Kmart decided to try on one of these coats. She slowly put her arm through the sleeve and didn't think much of the pricking sting she felt. When her arm started swelling several hours later, she was rushed to a hospital, where her whole arm had to be amputated."

The above story, overheard on the streets of Detroit, is an urban legend. Not one word in the story is true. There were no eggs in the shipment of newly made coats, and consequently no customer in Detroit claimed she was bitten by a snake. A reporter from a local radio station spent a day digging through hospital records but found no victim. Yet Kmart's publicity director received more than ten calls from news reporters who investigated the story after hearing it from people in the city.

Rumors are often based on people's most basic anxieties. Nobody knows where the rumor about Asian snakes started, but there is speculation that it was no accident it spread successfully in Detroit. It's possible that the rumor had its roots in Detroit's worries about Asian car imports.

What does this mean? Sometimes we talk to let off steam or to vent anger. The most common source of negative buzz comes from a negative experience a customer has had with a company. Unhappy customers will try to ease the internal tension they feel by "getting even." And they do! Studies have shown that negative information is given more weight in the purchase decision and spreads faster than positive information. (See box: "How Many People Do We Tell?"). The Internet gives customers the ability to tell even more people about their negative experiences. "Word of mouth is incredibly powerful online. A dissatisfied customer can tell 1,000 people in a few minutes," Amazon.com chief executive Jeff Bezos told *Time* magazine. By posting a story about a negative experience on a newsgroup or a personal Web site, customers can spread the word very effectively.

Tension is also often created as a side effect of the purchasing process. Especially with expensive products, customers may feel discomfort after making the purchase, a phenomenon known as "cognitive dissonance," or "buyer's remorse." To reduce the dissonance, they will talk to others and try to justify their decision. A person who has bought a new car is likely to tell others about the advantages of the particular brand and cite information from reliable sources that support his or her decision. By seeking information *before* they buy, customers increase their chances of feeling satisfied later on, thus reducing the potential for tension.

Reports in the media about the loss of community in Western society leave one with the image of millions who live in little boxes, glued to their TV screens and Nintendos. This image is not totally unfounded. Americans, for example, don't spend as much time with their neighbors as they used to. Participation in public life is declining, too. Fewer people sign up for the PTA or attend public meetings.

But that doesn't mean that we don't talk. We talk because *we are programmed to talk.* Fewer people may attend public meetings, but more express their opinions on the Net. People may spend less time with their neighbors, but even in the age of Nintendo and Walkman, human interaction is still a major part of our lives. We still have an almost unquenchable urge to sit around the fire like the Bedouins and talk. In the spring of 1997, Roper Starch Worldwide interviewed 35,000 adults and teenagers in 35 countries. One of the findings of this mega-survey was that spending time with family and friends is

# How Many People Do We Tell?

One of the few things that consistently show up in research about word of mouth is the fact that we tend to spread negative comments to more people than we do positive ones. A company that has conducted extensive research on the topic is TARP (now e-Satisfy) in Arlington, Virginia. John Goodman, president of TARP, got interested in the topic in the late seventies. It was commonly reported that when a customer had a positive experience, he told three other people about it, and when the customer had a negative experience, he shared it with seven other people. Goodman started looking at where these numbers came from. "I'd call up each source and say, 'Well, where did you get this data?' I found myself chasing my tail." Nobody knew the source of the numbers.

Goodman then approached the Coca-Cola Company and suggested a study to actually measure word of mouth. A mail survey was sent to about 1,700 Coca-Cola customers who had either complained or had made an inquiry to the company in previous months. TARP's findings in the Coca-Cola study and in consumer studies that followed confirmed the general belief that people talk about a bad experience with more of their acquaintances—although the actual number of people they talked to was different. In the Coca-Cola study, for example, consumers who were satisfied with the way Coca-Cola handled their complaint told 4 to 5 people about it, while those who felt that their complaint had not been satisfactorily resolved told 9 to 10 people. A study for General Motors found that the numbers for cars were 8 and 16. "Over the next fifteen hundred studies, anytime we did customer surveys, we would ask about word of mouth," Good-

high on the list of the most popular leisure activities: Seventy-three percent of adults and 63 percent of teenagers said that they frequently spend time with family. Thirty-two percent of adults and 62 percent of teenagers surveyed frequently spend time with friends. These numbers are higher than the percentages of time spent watching TV, playing sports, listening to music, or shopping. The United States was no exception. "People are extremely social," says Diane Crispell of Roper, "and [reaching] people through their relatives and friends is extremely powerful."

man says. "We do find that data varies rather dramatically. In certain industries we find that *one* person hears about a good experience and *six* hear about a bad experience. So we've found over the past few years that the two-to-one ratio that everyone always talks about isn't necessarily correct." In a study of electronic customer service conducted in late 1999, e-Satisfy found that dissatisfied on-line customers were almost four times more likely to discuss their experience in an on-line chat room than satisfied customers.

The emotional involvement a customer has with a product is a good predictor of how many people he or she will tell about an experience. Since many people have strong feelings about their cars, they may share related information with a higher number of friends. On the other hand, it isn't the same with grocery shopping. "Even if you got in-competent service at the local supermarket, you may not talk to as many people about that, because that's not as exciting," says Goodman. Another issue affecting the number of people to whom customers spread the word is privacy. People may tell fewer of their friends about financial services and health care. So buzz can be industry-specific.

Moreover, the number of other people we tell about a product can change over time. A 1999 survey sponsored by Priceline.com and conducted by Opinion Research Cor-poration International of Princeton, New Jersey, shows that on-line shoppers on average told 12 other people about their experience with on-line purchases. To give but one ex-ample: On average, a person who used an on-line travel service told 3.2 family members, 3.3 friends, 2 relatives, 2.5 co-workers, and 1.3 "others" about it. One can expect these numbers to go down as the novelty of booking a flight on-line wears off and customers begin to spread buzz about a new topic.

# Network

# Hubs

**4.** **Jim Thompson first heard about** the Palm-

Pilot from his colleague Glenn Kowalsky. "Walking down

the hallway in my hospital, he showed me this little machine he just

got, and it instantly grabbed me," he remembers. "I knew that this

was what I'd been waiting for."

Thompson got a PalmPilot right away, after checking a couple

of Web sites to see if the Palm could accommodate a programmable

calculator. Since then he has downloaded dozens of programs into his

Pilot. I was embarrassed to tell him that I had only downloaded one

game in my entire life as a Piloteer—what he calls us Palm users.

Thompson really uses his. He plays games on the Palm in the dentist's chair, keeps his mileage log on it, updates his expense account after he pays the bills in restaurants, makes notes riding in the elevator. He even downloads books to it and reads them on flights.

No wonder he's been talking with so many people about the Palm. Thompson has developed a fascination with the machine. And he finds that he's not the only person intrigued by it. Everywhere he goes, people ask him about it. In addition to friends, family, people at the dentist's office, cashiers, fellow diners and passengers, he's been spreading the word to several medical groups he's been part of in Sundre, Alberta (ninety minutes north of Calgary), southern Alberta, and Charlottetown.

And then there's the on-line world. Shortly after he bought the PalmPilot, Thompson started a Web site he called "Jim's Health Care Pilot Page." He announced the page on newsgroups and immediately started to get inquiries from physicians who were using the PalmPilot or wanted to get one. From his home in a rural town in Canada, Thompson was addressing inquiries from Australia, the United States, Japan, and other parts of the world. "I ended up being their tech support in a certain way," he says. He became recognized as an expert on the device's medical applications, and people turned to him for advice. And because he loves to help, he was happy to give it.

Jim Thompson is what I call a "network hub." Network hubs are individuals who communicate with more people about a certain product than the average person does. Researchers have traditionally referred to them as "opinion leaders." In industry they're called "influencers," "lead users," or sometimes "power users." (I prefer the neutral term "network hub" for reasons I'll explain later in the chapter. However, when specific research refers to such people as "opinion leaders," I use that terminology.)

The fact is, not much is definitively known about network hubs; moreover, the nature of network hubs may differ from industry to industry. You won't find their names and addresses in any directory—identifying network hubs is usually more complex than renting a mailing list. But the reward for paying attention to these people can be huge. Not only do they further the buzz about a new product—their central position sometimes allows them to change a message or even block it from spreading. In this chapter I explore who they are and why they matter. Later, in Chapter 9, I will outline how they can help you spread the word.

Network hubs exist in every category of conversation products. Certain kids spread the word about yo-yos; certain engineers spread the word about a new programming tool; certain readers spread the word about new books; and the payoff for capturing these special individuals' attention is high. "If you get them on a book, then twenty-five other people know about the book tomorrow," says David Unowsky of Ruminator Books, a bookstore in Saint Paul, Minnesota.

Think about the ultimate network again, those 6 billion dots on the huge screen. When you put a specific filter in front of the screen, you're able to see only the comments that flow about a certain product category. For example, if you put the "yo-yo" filter on, you'd see only the comments exchanged about yo-yos. Those individuals who talk with many others about yo-yos will stand out as network hubs. Switch to another filter—say, to the filter of medical devices—and you see on your screen the physicians who are especially knowledgeable and chatty about certain medical devices.

## The Four Types of "Network Hubs"

The first step in trying to find the individuals who act as hubs is to understand that such people come in many shapes, colors, and forms. In general, I've found they can be classified into four groups. First, I distinguish hubs based on the number of links they make with other individuals.

**Regular Hubs:** These are regular folks who serve as sources of information and influence in a certain product category. They may be connected to only a few other individuals or to several dozens. Jim Thompson, the PalmPilot early adopter, is one such hub.

**Mega-Hubs:** This term refers to the press, celebrities, analysts, politicians. These individuals have many two-way links like regular hubs, but in addition they have thousands of one-way links with people who listen to their message via mass media. Oprah Winfrey is one example. Traditionally these people have been categorized under labels such as "the media" or "the political heavyweights." In our context each is a member of the networks. On that huge screen I described earlier, Oprah Winfrey is a single node, just like you and me. What makes her so powerful in spreading the word is the fact she is able to link up with millions of other people.

In an informal survey that my assistant, Haim Zaltzman, and I conducted at a university on the West Coast, we asked students to report whether or not they had talked about a certain product—a music CD, *The Miseducation of Lauryn Hill*—and if so, to give the names of the people with whom they discussed it. From this survey a few people at the school emerged as network hubs. One network hub, whom I'll call Jane, talked with seven other students about the CD. She is a perfect example of a regular hub. An MTV veejay or a writer for *Rolling Stone* is an example of a *mega*-hub who is able to reach millions of people with his or her opinion.

Where do you draw the line between a regular hub and a mega-hub? The Internet is obviously blurring that line. On the Web, people can broadcast information in a way that makes them more than just a local expert. So instead of spreading the word to sixty people, a yo-yo enthusiast can put together a Web site about yo-yos and suddenly spread buzz to *thousands* of people. Sometimes such people gain mega-hub status. Harry Knowles, for example, an Austin-based

**Mega-Hub. An MTV veejay spreads the word to thousands or millions of people through one-way links.**

**Hub. This undergraduate has spread the word to seven other people through two-way links.**

movie fan who set up a Web site (www.aint-it-cool-news.com) to publish reviews of films reported by a network of "spies" who go to prescreenings of movies. He now estimates the readership of his Web site at more than 2 million people.

Even what I call a regular hub is a relative term. When 665 adults were asked by Maritz if they were the kind of people others come to for a recommendation on a new car, eleven percent answered "to a great extent." At the other end of the spectrum, 32 percent said "not at all." The remaining 57 percent were somewhere in the middle. Perhaps it is accurate to say that you start to be a network hub if you transmit comments about a certain product category to more people than the average person does. If an average Palm user tells twenty other people a year about the device, and another user tells eighty people about it, that second person is clearly a hub. Jim Thompson, for example, probably communicates with several hundred people. That's why researchers talk about an individual's *degree* of opinion leadership. Walt Mossberg, for example, who writes a column about technology for *The Wall Street Journal*, is at one extreme, with hundreds of thousands of one-way links with readers of his column. At the other extreme is a random guy who talks with just two to five of his friends about computers. Obviously there is an enormous range in between.

What's important to realize is that while that random guy may not be talking about computers much, if we switch to a different filter—say, the *Star Wars* filter or a filter that lets us see only the comments about jazz—he may be a network hub for this among his peers. Maybe even a mega-hub. Similarly, Walt Mossberg's opinion leadership may dwindle when the subject is education or dancing troupes.

It's also important to distinguish between hubs who are listened to because of what they know—expert hubs—and hubs who are listened to because of their social centrality—social hubs. I describe this feature of hubs as their source of influence.

**Expert Hubs:** Some people are listened to because they have demonstrated significant knowledge of a certain area (at the very least, they have convinced others of their authority on a subject). You probably know someone like this at work, who answers a lot of questions about software and computers. Expert hubs tend to specialize. You may have one friend who's up on all the latest movies, another one who you ask about cars, and a third one who is knowledgeable about computers, cooking, or sports.

**Social Hubs:** In every group there are those who are more central because they are charismatic, are trusted by their peers, or are simply more socially active. One such person in the city of Chicago is Lois Weisberg, who was profiled by Malcolm Gladwell in a 1999 article in *The New Yorker*. Weisberg makes friends easily and brings people together. Among other things she was director of special events for the city, owned a secondhand jewelry store, started an organization called Friends of the Parks, and ran a drama troupe. And she's made many friends along the way. Every town, every neighborhood, every company seems to have at least one person like that.

By looking at both the "scale of influence" and the "source of influence," we're able to identify four specific types of network hubs:

|  | Regular Hubs | Mega-Hubs |
| --- | --- | --- |
| **Expert Hubs** | Jim Thompson | Walt Mossberg |
| **Social Hubs** | Lois Weisberg | Oprah Winfrey |

Jim Thompson is a regular hub. So is the person at your company to whom everyone turns for advice on computers. They both derive their authority from their expertise. Walt Mossberg, too, is an expert about computers, someone who connects to more than a million people through his column in *The Wall Street Journal*. Lois Weisberg is a network hub because she loves people and knows so many of them in the city of Chicago. Oprah Winfrey derives her influence not from her expertise in a particular subject but from being trusted by millions of people. Although she doesn't know most of her viewers, many of *them* view her as a trusted friend.

The question is, how do you reach such people—these hubs? The tactics for reaching *mega*-hubs—"the media"—are well known by publicity people, and I have little new to offer here. What other books do not usually discuss is how to go about reaching the millions of regular hubs who can spread news about a product. So I will focus here on reaching *regular* hubs.

## Who Are These Regular Hubs?

I wish I could tell you that most people who are network hubs are easily identifiable—are thirty to forty-five years old, have an average household income of $55,075, and watch PBS every Wednesday night. Of course, it's impossible to give such exact characteristics, because there are all kinds of network hubs. A video games network hub could be a twelve-year-old boy with an annual disposable income of $613. A network hub for medical equipment will have a totally different profile. Still, several characteristics typical of network hubs emerge. Let me offer an easy acronym you can use to remember them: network hubs are ACTIVE. They are Ahead in adoption, Connected, Travelers, Information-hungry, Vocal, and Exposed to the media more than others.

**Ahead in adoption.** Network hubs are usually *not the first* to adopt new products, but they are at least slightly ahead of the rest in their networks. The term used by scholars to describe this characteristic is "innovativeness." It refers to the relative speed at which an individual adopts new ideas.

Roper Starch Worldwide (RSW), a New York–based marketing research firm, has been tracking a group they call "Influential Americans" for years. "We have learned that in fact those folks are leading-edge consumers in many ways. They are the first to do just about anything," says Diane Crispell of RSW. For example, in 1982, 8 percent of these individuals owned a PC, versus 3 percent of the total public. This trend has continued over the years. In 1995, 53 percent of influential Americans owned a PC, versus 24 percent of the total public.

**Connected.** Network hubs are by definition connected. *How* they are connected may vary. One hub may be heavily connected within her clique. Another may be connected just to several other clusters, serving in effect as an information broker among these different groups. Often hubs will have ties within a core group and also be connected to an *outside* source of information. Everett Rogers points out that opinion leaders are more "cosmopolite" than others, which means that they tend to be oriented to the world outside the local system. For example, network hubs in the high-tech industry tend to gravitate toward other network hubs from whom they can get more information (which they then will transmit within their cluster). To find these other network hubs, they go to trade shows, join user groups, and hang out in on-line forums that discuss the topics they are interested in. These activities result in additional links to the outside world.

**Travelers.** In a study done for the pharmaceutical company Pfizer in the 1950s, it was found that physicians who adopted tetracycline earlier than their peers attended more out-of-town scientific conferences and visited more out-of-town medical institutions. In another classic study that followed the adoption of hybrid corn among farmers in Iowa during the first half of the twentieth century, farmers who were early to adopt the innovation made more trips to Des Moines, Iowa's largest city. The RSW study of Influential Americans confirms that network hubs tend to travel: "At any given time, they are likely to be just coming off a plane from a personal vacation, business trip or weekend getaway," RSW reports.

This issue has not yet been studied systematically on the Internet. It will be interesting to see if network hubs tend also to travel *virtually* more than others. For example, do network hubs exchange e-mails with people from other countries more often than do people who are not network hubs?

**Information-hungry.** Because they often serve as "local experts," network hubs always want to learn more. This is especially true of expert hubs who are expected to provide answers to people in their groups or clusters. It is worthwhile to keep this in mind when you communicate with network hubs in *your* market. Colorful writing can help, but what's *really* important are hard facts about products. Ziff-Davis became a publishing empire around this idea—providing information to a core group of network hubs in each market: cars, stereo, computers. When you look at *PC Magazine,* one of Ziff's major publications, you see this focus on product information. Joe Gillespie, an executive at Ziff-Davis, put it succinctly: "Never has a book dared to be as dull yet appeal to so many people." *PC Magazine* gives network hubs in the computer industry what they love most: facts. Lots of facts.

**Vocal.** Jim Thompson is soft-spoken, but he's not shy about voicing his opinions. Roper Starch Worldwide found that when their Influential Americans like a product, they are much more vocal about it than the general public is. Thirty-seven percent of them made a recommendation about a car or a truck in the past year, while only 19 percent of the total public say they have done the same. Twenty-two percent of these influentials say that they have recommended a brand of liquor, wine, or beer to another person in the past year, while only 9 percent of the total public say they have done so. Being outspoken on the Internet is likely to be a good indication of being a network hub. These are the people who voice their opinions about issues and who are more likely to be heard.

**Exposed to media.** Because network hubs are information-hungry, they read more. Studies have shown that network hubs open themselves to more communication from mass media, and especially to print media. One study found that financial opinion leaders are more likely to read publications such as *Money, Barron's,* or *The Wall Street Journal* and watch TV programs such as *Wall Street Week*. Other studies have demonstrated similar results among network hubs who are interested in politics, fashion, and medical innovations. But buzz doesn't follow neat patterns, so don't expect all network hubs to learn about new products from mega-hubs in the media and then pass it on to their "followers." This "trickle-down" theory used to be the common belief among researchers, but it doesn't always work that way. Jim Thompson, for example, learned about the PalmPilot from Glenn Kowalsky—a colleague. After he learned about it, he went on-line to check a few Web sites and, as someone who's always hungry for more information, he read about the Palm in the media as well. So hubs may use the media, but they also rely on friends for information and feedback.

A common thread among all these characteristics is that network hubs create links between their local system and the outside world. Because they travel and are exposed to the media, they can

## Are Network Hubs Early Adopters?

One of the characteristics of network hubs is that they are usually at least slightly ahead of the rest of us in adopting innovations. But there are differences between early adopters and hubs.

### 1. Are All Network Hubs Early Adopters?

No. Network hubs are people who transmit information and who tend to influence other people's decisions about products. They don't automatically adopt every new product they come across. They can be early adopters of certain products and early *rejecters* of others. In marketing technology solutions, for example, you may find that the network hubs you're appealing to are already hooked on a different solution and unwilling to accept yours. John Sculley, former president of Apple Computer, admits, "It's not always easy to influence the influencers, who tend to potentially be your most informed audience. The powerful 10 percent, then, can work for or against you."

### 2. Are All Early Adopters Network Hubs?

No. Just because someone was one of your first customers, that doesn't mean he or she influences others. In fact, Everett Rogers points out that *the most* innovative individuals—people who are "totally into technology"—may have low credibility among the average members of a network and therefore will not be able to influence others. Also, some "early adopters" buy the product early because they *need* it, rather than because they are on the cutting edge. Two Harvard professors, Susan Fournier and John Deighton, have stud-

gather information that they can then broadcast within their clusters. Of course, hubs come in many shapes and colors. Some network hubs may be more locally oriented, while others may be more cosmopolitan. Consider two network hubs—John and Andrew—each with ties to ten other people. Although they have direct links to the same number of people, they can be dramatically different in their reach. John is linked to seven co-workers and has three ties outside the company. Andrew has just three strong ties within the company, but seven ties with individuals in seven separate clusters. They are both influential, but Andrew—the more cosmopolitan net-

ied the adoption of on-line grocery shopping by following twenty-six households that adopted the Peapod service early on. The idea behind this service is that instead of going to the grocery store yourself, you transmit your shopping list electronically to Peapod, which delivers the groceries to your home. "There are some people who jumped onto this service because they are very savvy, very cosmopolitan, very much into 'what's new,' and they came in through a hook of the attraction of the new technology," explains Susan Fournier. "But then there are these other people who are grocery shoppers, and they came into this because they just needed a better way to do their grocery shopping," she continues. An older woman, for example, who was having a hard time carrying her groceries upstairs adopted the service because it was the right solution for her. She doesn't even use a PC—her husband enters the shopping list for her. She's not necessarily an innovative person or a network hub, just a person who's tired of carrying grocery bags.

### 3. Is There a Correlation Between the Two?

Yes. Given all the foregoing, network hubs are often more innovative than other people. Often they are the first to adopt new products. Several studies that examined the relationship between innovativeness and opinion leadership found a positive relationship between the two. This is true in the political arena as well. In the late seventies John Black traced changes in opinions about various political issues by interviewing people every three months for a period of three years. He found that opinion leaders on national issues—people who reported that they were consulted for advice—were always the first to change; other people followed.

work hub—has a much broader reach both in terms of the diversity of the information he can gather and the number of people he would eventually be able to spread the word to. Being a network hub is not only about having lots of friends. It's also about who these friends are connected to.

To spread the word, you often need to talk to both Andrew and John. Andrew may be a good person to spread information from one cluster to another. But when it comes to adopting an actual innovation, the members of John's group may look to him more to hear what he has to say about it.

## What Hubs Are and Are Not

In marketing circles a whole alphabet soup of terms is used to describe concepts similar to the concept of network hubs: champions, happy customers, lead users, and so on. So it's important to make sure that we're talking about the same thing when we talk about network hubs.

Let's start with what network hubs *are*. Network hubs are what researchers call "opinion leaders." In the academic literature, opinion leadership is defined as "the degree to which an individual can informally influence other individuals' attitude or overt behavior in a desired way with relative frequency." The reason I prefer to use a network term is that the word "leader" immediately connotes someone whom others seek to follow. This implies something more grandiose than is often the case. Elihu Katz and Paul Lazarsfeld, who used the term "opinion leader" back in the 1950s, explained that "what we shall call opinion leadership, if we may call it leadership at all, is leadership at its simplest . . . not leadership on the high level of a Churchill, nor of a local politico, nor even of a local social elite," they wrote in 1955.

It's just as important to understand what hubs are not. Network hubs are not "champions," "lead users," or simply "happy customers." All these terms are used to describe customers who are especially satisfied with a product or service. An easy mistake companies can make is to jump to the conclusion that satisfied customers are also influential in their own networks. There is no evidence for any correlation between the two. Happy customers can (and should) be engaged in referral programs and special "champion programs." But a single customer's satisfaction has very little to do with his or her *centrality* in social networks. Suppose you're marketing software to a school. One of the teachers in that school is an enthusiastic customer of yours. You embrace and support him, but you can't understand why your sales in that school are so low.

He may not be a network hub at all, while another teacher who is using a competing product is influencing the usage patterns of other teachers.

## The Value Over Time of a Network Hub

**How much is** a network hub worth to you? It's impossible to attach an *exact* monetary value to any customer, but it is worth trying to estimate it. To illustrate how this can be done, let us look at a hypothetical hub who is spreading the word about luxury cars. In 1997, Market Probe International conducted a survey for *Car & Driver* among the magazine's readers. Those readers who reported giving advice about passenger cars said that, on average, they had advised 6.1 people about this category in the previous twelve months. Not all of these friends and family members subsequently bought a car—only an average of 2.9 people did. And not all those who bought followed the advice of the respondents, but 2.3 did. Let us arbitrarily assume that 30 percent of the friends would have bought the recommended brand anyway. We end up with 1.61 vehicles for which our hypothetical network hub is directly responsible every year.

If a car costs $25,000 and you add 10 percent parts and service to that, each new customer is expected to pay somewhere around $27,500. Multiplying that by 1.61, our hypothetical person is responsible for $44,275 a year in revenues, or $885,500 over a twenty-year period—*in addition to his or her own automotive purchases.* (That is, of course, if you can maintain this hub's high opinion of you or your product over twenty years). Notice that we're not including the lifetime values of these additional customers who may stay with the dealership for more than that one purchase. Nor are we including other customers *they* may have influenced. While this is just a hypothetical example, it shows why marketers have a huge deal to gain by cultivating network hubs.

# The History of Network Hubs

The recognition that opinion leaders are sprinkled throughout society and can be used to spread ideas is an ancient one. Gabriel Weimann, who has chronicled the history of the concept in *The Influentials: People Who Influence People,* traces this notion all the way back to the Bible. When Moses complained to God that he could no longer control the people of Israel, God told him to gather "seventy men of the elders of Israel" and use them to spread the word to the rest of the people.

In 1903 the French sociologist Gabriel Tarde, a pioneer in the field of the diffusion of innovations, recognized that "every herd of wild cattle has its leaders, its influential heads." But only in the last sixty years have researchers started to study the subject empirically. Like so many other discoveries, it all started as an accident. In 1940 mass media were a new and exciting phenomenon considered to be extremely powerful in that they directly reached each person in society. Paul Lazarsfeld of the Bureau of Applied Social Research and his staff at Columbia University conducted a study to measure the effect of mass media in the 1940 presidential election. They were ready to report how powerful the mass media were in influencing people's opinions. But what they found surprised them. When they asked people who changed their minds during the campaign what had contributed to their decision, the answer was *other people.* Lazarsfeld and his colleagues turned to look a little closer at these "other people," and in their 1944 book *The People's Choice* they defined them as "opinion leaders."

Right after World War II, Lazarsfeld decided to study the topic more closely. He and his team looked for a typical American town and chose Decatur, Illinois. They interviewed about eight hundred women in the town about fashion, public affairs, moviegoing, and the purchase of consumer products. Each one of these women was interviewed twice, with a two-month gap between the interviews. If a respondent changed her opinion during the second interview about any of the products or services discussed, the interviewer asked her several questions about why she changed her mind and to whom she had talked. Not every opinion change involved another person, but many did. Reporting on the results of the study in their book *Personal Influence,* Lazarsfeld and coauthor Elihu Katz were able to identify individuals who were more influential than others and to describe some of their characteristics. One finding was that each opinion leader had her specialty: While one woman was the opinion leader about fashion, another was the expert on movies, and a third was the person everyone asked about public affairs.

The pharmaceutical firm Pfizer became interested in the subject and budgeted $40,000 to study it (a significant amount back in 1955). They were just about to introduce a new type of antibiotic, tetracycline, and saw this as an opportunity to monitor how its usage spread. They turned to the Bureau of Applied Social Research, where Katz and two of his colleagues—Herbert Menzel and James S. Coleman—designed a study to analyze the process. The researchers traced the information flow among physicians in four Midwestern cities for about a year and a half. The team asked each doctor in the four cities for the names of colleagues whom the physician was talking with about medical issues, and to date the first time each doctor had prescribed the new drug. As a result they were able to draw a diagram of the links each physician had with his or her colleagues; several physicians emerged as network hubs and were shown to be influential in the diffusion process.

These early studies created a persistent interest in the field in the 1960s and 1970s. Additional studies examined the issue of opinion leadership and tried to find ways to classify and identify opinion leaders. Nonetheless, such studies have generated what may be seen as consistent opposition to the importance of word of mouth. To this day, "People are desperate to show that we are wrong," Elihu Katz says. There are several possible explanations for this. First, word of mouth represents an elusive concept. When you buy advertising, you see it in the newspaper. It's harder to see and measure buzz that spreads from network hubs to others. The second reason is that the concept contradicts a nice linear paradigm: the idea that by buying advertising, marketers can spread messages directly to an accepting public. It's hard for some marketers to accept the fact that information spreads in nonlinear ways they can't always control. Above all, much of what may seem to be opposition derives from people's desire to better understand an extremely complex phenomenon.

Measurement and sampling techniques, as well as new computing tools, are constantly being created that will help identify network hubs more accurately. As a result it's now possible to analyze how things happen in a small group. Analysis of the dynamic in large social structures, however—closer to the real world—is just beginning.

# It's a Small

# World.

# So What?

**5.**

**Some say that we're all** connected by a chain of no more than six mutual acquaintances. For example, I may discover that your physician went to school with someone who collaborated on a research paper with a colleague of my dentist. Or maybe a cousin of my neighbor works on the same floor as a good friend of your seventh-grade teacher. By talking together, presumably each one of us could find out exactly how we are linked. But what does the concept of "six degrees of separation"—better known among social scientists as "the small world phenomenon"—mean to marketers?

There are ten principles at work in social networks that affect buzz. In this chapter I present these principles or rules that networks live by.

## Principle 1:
## The Networks Are Invisible

In the same way we can't tell that the world is round by just walking on the surface of it, we don't have the right perspective to see the huge social networks of which we are a part. We know our friends, and we may know of our friends' friends, but that's about where our "social horizons" stop. The networks are just too complex. Even in a small network that consists of only 100 people, there are 4,950 possible links among them. In a network with just 1,000 members there are almost *half a million* possible links! As if this weren't enough, the networks keep changing. People in our society constantly form new friendships, change jobs, move—all factors contributing to the fluidity and invisibility of the networks.

Even in a close environment we don't seem to see the networks very clearly. Studies of informal networks at the workplace show that managers have a difficult time describing workplace networks. "Although they may be able to diagram accurately the social links of the five or six people closest to them, their assumptions about employees outside their immediate circle are usually off the mark," say David Krackhardt and Jeffrey Hanson, authors of a study on how informal networks operate in the workplace. This is true as well for on-line communities, as illustrated by Stacy Horn in her book *Cyberville*. A few members of Echo, the on-line community Horn founded, once complained to her about a clique they identified on Echo. So Horn asked them to name members of this "in" group. "The answers were amazing," she writes. The complainers pointed to members who barely communicated with each other. "They assumed friendships between people who were either indifferent or who actively disliked each other."

### Implications

The implications of this principle to customers is that customer privacy is protected because our social ties are not easily visible to the world. It also means that marketers are in the dark. If members of social networks can't see their own links to each other, these links are even more hidden to outsiders. The good news is that *marketing activities* in the networks can be invisible as well, a fact that can help companies gain market share under the radar screen of competitors. For example, hundreds of thousands of customers signed up on Hotmail before anyone in the high-tech industry paid attention to this start-up. Grassroots activities and the buzz they generate are much harder to detect than mainstream advertising or publicity. It may take months before the grassroots buzz gets picked up by the media.

## Principle 2: People Link with Others Who Are Similar to Them

Look at a family taking a stroll on a Sunday afternoon: mom, dad, teenage boy, young girl, and a dog. Now, here's another family coming from the other end of the street: another mom, dad, teenage boy, young girl, and a dog. They wave. Obviously the two families know each other. What do you think will happen when they meet? Most likely adults will talk to adults, the teenage boy will talk to the other teenage boy, and the two girls will talk to each other. Even the dogs will sniff each other before they do anything else.

It's human nature for people to make contact with others like themselves. Scientists love to talk with other scientists. Rich people associate with other rich people. If you're into mountain biking, you're likely to hang out with other bikers. This tendency for people to like and associate with those who are similar to them is called "homophily," and it is one of the fundamental principles of invisible networks.

As innocent as this principle may sound, it is the main factor that can limit the acceleration of buzz. When PowerBar was first introduced, the high-energy snack spread quickly among runners, cyclists, and swimmers. As a triathlete, cofounder Jennifer Biddulph knows people in these sports. Cofounder Brian Maxwell, a world-ranked marathoner, knows other leading athletes. "We'd talked to a lot of serious athletes that were our friends and had given them samples of the bars we were working on in our kitchen," he remembers. But each sport has its own social networks, and although some people help to link different sports, a company can't rely on them alone. Swimmers talk to swimmers, golfers talk to golfers, windsurfers talk to windsurfers. Maxwell realized that buzz about PowerBar wouldn't spread easily between runners and golfers, for example. "We really had to plant separate seeds in each area," he notes. When they marketed PowerBar to tennis players, they hired a tennis player. "She was not a marketer, but she knew tennis," Maxwell recalls. They gave her a certain number of complimentary bars and a marketing budget, and then they set her free to market to her network. She sent bars to tennis people she knew, called tournament directors, placed bars in tennis shops, and so on.

Maxwell's intuitive strategy is supported by research. One study, for example, found that insurance agents made sales more easily when they were similar to the customer in age, education, and income. This was true as well for belief systems, such as politics and religion, and even for physical characteristics, such as height. Another study conducted at a music store reinforced this. When a customer who was ready to purchase tapes approached the cash register, the salesperson would comment about her own experience with these tapes. Half the time she told the customer that she didn't listen to the type of music the customer was buying. The other half she told the customers that she owned the same tapes and listened to them frequently. The salesperson then asked the customers if they would buy a cleaning kit for their tape player. Out of sixty people who were told that the clerk listened to different music, only twenty bought the cleaning kit. Out of the sixty who were told that she listened to the same type of music, thirty-three bought the cleaning tape.

### Implications

The homophily principle has two basic implications. The first is that people who are similar to each other tend to form clusters (see Principle 3 below). The second implication is that the more similar your employees are to your customers, the easier the communication between them will be. Nintendo used this concept when hiring video game enthusiasts as "game counselors." These counselors, typically just a few years older than the children they advised, were well placed to understand the kids' feedback and to raise excitement about new games. The homophily principle also affects the type of people who apply to work for a company. "You'll find that in a running shoe company, a lot of people are what we call running geeks, people who just like to run 10Ks and hang out with runners," says Helen Rockey, a former executive at Nike and Brooks Sports.

## Principle 3: People Who Are
## Similar to Each Other Form Clusters

**Why do Hell's Angels** travel in packs? Why do the girls in second grade play together? Because people tend to interact with others who are similar to them. The results are clusters—sets of people who share similarities in some dimension of their lives and, as a result, who frequently communicate with one another. Millions of unique clusters are formed according to dimensions such as age, sex, education, occupation, social class, area of interest, geography, and ethnic background.

Clusters and cliques are so common, in fact, that when we don't see them, we're perplexed. A study of social networks in a prison found that the inmate networks always clustered around race, geographical origin, and the type of crime the inmates had committed. Russ Bernard, one of the researchers, says, "In the hundreds of groups among the living units we studied, the cliques always made sense." They did come across one exception: The researchers discovered three men who formed a tight network despite the fact that they didn't seem to have anything in common. As the researchers and the prison staff were contemplating this special case, the three prisoners escaped together. Common goals can also tie people to each other.

Clusters can informally adopt products together. At Buck's restaurant in Woodside, California, one of the in breakfast spots in Silicon Valley, you will see Palm handhelds on almost every table. One morning in December 1998, CNN came to Buck's to film a story about the Palm. When a reporter from CNN asked everyone who had a Palm device to raise his or her hand (or Palm), you could see the power of clustering. "There were PalmPilots everywhere," says Steve Jurvetson, a venture capitalist who witnessed the scene. "When they asked, 'How many of you have Windows CE devices?' one hand went up." (Palm organizers don't use the Windows CE operating system.)

Such clusters can be found everywhere. In marketing End-Note to the academic market, our company often came across university departments that were defined as "All Macintosh" or "All PC." Software usage followed the same pattern: You could find a cluster of WordPerfect users in one building at a university and a cluster of Microsoft Word users in another building. Everett Rogers and Lawrence Kincaid observed this same phenomenon when they studied the adoption of family-planning methods in Korea. The Korean government promoted three types of family planning: oral contraceptive

pills, vasectomy, and IUD. In surveying twenty-five villages, Rogers
and Kincaid found that villages tended to unofficially select one particular method. In fact, the researchers started referring to some villages as "pill villages," to some as "IUD villages," and to one as "the
vasectomy village." Explaining these clusters was easy: After one local network hub chose a method, she began to spread the word about
the advantages of that method and consequently influenced the rest
of her village.

### Implications

The good news for companies is that if your product becomes
the standard within a cluster, it makes it very difficult for competitors
to uproot you from this position. There is a reinforcing effect, as network members tell each other about the product and as your company develops relationships with members of the network. Of course,
this is *bad* news when it's your competitor's product that has been
adopted.

Another implication of this principle is that sometimes a
product becomes so closely associated with a certain cluster that people in other clusters hesitate to adopt it. In the early 1970s, for example, the Birkenstock brand was adopted in alternative-lifestyle
clusters, so much so that wearing Birkenstocks became a political
statement. It took the company years to convince mainstream customers to wear the sandals.

## Principle 4:
## Buzz Spreads Through Common Nodes

We all belong to more than one cluster or clique, which is one
way buzz spreads. To understand this idea, we need to examine the
"small world" or "six degrees of separation" concept, the belief that

any two people are linked through a chain of no more than six other people. The focus here shouldn't be on the number six. The main point is that experiments have demonstrated that any person can be reached through *a limited number* of steps. The key reason for this is that none of us knows exactly the same people. We are usually connected to our family through one cluster, to our colleagues at work through another, and to our friends from college through yet another cluster. In this way clusters are connected to larger networks, ultimately linking people who belong to distant clusters.

The social psychologist Stanley Milgram was one of the first people to study how people are linked to each other. Milgram asked people from Wichita, Kansas, and Omaha, Nebraska, to pass on an envelope to a target person, a wife of a divinity school student in Cambridge, Massachusetts. Each participant in the experiment was given an envelope and a brief description of the target person (where she lived, what she did, etc.). If the participant knew the target person on a personal basis, he or she could mail or give her the envelope directly (none did). Otherwise, the participant was asked to pass it on to someone who they thought was likely to know her or get the envelope closer to her. Four days after the experiment started, someone stopped the target person on the street in Cambridge, handed her an envelope, and said, "Alice, this is for you." This particular envelope originated with a wheat farmer in Kansas, who passed it on to the Episcopalian minister in his hometown, who forwarded it to an instructor at the Episcopal Theological Seminary in Cambridge, who handed the envelope to Alice. Most envelopes in this and in later studies had a longer trip. In one study where people were asked to pass on an envelope from Omaha, Nebraska, to someone in Sharon, Massachusetts, it took, on average, about five intermediate people to get the envelope to the target person.

To see how the small-world phenomenon helps buzz to spread, let's focus on one tiny section of a network. In following the buzz about the book *Cold Mountain* (a book I discuss in the next chap-

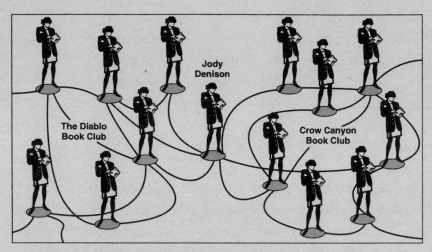

**How Jody Denison helped to spread the word about *Cold Mountain*.**

ter), I met Jody Denison, who lives in the San Francisco Bay Area. She loves books and belongs to two book clubs. Denison heard about *Cold Mountain* from members of one club—the Diablo Book Club—and relayed the information about the book to her friends at the second club—the Crow Canyon Book Club. Essentially she served as the link between the two clusters. "I know that it was dispensed from there to daughters and daughters-in-law and friends," she reports.

## Implications

While it is true that buzz spreads through mutual acquaintances, the degree of control that marketers have on this process is very limited. Let's assume that the following path exists between you and me: Your physician went to school with someone who collaborated on a research paper with a colleague of my dentist. Could I have gotten the word about *The Anatomy of Buzz* to you through our mutual acquaintances? I doubt it. When you first hear the concept of five or six degrees of separation, it doesn't sound like much of a separation, but it is. "When we speak of five intermediaries, we are talking about an enormous psychological distance between the starting and target points," Milgram wrote in 1967. "We should think of the five points as being not five persons apart, but 'five circles of acquaintances' apart— five 'structures' apart. This helps to set it in its proper perspective."

## Principle 5:
## Information Gets Trapped in Clusters

I once promised a new customer of EndNote that I would give her a quick demo of our software and help her install the software on her computer. On the designated day I arrived at her office and quickly installed the software on her Mac. We had hundreds of users already at the university where she worked, so I was a little surprised when she asked me if anyone else around there was using EndNote. She was equally surprised to hear that hundreds of people in the same university were already using the software. The mystery was resolved after we talked further. She was a surgeon involved mostly in clinical work, rather than in basic research. Most of the users of EndNote at that university at the time were Ph.D.'s who did only basic research. There was a significant gap between them.

When we look at a diagram of a network, we first notice the connections. But sometimes you can learn just as much from paying attention to the *absence* of ties. Assume, for example, that you need to spread the word about your product to all the people in the illustration that follows. Although ultimately everyone in the graph is connected, there are two separate clusters in the picture, separated by a void around the letter H (for "hole"). Ronald Burt of the University of Chicago defines this type of a gap as a "structural hole"—"a separation between nonredundant contacts." It is important to realize that often-times different information circulates on either side of a structural hole. The surgeon with whom I talked about EndNote certainly knew of the Ph.D.'s at her facility, and may have occasionally interacted with them. But most of her daily contacts were with other surgeons.

Although these people are linked to each other, they are organized in two clusters separated by a structural hole (H).

## Implications

It is important to identify the gaps between different clusters and to find ways to spread the word about a product to people on both sides of any structural holes. Of course, in real life this neat theory is complicated by the fact that no one is handed a chart of such social networks. All you see is people. Still, trying to identify these gaps—even just knowing that they exist—can be valuable.

### Principle 6:
### Network Hubs and "Connectors"
### Create "Shortcuts"

**Imagine a woman** from California traveling to Germany for her vacation. She stays at a health spa, where she takes yoga classes. One morning she asks her yoga teacher about a certain brand of Scandinavian wooden sandals that she believes would be good for her feet. The yoga teacher tells her about another kind of sandal, with a *cork* sole instead of a wooden one. The woman finds these sandals, buys them, and discovers that they're exactly what she was looking for. When she returns to America, she tells others about the sandals' benefits.

While no one had planned this link, this shortcut was a significant event in the history of the German manufacturer of Birkenstock sandals. The woman who made that trip to Germany is Margot Fraser, who became not only a satisfied customer but also the company's exclusive distributor in the United States, with estimated sales of more than $90 million. Margot Fraser's tie with that yoga trainer is an example of a spontaneous shortcut that connected two clusters and accelerated the diffusion of the product.

Shortcuts that connect clusters may explain the small-world phenomenon, according to Duncan J. Watts and Steven H. Strogatz, who have used computer simulation to analyze this phenomenon. What's surprising, according to Watts, is that it takes very few shortcuts between nodes and clusters to turn a big world into a small world. It only took one person to connect two clusters in Germany and in California, and dramatically accelerate the diffusion of Birkenstock shoes. The point is, however, that without these kinds of shortcuts, the networks would be much slower to spread the word.

**The tie between Margot Fraser and her German yoga teacher accelerated the rate of adoption of Birkenstocks in the United States.**

Margot Fraser served as a "connector," creating a shortcut between clusters. Connectors are not necessarily directly linked to a lot of people. What distinguishes them from hubs is that they can connect two or more clusters. Fraser was originally from Germany, so she was well suited to serve as a connector in this instance—she speaks both languages and is familiar with both cultures. Connectors like Fraser who straddle the worlds are best positioned to create shortcuts.

Another example of people who tend to create shortcuts are venture capitalists. To spread the word about a product to start-up companies in Silicon Valley, try getting the attention of local venture capital firms. The partners in these companies work with many start-ups and serve as a communication channel among them. A message that they value will find its way to their contacts quickly.

### Implications

The first implication of this principle is that companies can deliberately *create* shortcuts by using people within the company to link with individuals in remote networks. In doing so, companies accelerate the natural diffusion process. I expand on this idea in Chapter 8. The other implication is that companies can identify people who have the most potential to create shortcuts. The automotive industry, for example, has been aware for years of the importance of accountants, realtors, and lawyers in spreading the word about their cars. These people, because of the nature of their daily work, often serve as a bridge between cliques and clusters in the local community.

## Principle 7:
## We Talk to Those Around Us

The Internet *does* cross geographical boundaries, but this does not mean that geography doesn't matter anymore. Even in the new era of chat rooms and newsgroups, physical proximity is still key in the way buzz spreads.

My assistant, Haim Zaltzman, asked students to name three people with whom they discussed the singer Lauryn Hill. The vast majority of communications were with people who were close by. There was relatively little communication about Lauryn Hill with people off campus, although all the students have e-mail accounts and access to a phone.

Barry Wellman and David B. Tindall of the University of Toronto reported that while residents of Toronto had global ties, *most* of their ties were still in or near metropolitan Toronto. Thomas J. Allen from MIT, who studied communication among employees in seven R&D labs, measured the walking distances between each of the technical people in these labs and asked them to keep track of whom they communicated with for several months. The results showed that the closer people were to one another, the more likely they were to talk. Although these two studies were conducted before the Internet era, I would be very surprised if this fundamental aspect of human behavior has changed. It's simply so convenient and natural to talk most with those who are around us.

When you think about it, this makes perfect sense. First, remember that most people hang out with people like themselves—perfect candidates for a conversation. Add to that the fact that it's still easier to talk than to type e-mail, and then factor in the fact that much "product talk" is incidental. (Remember that some of our talking is motivated by a grooming instinct). Although the Internet allows people to connect with anyone around the world, and many do, physical proximity is still an excellent predictor of those with whom you will share information.

## Implications

In the same way that regional dialects continue to live on in the United States despite decades of national TV, local and regional influences remain important, despite the Internet. Since people talk to those around them, in marketing a product or service it is important to create a presence in every geographical location. This means that traditional marketing focused on ZIP codes, database marketing, and brick and mortar sales outlets are still key in spreading the word. The networks are still (and I believe always will be) pulled by social gravity to the ground around us.

## Principle 8:
## Weak Ties Are Surprisingly Strong

In the late 1960s Mark Granovetter, a graduate student at Harvard, was interested in how people found out about their jobs. He conducted a pilot study to explore the topic. One question that sparked Granovetter's curiosity was how the shape of people's close networks helped them in their job search. He asked his interviewees to name the five people with whom they spent the most amount of time and to draw a diagram of how these people were linked to each other. It was basic knowledge that most people find out about jobs from other people rather than from advertising, so Granovetter asked his interviewees to identify the person who referred them to their last job. To his surprise, that person was never on the diagram of close friends. When he asked them to tell him about the friend who *did* refer them to the job, they would often correct him by saying, "Not a friend, an acquaintance."

Granovetter was intrigued. As a result of that pilot study, he surveyed 282 professional, technical, and managerial workers in the Boston suburb of Newton. He found that most of these people—about 56 percent—found their jobs through a personal contact and, as in the original study, this personal contact was usually *not* a close friend. In fact, of those who found their job through a personal connection, only about 17 percent learned about their last position from close friends or family. Most people found out about it from people *outside* their immediate close network—people they would see occasionally or rarely, such as former workmates or old college friends.

This phenomenon, which Granovetter called "the strength of weak ties," goes well beyond just the job market. Your closest friends—those who move in the same social circles as you do—are likely to be exposed to the same sources of information as you are. Therefore, they don't usually bring you fresh news. On the other hand, people outside this group are much more likely to hear things that you do not. In this way, weak ties with distant acquaintances are most apt to bring in information that is new.

When Elon and Kimbal Musk tried to raise money for their start-up, they began by talking to other young entrepreneurs in Silicon Valley, as well as to venture capitalists. These conversations, they found, usually got them nowhere. "We had a good story, a good product, a good team. Everything was in place, but we couldn't get them to listen to us. So we said we'll do it ourselves, and we tried to find people in the community to give us a little bit of money." They talked to anyone who would listen, and they went outside the obvious networks of entrepreneurs and computer enthusiasts.

It was the founders' landlady who finally put them in touch with an angel investor who provided part of the seed investment. She was the weak tie. A few months later it was one of their commission-based salespeople who put them in touch with venture capitalists, "who were all over us to give us money." The deal was closed within two weeks and their Web technology company, Zip2, was on its way, with several million dollars to finance its development efforts. "Some of the people who you think will not be able to help you in any way know people who can help you in ways you cannot believe," says Kimbal Musk.

## Implications

Since people tend to form networks with individuals just like themselves, who are likely to be exposed to the same sources of information, people *outside* these networks are important in bringing in fresh data. The implication to businesspeople is clear: Don't listen only to your close network—it is likely to rehash what you already know. Diversify your connections.

# Principle 9:
# The Net Nurtures Weak Ties

**It's easy to** maintain weak ties on the Internet, or at least *easier* on the Net than by phone. Calling someone on the phone is somewhat intrusive. Dropping the person a friendly note via e-mail is an easy way to keep in touch without too much obligation. You can also quickly create new ties on the Net and use these ties to acquire information. Barry Wellman and Milena Gulia of the University of Toronto argue that there is "ample evidence of the usefulness of acquiring new information from weak ties on the Net." Many people in newsgroups and on-line forums either maintain very weak ties or don't know each other at all. "Our weak ties will explode tremendously with the Internet," says Valdis Krebs, an expert on social networks. "I can have hundreds and thousands of these kinds of connections because they don't take a lot of time and energy to maintain."

This explosion in weak ties, however, should not lead us to the conclusion that technology is on the verge of linking everyone on the planet. Our own operating system, the brain, is capable of managing only so many links at any given time. The fact is that we can't (and probably don't want to) maintain links to an unlimited number of people. One proof is that despite the fact that many of us live among millions of other people in major metropolitan areas, "we still know only about the same number of people as our long-distant ancestors did when they roamed the plains of the American Midwest or the savannahs of eastern Africa," psychologist Robin Dunbar says.

It is difficult to determine how many links each one of us *can* handle. It's even hard to figure out how many links we actually do maintain. Scientists have delineated three levels of links. At the most intimate level the number seems to be 11 to 12. These numbers consistently come up when people are asked to list the names of those whose death they would find devastating. At the next level you can find people with whom you feel comfortable—people you wouldn't be "embarrassed about joining uninvited for a drink, if you happened to bump into them in a bar" as Dunbar puts it. Dunbar argues that "the figure of 150 seems to represent the maximum number of individuals with whom we can have a genuinely social relationship." Finally there are acquaintances, people you know but are not too close to. The average of those seems to be between 500 and 1,500 although the results of specific studies vary greatly and the question is still considered open by most scholars.

## Implications

The increase in weak ties on the Net can explain why information travels much faster today. The Internet creates millions of shortcuts of weak ties across clusters. There are many pieces of information that wouldn't warrant a special phone call to distant friends, but that you may put in an e-mail message and send to several of your acquaintances.

The fact that there is a limit to the number of ties one can maintain means that clusters are here to stay. Because we can manage just so many links, and because we prefer to form links with those similar to us, we will continue to cluster around people like us.

# Principle 10:
## Networks Go Across Markets

Bill McGowan, the founder of MCI once said, "No matter how hard we service our national accounts, when a top executive goes home, he's just another consumer. We can either lose or find ourselves in jeopardy on an account because a client can't get a clear connection to his or her mother . . ." McGowan recognized something simple: A top executive who uses MCI at his company—the business market—also wants good service on his home line—the home market. People belong to more than one market, and they are connected to people who are part of other markets. Take Joe, who is shopping for some new software for his home computer at CompUSA. He also has a PC at the office, and his daughter Jane has a PC at college. The computer industry has traditionally viewed the world as divided into three distinct markets: home, business, and educational. But Joe plays a role in all three—and he's not alone.

Again it's important to adopt a network point of view. Markets are often defined by categories. For example, marketers target men ages twenty-one to twenty-six. But we need to also remember that "men twenty-one to twenty-six" usually have ties to women twenty-one to twenty-six, as well as ties to men and women twenty-one to sixty-five at their workplace.

Going back to our image of the invisible networks, you can think of such networks as the basic foundation—individuals who are connected through social networks. Imagine a market category as a transparency put over the networks. On this transparency you circle those individuals who are in the market for a particular product.

### Implications

You never know how people in one market category are linked to people in other categories. Messages that you try to direct to one group of people can easily find their ways to other people. As a result, stories about bad service experienced at your "low-end" segment, for example, can move to your "high-end" customers.

There is a common thread running through many of these principles. It's the tension between networks. The close-by networks that you can see versus the distant invisible ones. The networks of those who are similar to us versus networks of people who are different. Strong ties with those who don't tell us much that we don't already know versus weak ties that provide us with fresh information. Local networks versus the Internet.

When I think about invisible networks, those thin glowing lines that link 6 billion people, I see them floating above the earth. Thousands of years ago, when the only connections among human beings were made face to face, these thin blue lines could be drawn on the ground. The first human being to jump on the back of a horse elevated the networks. So did the people who started sailing, driving, and flying. Every technological breakthrough allowed people to create links that were not bound by geographical origin. The telegraph, the car, the phone, the Internet have elevated the networks even further—to a point where geography doesn't matter as much as it did just a few years earlier.

But while some forces are pulling the networks up, others keep drawing them back to the ground: the human desire for physical connection, nationalism, ethnicity, our desire to be around people who are similar to us, our brain's capacity to keep track of only a limited number of connections. All these forces are stronger than any technology. The Internet gives people the ability to talk with others across the ocean about topics they share an interest in. And people love that. But we also like to go to local churches, farmers' markets, and bookstores and rub elbows with other people. As a result, like a piece of metal caught between two magnets, the networks float just above ground level.

# The Busy Network Paradox

Like all other people, marketers are members of some clusters and geographically or mentally distant from others. Unless they make a conscious effort to look beyond their social horizons, often networks remain invisible to them. We tend to pay attention to the networks that are "happening"—the active clusters where we sell a lot of product—and ignore those where our product is not popular. Managers, especially successful ones, are inundated with feedback from active clusters and industry circles. This creates an illusion in their minds that all clusters are covered, due to what I call "the busy network paradox": The more successful a company is, the more likely it is to be flooded by messages from its existing networks. Its managers, as a result, may fail to notice the nonactive networks.

Makers of hard drives in the early eighties, for example, were busy marketing to networks of mainframe manufacturers who bought 8-inch hard drives. They ignored new emerging networks of PC makers who were looking for 5.25-inch drives. The same story repeated itself a few years later, when the computer industry slowly switched from 5.25-inch drives to 3.5-inch drives. Clayton Christensen, describing this phenomenon in *The Innovator's Dilemma*, indicates that it happened again to some hard-drive manufacturers with the switch to even smaller drives. This time the hard drive makers actually produced prototypes for the smaller disks but couldn't find any buyers. Christensen describes a visit he had with a CEO of a large disk-drive manufacturer around that time. The man pointed to a prototype on the shelf and told the Harvard professor that it was the fourth generation of a 1.8-inch drive, but that his company hadn't sold any. Chris-

What does all this mean to you as a marketer? It means that if you market a conversation product, your customers are very likely to be talking about it—maybe even as you're reading this paragraph. Some are talking with their neighbors, co-workers, and friends— good old word-of-mouth marketing. Some are communicating over the Internet with people in other states, countries, or continents. And this combination of local and global networks is what makes buzz so important now. Understanding these rules can give you a hint as to what you can do to stimulate the flow of buzz—the subject of chapters to follow.

tensen cited market research that demonstrated sizable market potential. But the CEO insisted that there wasn't a market: "We've had that drive in our catalog for eighteen months. Everyone knows we've got it, but nobody wants it."

About a month later Christensen met someone who had previously worked on a mapping and navigating systems for Honda. Christensen was curious about how they stored the data for that system and was told they used a 1.8-inch disk drive.

"Who do you buy them from?" Christensen asked.

"It's kind of funny," the person replied. "You can't buy them from any of the big disk-drive companies. We get them from a little start-up company in Colorado."

Christensen describes the CEO of the disk drive company as one of the most astute managers he had ever met. Yet when the CEO said, "Everyone knows we've got it, but nobody wants it," it was clear that even he was misled. The CEO was too busy focusing on the network of computer manufacturers (the traditional customers for hard drives). He failed to notice the existence of other networks. This is a prime example of the busy-network paradox.

It's hard to break out of it, because we *are* busy taking care of issues in the active networks, supporting our supporters. It's hard also because it means we have to leave a comfortable environment we are familiar with and move to one that isn't. But by being aware of the busy-network paradox, companies will realize it's essential to fight our natural tendency to hang out in our comfort zone. Only by mingling in a variety of networks can we get a sense of what's happening beyond our immediate frame of reference.

A song went around from fiddler to
fiddler and each one added something
and took something away.
—Charles Frazier, *Cold Mountain*

# How Buzz

# Spreads

**6.** **Now that you understand the** structure of the networks—the highway system, if you will—it's time to examine how buzz—the traffic—spreads through the system. To do this, I first want to examine the buzz about one product, the publication of the novel *Cold Mountain,* which became a surprise blockbuster bestseller. It's impossible, of course, to expose *all* the buzz about such a book, since millions of comments related to the book have leaped from brain to brain. But analyzing *Cold Mountain* will allow us to peek at the invisible networks and try to use this snapshot to figure out how buzz spreads.

One thing needs to be pointed out before we start. Buzz is not water and it doesn't flow like water. Yet it is very tempting (and I, too, give in to the temptation from time to time) to use water as a metaphor to describe the process. When the French sociologist Gabriel Tarde described how fashion spread in France at the turn of the century, he used the metaphor of a water tower. Fashion, he believed, originated in the highest social class and flowed downward through a "waterfall of imitation": Upper-class women adopted the new fashion first, middle-class women observed them and started adopting the new fashion, and so on. Others who have studied this over the years have used terms such as "trickle-down" or the "two-step flow" model to describe the process. These concepts are not necessarily wrong—in fact, I believe that they describe important *components* of the process—but these terms immediately suggest that the source is in some way more important than the receiving end. Adopting this view, you assume that a French woman who has a new dress is superior to the one who doesn't. A journalist who writes about a new computer is above the reader who isn't yet aware of the new gadget. A publisher of a book is somehow more important than the bookstore, which is somehow above the customer. The water metaphor also assumes that information flows only in one direction, ignoring the fact that there's often a *dialogue* between people who spread the word about a product and those who are on the receiving end.

While I recognize that some hierarchy always exists in the way information spreads in the networks, the spread is not as hierarchical as some people think. If I were forced to use a water metaphor, I would say that buzz is more like underground water. It may trickle any which way: down, sideways, or even up. But I'd rather stick to the concept expressed throughout the book: the perspective of the invisible networks, those 6 billion nodes spread all around the planet. At some point somewhere in the vast networks, an idea is cooked up in the brain of one person, or sometimes of a few people—a node or a small cluster of them. And it starts spreading from there.

## Where Did It All Start?

**In the case** of *Cold Mountain*, author Charles Frazier first heard the story that would become the book's backbone from his father in the late eighties. Frazier's father, a retired high school principal in Franklin, North Carolina, was researching their family history at the time. He told his son about a great-great-uncle, a Confederate soldier by the name of W. P. Inman, who deserted the army while recovering from his battle wounds. "It's like someone saying, 'Here's a brief outline for a book; what do you think?' " Frazier told the *Washington Post* years later. Frazier couldn't find much more about that great-great-uncle, but the idea was planted in his mind. Over the next seven or so years he developed this very thin outline into a 449-page novel.

At what point does an idea leave the brain of its creator and start traveling in the invisible networks? In the case of Frazier, this would have probably taken a long time if it weren't for his wife, Katherine, who threatened to smuggle part of the manuscript to Kaye Gibbons, a bestselling local author whom the Fraziers knew through their children. Frazier proved willing to part with a hundred or so pages, and Gibbons was impressed with his work. She referred him to Leigh Feldman, a literary agent in New York City who works with Liz Darhansoff, Gibbons's agent. Feldman remembers receiving three outstanding chapters. "I wrote him and said that I loved it," she recalls. Months later she received a large part of the manuscript.

Feldman showed the manuscript to several editors in book publishing houses. She also showed it to a friend, Elisabeth Schmitz, who was the head of subrights at Grove/Atlantic, a midsize independent publisher. Schmitz's job at Grove was to deal with foreign and domestic rights. She had never edited a book before, but she fell in love with *Cold Mountain*.

We haven't talked yet about passion. We haven't talked about energy. But these forces started to form behind *Cold Mountain*. "I walked into my boss's office, Morgan Entrekin, and said, 'This is the most incredible thing I've read since I've come to work for you,'" Elisabeth Schmitz remembers. "'And I know you have a Christmas party tonight, and I know you usually go and stay up all night, but you *have* to read this tonight.'" Entrekin read the manuscript that night. He called Schmitz first thing in the morning and asked, "What do we have to do to get it?" A few days later Grove/Atlantic owned the world rights to the novel.

Only so much buzz can be generated in an industry at any particular point in time, and everyone knows that. Therefore, when left alone, most new products and ideas encounter objection or indifference in their industries. There is no buzz. The industry raises its head, mutters to itself, and gets back to its usual business. At first *Cold Mountain* was no exception. "Nobody even gave it two thoughts. It was a first literary Southern novel," says Feldman. It would take significant efforts to change that.

## How the First People
## Outside the Industry Heard About It

**We'll jump about** eighteen months ahead, to around the time when the book was actually published. The first printing of the book was 26,000 copies. As soon as it was published, it started to sell well. "It went on the bestseller list within about six weeks, and it was not from big media attention. It was from word of mouth and old-fashioned bookselling," says Morgan Entrekin, president of Grove/Atlantic.

Mike Jordan, a professor of social psychology at Francis Marion University (near Florence, South Carolina), first read about the book in a prepublication review in the *Charlotte Observer*. He was fascinated by the review and asked the people at his local store, Booksamillion, to give him a call when the book became available. Once he and his wife read the book, they were so excited that they bought three more copies and gave them to their parents and to a good friend. In addition to telling people about the book, Jordan posted a review on Amazon.com, participated in a panel discussion about the book that was aired on the local-access television station, and, although he is not a literature professor, gave *Cold Mountain* as one of the options for a graduate-student project. Six students chose the book, and "all but one of them loved it and then passed it on and talked about it with other people," he says. Seeing the activities of a network hub such as Jordan, you start to realize how powerful individual "hubs" can be in promoting a product they like.

Researchers who study communication refer to what happened in Jordan's case as an example of the "two-step flow model": Information flows from mass media to network hubs and from the hubs to the rest of the population. I talked to several network hubs who learned about the book in this way. Lynne Jenkins first read about the novel in *Southern Living.* "It sounded like something I'd like, because my family came from that area," she says. Like Jordan, Jenkins went to a bookstore right away, but they didn't have the book in stock yet. When she finally found it, she skimmed it at the store and decided she liked Frazier's style. "He used a lot of the old-fashioned terms like I remember my grandmother used. Definitely regional lingo and slang for different things in the kitchen, different types of herbs . . ." Jenkins bought the book and loved it. She estimates that she told ten people about it. She also gave the book to a relative who lives in the area where the action takes place. She, too, posted a review on Amazon.com.

## Buzz Spreads in All Directions

While the two-step flow model obviously describes part of how buzz spreads, buzz refuses to follow neat patterns. The word about products doesn't disseminate only from the media to opinion leaders and from them to the rest of us. Jo Alice Canterbury, for example, a reader from the San Francisco Bay Area, heard about *Cold Mountain* from a friend, *not* from the media. She went on to tell at least fifty people about the book. First she recommended it to her husband. This was an important side current within families—a lot of women felt that *Cold Mountain* was a book that they could pass on to their husbands. She also remembers telling family and friends in New Orleans, Arkansas, Texas, Colorado, and Washington. A flight attendant who crossed the Pacific three times a month, Canterbury took advantage of dozens of opportunities to tell passengers about the book.

Some readers heard about *Cold Mountain* from friends who aren't network hubs—just folks who tell a friend or two about a book. Others heard about it from clerks at the bookstore. And in a case of "reverse flow," some clerks got excited about the book only after hearing early readers' reactions. This reverse flow happens at another level of the distribution channel as well. Patricia Kelly, a sales representative for Publishers Group West (PGW, the company that distributed *Cold Mountain* to bookstores), said that she became intrigued about the book after talking with several independent bookstore owners who had already gotten galleys from the publisher.

A lot of information about the book was spread over the Internet. Last time I counted, there were more than nine hundred reviews of *Cold Mountain* on Amazon.com. It's no longer one review in the *New York Times* that gets everyone talking. And the media's glowing reviews don't immediately translate into enthusiastic reaction among today's skeptical customers, as one reader indicated: "You know, when reviewers start talking about an almost-perfect book, you're bound to be disappointed. I wasn't." Another reader said he simply found *Cold Mountain* at a bookstore without talking to anyone: "I was killing time waiting for a train and picked it up off a front display table in the train station bookstore. I judge books by the quality of the writing, period. I'd never heard of Frazier (how could I have?), but I could immediately tell that the prose was gifted. I almost never buy novels in hardback, but I was so taken in by the first couple of pages, that I bought it. There is no marketing substitute for good writing."

The last point is a key one and one that's not always taken into consideration in studying buzz. The flow of information about a product cannot be separated from the quality of the product itself. *Cold Mountain* traveled in the invisible networks and directly interacted with each reader. Over the course of reading 449 pages, something happens between a reader and a book that determines whether the reader will pass the word on, to how many others, and how enthusiastically. As I argue in the next chapter, "contagious attributes" built into the product—including the extent to which expectations are met or exceeded—are the biggest factors in determining how much buzz a product gets.

## What Made the Word Spread

Of course, I could end the discussion right here and explain buzz by focusing on the quality of the book itself. But we have all seen excellent books that did *not* become bestsellers. The quality of the writing in a book can only partially explain buzz. What was it then that made people talk about this book out of all the books they could talk about?

### Energy

The first observation is that it didn't happen by itself. A tremendous amount of energy was put behind this book. First, the comments that traveled in the networks about *Cold Mountain* were charged with energy. The people at Grove and PGW deeply believed in this book and warmly recommended it. Kim Wylie, a senior vice president at PGW, was one of the people "infected" by *Cold Mountain* early on. She became one of the biggest forces pushing the book, telling everyone around her about it, including buyers at Barnes & Noble and other accounts she manages. Everyone at PGW started talking about it as more and more sales reps read the book. These salespeople in turn spread the word to a network of independent bookstores, who in turn backed the book by giving it special attention: telling customers about it, featuring it in their newsletters, displaying it in a prominent place at the store.

Beyond just passion, energy is about the time and money put behind a product. Entrekin and Schmitz spent hours walking through the stacks at a Barnes & Noble with a pad and pen, writing down about 150 names of writers around the country who they felt would be interested in reading *Cold Mountain*. "We weren't necessarily asking them to give us a quote that we would use. It was more just 'Here's a great book, we want to share it with you,'" says Entrekin. Some of these authors in turn started talking about the book within their networks.

Grove/Atlantic also knew how to keep fueling the book's success by putting more of their time and money behind it every step of the way. For example, the first run of galleys was 500. When they noticed that the reaction to the advance copies was outstanding, they immediately printed an additional 1,000 copies. And as these copies started to generate even greater buzz, they printed another 2,500 to 3,000 more. Altogether they sent out in excess of 4,000 advance copies to bookstore owners, buyers, and anyone who could help spread the word, starting buzz in numerous networks. "We believe that taking the time and spending the money on making advance galleys, which a lot of publishers don't do, is one of the best ways to promote a well-written book," says Elisabeth Schmitz. Of course, every publisher sends out galleys, but the number that Grove sent out— 4,000—was particularly high, especially for a literary novel. Because these copies were produced in small print runs, the unit cost was relatively high (about $8 to $10 per copy), a cost Grove willingly absorbed.

Everyone involved in selling the book—including its author—put time and effort into promoting it. Months before publication, Entrekin took Frazier to meet some bookstore owners, buyers, and clerks. As soon as the publisher noticed that this book went beyond just the regionalism of the Southeast, Entrekin extended Frazier's tour to other parts of the country. Reaching out to retailers and readers this way sparked thousands of shortcuts into small cliques and remote clusters that allowed buzz about the book, and the book itself, to spread as it did.

Such energy can be contagious. Grove demonstrated so much enthusiasm and confidence in the book that the rest of the industry responded. Grove even sent galleys to sales reps of *competing* publishing houses, feeling that they would take an interest in a book of such quality. "People are supportive of a good piece of work even if it's not coming from their company. Everybody in book publishing loves reading a good book," Entrekin says.

At a certain point the book's popularity exploded. A first-time author who creates a serious literary novel that gets on the bestseller list . . . We all love a success story like this. A lot of goodwill surrounded the book. "Everyone in the publishing industry said, 'Go! Go! Go! Go!'" agent Leigh Feldman remembers. Carl Lennertz of Random House, who published a weekly newsletter for independent bookstores, featured the book enthusiastically. Larry Kirshbaum, CEO of Warner Books, became an unofficial spokesperson for *Cold Mountain*.

Entrekin is the first to emphasize the importance of the quality of the book itself in the buzz that it created. "You couldn't just try to do this for any kind of book. It has to be a special book," he says. "What you're trying to do is get the book in a position where it can make its own fate." Nobody can say for sure what would have happened to *Cold Mountain* if the energy of Entrekin, Schmitz, and their colleagues hadn't been marshaled behind the title. But we know what happened when it was. The book sold 1.6 million copies of the hardcover edition alone, an astounding number.

## Credibility

Buzz travels most smoothly through channels built on trust. Customers of many independent bookstores have learned to trust the clerks behind the counter. One customer in Danville, California, for example, told me how much she trusts Michael Barnard, the owner of Rakestraw, a local bookstore. "Many times he'll recommend a book, and I don't even have to read the cover," she said. When Barnard recommended *Cold Mountain*, that was all she needed to know.

Mike Barnard first heard about *Cold Mountain* from Patricia Kelly of Publishers Group West. "She said that there was one book on the spring list that I really had to pay attention to," he remembers. She gave him the galleys, and he read it. Kelly enjoys tremendous credibility among her clients. In 1999 she was named "Publishers Weekly Rep of the Year." And in an article profiling her, one store owner said, "If she tells you that this book is something she really likes, you know she's not making that up."

I heard almost the exact same remarks about Morgan Entrekin from two people. Entrekin was telling people that this was going to be one of the best books he would ever publish, "and he doesn't throw that around freely," one of them commented. About a month before publication, Grove/Atlantic had a dinner for leading booksellers in the San Francisco Bay Area to promote the book. It was the first time that Barnard met Entrekin, and he was impressed—by the way the publisher read, by his enthusiasm, by his commitment to a title that had none of the hallmarks of a book destined to become a bestseller.

People who spread the word effectively are not necessarily

loud, and you won't always see them gesticulating furiously. They are people whom we trust. Most of them understand that trust can be fragile. They enjoy their credibility, and when they back a product, they know that they're putting their reputation on the line. "I would not do this for a book that I was not as enthusiastic about, because I just couldn't afford to," Entrekin explains.

There is another important point about credibility. No matter how much credibility one has, the best buzz comes from *third* parties—not from the manufacturer itself. In a paradoxical way, your competitors often are the ones who signal to the industry whether what you're doing is worth talking about. "The really interesting thing in the word-of-mouth process is that the very first place that a product has to gain acceptance is from its competitors," says Stewart Alsop, a venture capitalist in Silicon Valley and former editor of *Infoworld*. A new technology product that is not recognized by its competitors (by their reacting to it) is immediately dismissed in the industry.

In the case of *Cold Mountain* the recognition was positive and came from other publishers who bought the rights to publish the book in additional languages or formats. When Grove/Atlantic sold the paperback rights before hardcover publication to Vintage (a Random House imprint) for $300,000, that sent a clear message to people in the publishing industry. Such an amount for a first novel by an unknown author made people in the industry talk. In addition, bookstore buyers started to hear about the book not only from the sales reps of Publishers Group West but also from the Vintage reps, who were going to sell the paperback many months later.

## How Buzz Became Buying

Let's assume you have not read *Cold Mountain*. Suppose you meet a friend at a party—let's call him Alex—and you start talking about books. And suppose Alex mentions *Cold Mountain,* saying, "Oh, you ought to read this book." Let's examine what happens as a result of this molecule of buzz.

During the first few moments of conversation Alex's comments will go through some initial tests in your brain. One is the relevance test: Are you in the market for a book like *Cold Mountain?* This will greatly affect your level of interest. Typically, people are much more receptive to hearing about products they think they might want to buy. If you are interested, you're likely to ask a question about the book, such as "What's it about?" Alex might tell you that it takes place during the Civil War. You may get turned off, pointing out that you don't usually read books about the Civil War era. Alex would then quickly point out that it's not a typical war book. The conversation that develops shows what makes buzz so powerful. Unlike mass media, word of mouth allows you and Alex to exchange information so that you can make sure you understand each other.

Credibility is the next test that Alex's comment will have to pass. How much credibility he has with you depends on your mutual history, his reputation, and your overall impression of him. For example, if he has recommended ten books to you in the past and you loved every single one of them, you would be likely to trust his recommendation.

Another factor that will determine what happens to that comment is the energy behind it. If Alex says, "*Cold Mountain* is the best book I've ever read. You *must* read it!" while raising his martini in the air, there would be more energy in his comment and therefore the probability that it would be passed on would be higher than if he just said, "I really liked it."

What will happen next? Any number of things could happen. A waiter may pass by with a plate of mini–sausage rolls, or someone may join you and you'll move to a different topic, or maybe the party will be over and it will be time to go home. My point is that a comment is just a comment. Millions of other things in a customer's life will distract him or her from information about a product. This is the environment in which Alex's comment will live in your brain—surrounded by constant distractions.

Although it is possible that you'll go to the bookstore first thing the next morning and buy the book, it is also possible that you'll store the comment for future reference or that you'll let it evaporate from your memory altogether.

Up until now we assumed that you and Alex are having a conversation in a vacuum. We ignored the networks around you. But your decision is influenced not only by Alex but by others in your social network. In examining this effect, let me digress for a moment and tell you about something I saw on a sweltering day in a small town in Italy. It was unbearably hot. My wife and I were walking down the street when we noticed a young woman who had dragged a plastic chair away from a nearby café and placed it so that she was facing an archway. After a few moments a man saw her and brought over another chair. He placed it next to the woman and sat down. Not a word was said, just a sigh from the young woman. It didn't take long before an older lady grabbed a chair and joined them. Now the three

Each of us has a threshold level that determines how many people in our network need to adopt a certain behavior before we do.

were sitting there. Too curious to go on, we went to stand behind them and felt the cool breeze that came through the opening between two houses.

The same sequence of events takes place in every small group that faces a new idea or a new product. There are always people who come up with the idea or who are fast to adopt it. Then there are those who follow. Finally those who lag behind (like those you don't see in this picture, who stayed to sit in the café). "Some people adopt when few in their network adopt, and some people wait until most of their network adopt," says Tom Valente of the University of Southern California.

To return to *Cold Mountain:* In addition to Alex's credibility, the energy of his comment, and whether you are in the market or not, your behavior depends to a large extent on your adoption threshold and on how many people in *your* network have already bought and read the book. Once enough people in your network have read *Cold Mountain* to surpass your threshold point, you will probably follow their lead.

Let us assume that you bought the book and read it. Based on your experience reading the book, you will form an opinion about it. The quality of the product is key. Whether or not you will pass on comments to other people depends to a large extent on how *you* judge the book. This is the beauty of the word-of-mouth phenomenon. Every node in the network who decides to try a product ultimately performs his or her own quality-control test and, based on the results, decides whether to pass the word further. As a marketer, you can't force customers to say anything positive about your product, just as you can't order people to love you. Even if they say the words, they won't mean them. Buzz is authentic because it is uncoerced.

# How Risk Affects Buzz

Suppose that you're a cardiologist who is considering a new device for use in heart surgery. A lot more is at stake when you make this decision than when a consumer buys *Cold Mountain*. The worst that can happen if you choose a bad book is that you will be bored and lose a few dollars. By choosing the wrong medical device, you could kill one of your patients.

The increased risk affects how buzz spreads. In risky situations people turn to mega-hubs for help. As a reader, you may not care that much about what a prestigious critic writing for the *New York Times Book Review* thinks about *Cold Mountain*. As a cardiologist, you care a lot about what the top professor in the country's best medical center says about the device you're going to use on Thursday in Operating Room 3.

In planning the marketing strategy for a new product, you should think about whether information flow in your industry tends to be centralized. Is your product associated with risk? Is it highly innovative in a largely conservative industry? Is it the kind of product that will be adopted at first by a small number of forward-thinking individuals and only later by a wider circle of people? Or will it be adopted by people all around the networks simultaneously?

The higher the monetary or psychological risks involved in the consumer's decision to buy, the more the classic adoption patterns will apply. Scholars who study the diffusion of innovations have traditionally classified the population into five adoption categories: innovators, early adopters, early majority, late majority, and laggards.

At first a few innovators who are willing to take risks will adopt an innovation. This group is usually considered to be about 2.5 percent of the population. They will be followed by the early adopters, a group that is usually about 13.5 percent of the population. Then the first mainstream group, the early majority (34 percent), will start to adopt the innovation, followed by the late majority (34 percent). Finally the laggards (16 percent) will adopt the innovation. This model has its roots in a classic study by Ryan and Gross, who examined how an innovation was adopted among farmers in Iowa. Since 1962 it has been described extensively by Everett Rogers in the four editions of his classic work *Diffusion of Innovations*. In the early 1990s Geoffrey Moore brought the model to the attention of technology marketers by arguing that there is a chasm between the early adopters (who are interested in the technology) and the early majority, a mainstream group that is more pragmatic about technology.

This model was designed to describe actual adoption rather than just buzz about

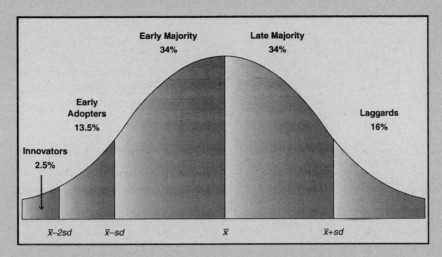

an innovation. Buzz spreads in a somewhat similar way, but there are certain differences that are worth pointing out. Since the risk in *hearing* about an innovation is much lower than the risk in adopting it, buzz spreads at a faster rate than actual adoption. For early adopters we can expect to see a shorter gap between awareness and adoption, whereas later adopters may take longer between the time they hear about something and when they actually buy it.

What companies like Hotmail did that revolutionized the adoption process was to reduce the risk to almost zero. The service was free, so the monetary risk was nil. Hotmail was also extremely easy to use—it just took an Internet connection and forty-five seconds of the customer's time to get started—so the risk of wasting time was minimal. That meant that even someone who might normally wait for others to try it first was willing to jump right in.

When the risk is high, we can expect a slow adoption spread that starts from centers of influence. A mission-critical piece of software is likely to be adopted much more carefully than a personal e-mail account. Customers will tend to take their time, letting the innovators adopt products first and learning from their mistakes. This is true for most products essential to getting a job done.

Other products, too, are judged from the perspective of risk. For example, the risk of appearing ridiculous affects what clothes people are willing to wear. Most items that affect one's personal appearance come under great scrutiny. Adopting a new kind of sunglasses, a style that is visually outrageous, is something mainstream dressers will do only after significant prompting. So if you make sunglasses, it's important for you to make sure that visible, influential people—whose sense of style is respected—wear your product. Luxottica, a large manufacturer and distributor of sunglasses, home to such brands as Yves Saint Laurent and Giorgio Armani, tries to place their cutting-edge styles in the movies. They view celebrities as innovators who can lead the way in transmitting the new look to early adopters and, from there, to mainstream groups. "As someone wears it in the movies, it goes right down to early adopters, early majority, late majority, and eventually it becomes an accepted thing and part of conservative style and fashion," says Steve Hollander, VP of marketing for the company.

## Understanding How Buzz Spreads

**The flow of** information is unique to each market, product, and niche. So how does information spread among *your* customers? Marketing research studies often focus on the individual's beliefs and attitudes. They tell you, for example, that 23 percent of your customers are males over 40, that 63 percent of them are aware of your competition, and that speed is the most important product attribute for 32 percent of them. This is important. But how do these individuals interact with one another? Who influences them? How many other customers are they connected to? What do they tell them? The spread of buzz, since it is not always easy to trace, tends to be neglected. To learn how to help create buzz, you should be able to answer questions like these:

■ From whom do your clients or customers typically learn about your product?

■ What do people say when they recommend your product?

■ How fast does information about your product spread compared with other products?

■ Who are the network hubs?

■  **Where does the information hit a roadblock?**

■  **How many sources of information does a customer rely on? Which ones are more important?**

■  **What other kinds of information spread through the same networks?**

Most likely your research already addresses some of these questions, and you may have some assumptions about the answers to others. But isn't it important to know for sure?

It's crucial to understand that buzz about a product never spreads as simply as the two-step flow model would indicate—from company to media and mega-hubs and from these hubs to the public. Yet the two-step model has been blithely assumed by countless companies over the years. It's easy to see why. It's tempting to think about the communication process between a company and potential customers as a linear process. Just send a press release to the media influencers, meet them at a cocktail party, and they'll do the work for you. Another version of this model assumes that the distribution channel is king. Just fax the latest news to the company's distributors, and the distributors will rush to tell the dealers, who in turn will communicate the news, enthusiastically of course, to their customers. But real networks are not linear or predictable. People talk to each other unpredictably. For example, a mega-hub may sit down next to a customer at the airport, who tells him or her how lousy your service is. Customer A surfs the Net and finds a discussion group in which Customer B warmly endorses your company. The fact is, dealers often hear about new products from customers, not the other way around. The trickle-down effect looks nice and neat on paper, but networks aren't organizational charts.

Why is this important to marketers? Because there are two traps companies can fall into. The first is thinking that creating buzz is all about network hubs. If you exclusively focus on the two-step

## Industry Buzz Versus Customer Buzz

A common mistake companies make is to pay attention to what is being said in industry circles and to assume that they are getting all the buzz they need. They are not. Industry buzz and customer buzz are two different things. Both are important. Industry buzz tends to focus on the future. A rumor you hear over lunch with an industry analyst may prove to be a fact in six months. Customer buzz, on the other hand, centers on the present: Comments read on the Net or heard on the street can tell you what people think about your product today. You should be listening to both.

Why are the two types of buzz different? The first reason is in the level of involvement. Although customers can become highly involved with certain types of products, they usually don't reach the level of involvement of industry networks, where everyone has a lot at stake: money, career, ego, dreams. The second difference is geographical concentration. While customers are often spread all over the world, industries tend to cluster. Silicon Valley, Detroit, New York City, and Hollywood are well-known examples of industry clusters, but the phenomenon is much more universal. "Clusters are a striking feature of virtually every national, regional, state, and even metropolitan economy, especially in more economically advanced nations," says Michael Porter of Harvard Business School.

flow model, you can leap to the dangerous conclusion that direct communication with your customers is not important. The second potential trap lies in a narrow interpretation of the term "network hubs." Almost all companies try to go after network hubs. But there's a big difference between going after an elite group of forty influencers and going after a broad, less visible population of four thousand of them. Numbers make a big difference in getting the word out. Many experts agree that the percentage of opinion leaders on average in the population is about 10 to 15 percent. Silicon Valley marketing guru Regis McKenna, who pioneered the "influence the influencers" model, wrote, "If a company can reach the critical 10 percent, it will indirectly influence all the others. The word-of-mouth message will grow like a snowball rolling downhill, as the critical 10 percent pass

All this explains why industry buzz can be so frenetic. If you want to hear the industry buzz in Silicon Valley, you go to Il Fornaio in Palo Alto or Buck's in Woodside for breakfast. You'll actually hear the humming buzz of dozens of men and women, all talking at the same time about different aspects of the same industry. Tell someone at one table that Microsoft intends to buy Company X, and within minutes you can be sure most of the restaurant will know it. Give it another hour and the word will spread by cellular phones and e-mail to the rest of the Valley, where some seven thousand technology companies are concentrated in a fifty-mile corridor. But what excites the crowd at Il Fornaio or Buck's may be met with a yawn by actual customers.

Let me use the example of pen-computing. In the late eighties if you had a product associated with pen-computing, your company was the talk of the Valley. But if you went out to listen to what customers were saying, you'd hear very little buzz, and the few comments that were circling weren't necessarily good. The same thing happened in the 1990s with push-technology, which was supposed to feed customized information directly to people's computers. Companies associated with this concept got deafening buzz within the high-tech industry, but very little from customers.

If your product gets a lot of talk within your industry, that's good. But if at a certain point this industry buzz doesn't become customer buzz, you may have a problem. Ultimately *customers* are the people who have to recommend your product to their friends.

the word to others." But in practice, marketers sometimes target just a handful of "influencers"—not the full 10 percent.

The spread of buzz is complex. People don't rely on any one source of information, whether it be their friends, the media, or manufacturers. They use all of the above. The way all these different sources interact is still unclear. But the fact that such sources of information may be a bit of a puzzle shouldn't stop us from using what we *do* know to stimulate the networks. And this takes us to the second part of *The Anatomy of Buzz.*

# Success in the Networks

Part
Two

# Contagious

# Products

**7.** **I'm not a car enthusiast**, but when I first saw the BMW Z3 Roadster, I was stunned. I doubt if anyone could just walk by this car seeing it for the first time without making a comment. "I watched the driver of a Jeep Grand Cherokee drive up on the sidewalk while ogling the Z3," said Fred Kern, who owned one of the first Z3s. At one point Kern was so tired of answering the same questions about the car, over and over again, that he considered putting a sign on it:

YES, IT'S THE CAR FROM THE MOVIE.
$28,750, BUT THE LEATHER WAS MORE—ABOUT $32,000.
ABOUT FOUR MONTHS.

A lot of the buzz about the BMW Z3 roadster originated from the car's striking design.

Some products just make people talk, and the Z3 is such a product. The talk was enhanced by a clever launch campaign, which I discuss in a later chapter (placement in the movie *GoldenEye* was part of it). But first and foremost it's the car's stunning design that generated so much buzz.

This chapter focuses on products—the products that have what it takes to create good buzz—*genuine long-term buzz* that leads to sales. This is ground zero of any buzz campaign. I call these "contagious products." They possess a tendency to propagate themselves somehow and to generate talk. The best buzz comes not from clever PR or advertising but rather from attributes *inherent* to the product itself. Contagious products can be grouped into six categories.

## Products That Evoke an Emotional Response

**When I got** out of the theater after seeing the movie *Psycho*, I couldn't stop talking about the movie for days. Neither could my teenage friends. Why? Because we were scared. This is exactly what happened with *The Blair Witch Project*. The movie was also marketed in a clever way, but buzz was driven by the fear that the movie evoked among viewers. This was especially true in the first few weeks after the release, when some people still believed that what they were seeing on the screen was actual footage taken by three students who disappeared in the forest.

Fear, of course, is an emotion that evokes positive buzz only for very few products, such as horror films. For most products and services it is usually the feeling of excitement and delight you get when your expectations are exceeded. Take the case of the PalmPilot. When this product was introduced, people in the high-tech industry didn't expect much from personal digital assistants (PDAs), a category that after a long history of failures was essentially considered dead. The PalmPilot team didn't try to change these low expectations. This is in stark contrast to the launch of Momenta, which I described in Chapter 2. Momenta was advertised months before the product launch. The PalmPilot wasn't. Momenta had a stunning booth at Comdex. The Palm was launched at a little show of industry influencers called Demo, where new products are presented to an audience of several hundred industry people.

"It wasn't some big company coming out saying, 'We've invented this thing and it's awesome and you'd better like it,'" says Ed Colligan, former VP of marketing at Palm Computing. This humble attitude, coupled with a *superb* product, created true excitement among people. "When I saw the PalmPilot, there was one of those 'aha' moments," says Andy Reinhardt, a *BusinessWeek* reporter who was news editor for *PC World* at the time. "It was fantastic! After all the other failures in handhelds, Palm had really gotten it right."

Colligan sounds apologetic when he explains Palm's positive buzz. "The product just works, you know? I know that's really simple, but there were just a lot of fundamental flaws about everything else that was done." The initial experience a customer has with a product is critical to buzz. "We're so used to having terrible experiences that when we have a good, easy experience, we tell our friends," says Patricia Seybold, president of the Patricia Seybold Group, and author of the bestselling book *Customers.com*.

This is part of what made EndNote a contagious product: Customers would so often say, "I was up and running in less than ten minutes" or "It really worked the first time!" These people began to tell their friends about the software, sometimes just minutes after they had installed it. They were pleasantly surprised, so they told others about the product.

## Products That Advertise Themselves

**Another type of** contagious product is the one that creates visual buzz. Imagine that it's the year 1888. You walk in the park on a Saturday morning and suddenly notice a man who's holding a box to his waist, pointing it at his wife and two children, and asking them to smile. You're terribly curious to find out what he's doing. A small group of people gathers nearby, and you overhear that the box he's holding is called a Kodak camera. It's almost as if the camera were using this man's family just to show itself off in public. In the following weeks some of the people who observed the man in the park will buy their own Kodak cameras, and they in turn will be seen pointing it in public.

That's how many new products spread. Think of the first time you saw one of those wheeled suitcases. The suitcase first advertised itself as it rolled behind flight crew members in airports all around the world. Then, when passengers started using it, the product triggered thousands of conversations: "Do they really consider this carry-on?" "I heard that it was invented by a retired pilot." "Where do you get those?" A great deal of fashion products spread in a similar way. More than half of the respondents who were asked by market research firm Yankelovich to specify sources of information about new styles said they learn about fashion by observing what others are wearing.

Social learning of this kind plays a major role in buzz among younger customers. Barry Schwartz, owner of three toy stores in New York State, describes how buzz about Beanie Babies started in his area. Schwartz first saw the toy at a toy fair, and in mid-1994 he displayed some in his stores. A son of one of the stores' employees got excited about a pig Beanie Baby. The child took the pig home, and on the following day he got on the bus with the pig stuffed in his shirt pocket. "Where'd ya get the pig?" the other children on the bus wanted to know the moment they noticed it. "That afternoon we might have had thirty-six pieces. They were gone. The following day we had a waiting list. In the first six weeks that we had it, we sold fifteen hundred pieces."

What are the implications for companies? Awareness of this effect at the design stage is key: If you design a new digital camera to look like the traditional film-based camera, for example, you are forgoing an opportunity to stimulate discussion. If you design it to look *different*, you can help the product stir conversation and thus advertise itself. This is exactly what the people at Apple had in mind when they designed the iMac. They wanted to make it look unlike any other computer.

Color is an effective tool in helping products advertise themselves. Distinctive blue bags in driveways tell people that their neighbors read the *New York Times*. A transparent bag would have not done the trick. Perhaps to counter this visual buzz in the San Francisco Bay Area, the *San Francisco Chronicle* in 1998 started to be delivered in yellow bags. Again, very noticeable.

## Products that Leave Traces

**Another way some** contagious products self-propagate is by leaving traces of themselves behind. This is especially true for products that allow their users to express themselves. In the early days of desktop publishing, the message "I used Photoshop" or "I used Illustrator" or the more generic "I used my Mac," often came along with the artwork. The same effect helped the spread of the Kodak camera. Not only did the camera capitalize on its observability as an object; its products—photos printed on Kodak paper—were specifically designed to be shown to friends and family.

A product that took this idea to the next level is the I-Zone pocket camera, which became an instant success at the end of 1999. The secret? The mini-camera can be loaded with Polaroid's Sticker Film, so it leaves its traces not only in photo albums but on school notebooks, lockers, skateboards, anything. Teenagers take pictures of their friends and stick the postage-size photos all around them, provoking thousands of conversations about the camera, in addition to visual buzz. Within two months of its release, the I-Zone became the bestselling camera in the United States.

Another product that has spread this way in recent years is Magnetic Poetry. Dave Kapell invented Magnetic Poetry to help him with his own writing—he would cut out words, paste them on magnets, and arrange them on his refrigerator. "When friends would come over, they'd gather around the fridge and play with it and leave these bizarre messages, and eventually people said, 'Hey, you should start selling this,'" Kapell says. He made some kits, took them to craft

**Magnetic Poetry spread by way of refrigerators in homes and offices.**

shows, and found that what happened at his house happened at his customers' houses—people saw it on their friends' refrigerators, started playing with the magnets, and left their own interesting messages. "For the first couple of years it was all pretty much word of mouth that sold this product," he says. To accelerate the process, Kapell hired sales reps and got into traditional distribution channels, where his product is exposed to many more eyes. But he still has people tell him that they first encounter it at someone's house. More than a million kits have been sold so far.

But this effect is not limited to products that facilitate creativity. When laser printers first came out, they left a long trail of reports and letters that simply looked more professional than those printed on dot-matrix printers. These documents advertised the printers that produced them in two ways: They established a tacit new standard for business documents, and sometimes they triggered discussion of printing techniques.

## Products That Become More Useful as More People Use Them

**Some contagious products** reward you if you talk about them. Suppose you're in a hotel and you've run out of ways to amuse yourself. Walking through the gym, you find a room with a Ping-Pong table, but you don't have anyone to play with. A Ping-Pong table is almost useless if you don't have a partner, so you go around the hotel and spread the word about the availability of the table. You do it not because you're such a good person (which you are), but because by spreading the word you increase your chances of achieving your goal: playing. This need for partnership is the basic building block of the network effects described in Chapter 3. Telephone, fax, and e-mail are examples of products that increase their value the more people use them—as do most communications tools.

This is how ICQ software spread. The idea for this instant-messaging service (which according to some reports popped up during a Ping-Pong game in 1996) grew out of the fact that users on the Net want to know which of their friends are on-line at the same time as they are. Once a user knows who's on-line, this service lets him or her chat with a partner in real time. Now, if you're the only person in your social network who has this piece of software, it's not very useful. By encouraging your friends to download it as well, it becomes far more useful for you. Mirabilis, the small Israeli company that produces the software, reported that over 10 million people downloaded ICQ between its introduction in November 1996 and the sale of the company to America Online in the summer of 1998.

Another service that spreads in a similar way is Accompany.com. This is a group buying service that allows consumers to get together on-line in order to receive volume discounts from manufacturers. If you're trying to buy a digital camera through this service and you know that the price will drop another forty dollars if you have additional people sign up, you are likely to tell your friends about the service. Again, the service is more valuable to *you* as more people use it.

## Products That Are Compatible

Researchers theorize that there may be a "preexisting structure" in our minds that determines what messages we will accept and spread. People are more open to ideas that match their existing set of beliefs, and because of that, ideas that fit their preexisting beliefs will spread faster. One reason for the intense buzz about the Palm was that it was compatible with expectations that many people had. "We have all the lists made out in our head," one customer said, explaining why he bought the Palm handheld. "[I had] in my brain a mental list of kinds of things that I would like an information organizer to do, and then when I saw it, it was just 'click.' " This customer went on to tell dozens of other people about the Palm.

Your product also needs to be compatible with the way potential users already do things. Several previously developed devices ignored that. But the Palm team understood that the first people likely to adopt a PDA used a PC and already had a way of keeping track of their contacts and schedules on their PC. Compatibility therefore became a top priority. While other devices allowed you to back up to a PC, the Palm handheld was designed as a PC device—as an extension of your personal computer. Pressing one button synchronized the data on the Palm and your computer.

Incompatibility blocks buzz from spreading. We first introduced EndNote for the Macintosh operating system. We used to promote our software at scientific meetings, where we'd often overhear the following conversation between customers who would stop by our booth:

> CUSTOMER A: Hey Joe, you have to check this out. An incredible piece of software.
>
> CUSTOMER B: *(notices the Apple logo on our computer)* Do they have it for DOS?
>
> CUSTOMER A: Hmmm . . . I don't think so, actually.
> End of story. Customer B's attention would usually shut down at this point.

We would of course take their names and promise to let them know when we created a DOS and Windows version (which we later did). But notice how incompatibility can block buzz from spreading. Even though the enthusiasm was there, the product wasn't appropriate for Customer B, and therefore he would not spread the word further.

Compatibility often is a matter of cultural traditions and of what is socially acceptable in a particular community. To improve the health of people in Los Molinos, a small village in Peru, the Peruvian government attempted to educate women in the village about general sanitation principles. They encouraged villagers to start boiling their drinking water. Most villagers, however, despite the two-year campaign, refused to adopt the practice, which was found to conflict with their basic belief system about food and drink. Everett Rogers, who describes this example in *Diffusion of Innovations*, makes the point that "the compatibility of an innovation, as perceived by members of a social system, is positively related to its rate of adoption."

## Products That "Do the Rest"

**Cameras were invented** in the 1820s. Why did it take roughly sixty years for them to become popular? The answer, I believe, is embedded in the slogan used by Kodak to introduce their first camera in 1888: "You press the button—we do the rest." Buzz about products that can make this claim (and deliver) spreads fast. When they were first invented, cameras were very complicated to operate. Then George Eastman reduced their operation to a three-step process: pull the cord, advance the key, and press the button. Eastman also understood that to appeal to mass markets, he needed to offer a simple development process. So the Kodak camera came loaded with film for a hundred exposures, and when the roll was done, the customer just mailed the whole camera to the company for development. Eastman demystified the process for thousands of people who knew about photography but previously perceived it as a complex process for only professional photographers and serious hobbyists. Eastman also understood the importance of communicating the simplicity of the innovation. To write the product manual, he hired a New York advertising man but ended up crafting the copy himself (in less than five hours), because the advertising executive, according to Eastman, "utterly ignored" the simplicity of the camera. By the mid-1890s, just a few years after its introduction, one hundred thousand Kodak cameras had been sold. "The craze is spreading fearfully," the *Chicago Tribune* wrote about the new camera.

Technology products are not the only products that simplify things in an appealing way. Look at the publication of a book like *In Search of Excellence*. What the Kodak camera did for photography, *In Search of Excellence* did for management theory: It demystified it. Lots of research went into the *Excellence* project, but the results were digested in several straightforward characteristics that excellent companies have in common. The authors gave basic advice, like "stick to the knitting" or "be close to the customer" and made it simple for people to tell their friends about the book.

Products that are easy to use spread faster because customers are hungry for simplicity. Buzz about these products travels more quickly, too. Here's why: When customers explain to their friends how they use a product, every extra step they describe—if it adds confusion—could serve to block the word from spreading. When a customer has to explain just one step, her likelihood of completing the "sales pitch" successfully is much higher than if she had to describe seven steps.

## Buzz and Balance

I want to go back to the subject discussed at the beginning of the chapter and talk some more about the emotional reaction people have to products. This reaction is affected to a large extent by people's expectations.

When you stimulate buzz, you raise expectations. If you raise expectations too much without being able to deliver, you will create disappointment. The key to creating good buzz is balance, and the rule of buzz and balance is very simple: Always exceed expectations. Falling below customers' expectations will create negative buzz.

If you have a product that you know is a real winner, you can afford to build high expectations. The BMW Z3 Roadster was promoted months before it was available. But the car's design was so striking that customers' expectations were met and often exceeded. If you promote a product that is just "very good," be careful. If you tell somebody that a movie will be the funniest comedy they've ever seen, and they laugh 25 percent of the time, they will feel cheated. If their expectations are moderate and they laugh the exact same amount, they will be delighted.

Another way to exceed expectations is to price the product below what customers anticipate. Young couples who were invited to see the Ford Mustang before its 1964 launch loved the car. But they developed reservations because they felt it was probably going to be beyond their financial reach. When told that the Mustang would cost only about $2,500, they wanted it badly. Something similar happened with the PalmPilot. Several people told me how they fell in love with the Palm when a friend showed it to them. Then, when they heard the price—"a price you could hide on an expense report," as someone put it—they *had* to have it, and they went on to tell their friends about the great value they'd found.

# The Power of Gossip

— "What's the deal with Carmela and Tony? Is their relationship this bad?"

— "Notice how Carmela scowled at Tony all during the barbecue, but smiled whenever others might have seen her."

— "I think Charmaine slept with Tony before Tony and Carmela were married."

These snippets from actual on-line conversations may sound like simple gossip. In fact, they are part of the buzz about one of the most talked-about television programs in recent years: *The Sopranos*.

We *love* to talk about people, and when a product somehow plugs into this fascination of ours, the result is big buzz. Tony and Carmela Soprano, as well as other characters from the HBO series, are part of thousands of conversations both on-line and off-line.

What other products and services can take advantage of our fascination with people? Buzz about certain restaurants focuses on the people who eat there. Word of mouth about some books derives from talk about the characters (just listen to kids talk about Harry Potter). A lot of movie buzz is about the stars who play in the film. Buzz about industry conferences is often about who will be there. *The Sopranos* is an example of a product that brilliantly uses our interest in people to generate talk. It's worth paying attention to what the creators of the program have done.

First, they realize that we all have met enough boring people in our lives, so we usually don't bother telling others about them. We do, however, talk about colorful and unusual people and we certainly find those on *The Sopranos*. Tony Soprano is such a character. On the surface, he's a waste management consultant. Scratch that surface lightly and you find that he's a mobster. Go a little deeper and you find a mobster on Prozac. Tony suffers from depression and midlife crisis and gives us a glimpse at what it means to be a Mafia Wiseguy in our times. Or meet Livia, Tony's old mother. "Oh my God! Am I sick of that old bag!" one viewer wrote in an on-line forum. Interesting characters aren't necessarily lovable. In fact, we all know that annoying people often trigger the most interesting conversations.

*The Sopranos* characters aren't lovable, but they are very relevant. It all starts with the fact that they feel so real and authentic that we treat them like people we know. In a way, they become an extension of our social network. As we meet them week after week and learn about their daily struggles, we become more involved with their lives. The issues that they deal with are very relevant to many of us: relationships, midlife crisis, power struggles, social status. Tony and Carmela have to choose a college for their daughter, convince Tony's mother to move to a nursing home, and deal with a problematic soccer coach. How much this relevance drives buzz becomes evident when you read discussions about *The Sopranos* in on-line forums. Many conversations are about relationships, about who did what to whom and what they should do next.

To stimulate talk even further, the creators of *The Sopranos* use an ancient method—shock treatment. When people we know are involved in outrageous things, we have to relieve the tension—we talk. Listening to a *Sopranos* fan list the day after Tony's sister shot her fiancé, you see just that. The cries of shock and disbelief were amazing. "I can't believe Janice capped Richie!!!!!" one fan posted shortly after he saw the program. Another reported, "I was watching the show with about seven *Sopranos* addicts, and when Janice shot Richie there was some serious 'Holy S———!' being screamed." Such emotional reactions are likely to stimulate additional talk.

There's something powerful that is unique to buzz about a series. A good movie can present us with interesting characters that face relevant problems. A good television series leaves us a whole week to wonder what will happen next. When we develop ongoing relationships with certain characters, our involvement rises. We look for other people we can talk with about the characters. If we miss an episode, we ask our friends what happened.

This generates many viewer-to-viewer discussions, but also involves nonviewers. Imagine that you stand by the water cooler at work and you hear two of your co-workers:

"You think his mother's in on this?"

"It's his uncle. He's so pissed at him."

"I can't believe that a mother—even Livia—would try to kill her own son . . ."

You're likely to ask what they're talking about. They'll tell you that they're talking about *The Sopranos*. It's on HBO. Someone tried to kill Tony last night. You don't get HBO?

HBO expects to add between 1 and 2 million new subscribers during the year 2000. Not all this projected growth is attributed to *The Sopranos*, "but it certainly helps," HBO's chairman, Jeffrey L. Bewkes, told the *New York Times*. The company does many things to enhance buzz about the program. Running a weeklong marathon of last year's episodes is one way to reignite discussion. So is a traveling "waste management" truck that parks in central locations. (Fans can pose next to a cardboard cutout of their favorite character.) Viewers can also vote for their favorite line on HBO's Web site.

At the core of the extensive buzz about *The Sopranos* you find a high-quality program, brilliantly written and executed. The reason why it gets so much buzz seems to be that the Sopranos are exactly the people that we love to talk about.

# Accelerating Natural Contagion

**8.** **Trees have an interesting marketing** problem. They need to spread their seeds widely to avoid competing with their own offspring for sun, water, and food. But the problem is that they are rooted to one place. If you've ever been grounded for a week, you know the feeling.

So trees have had to develop other ways to help spread seeds. One of the techniques involves seduction and hitchhiking. The tree seeds start developing inside a green and not very attractive fruit, nut, or cone; as the seeds mature, the fruit around them becomes ripe, making it more attractive, sweet, colorful, and juicy. That's when the seduction happens. Animals see the colorful fruit, taste it, and take it with them to eat. In their travels they disperse the seeds, sometimes miles away from the source tree.

Nature has devised a clever strategy. But what works for trees doesn't work in business. There's an obvious reason: Companies operate in a more competitive environment, one where their survival often depends on their dominance. The strategy adopted by trees is too limited. Yet some companies adopt it by default. They develop beautiful "fruit" and wait for customers to come and find it and carry it around to wherever they happen to go. They believe that having a good product or providing a good service is all that's needed. These companies are not utilizing a significant advantage that we, as humans, have over trees: We can walk to the other end of the forest and plant the seed ourselves.

Two things are needed to create buzz successfully. The first one, as discussed in the last chapter, is to have a contagious product. But having such a product alone is not enough. Companies that get good buzz also *accelerate* natural contagion.

The game Trivial Pursuit sold 20 million copies in 1984. Contagion played an important role in buzz about this product. People who played the game were compelled to demonstrate their knowledge of trivia to others at work, school, or home. But word about the product didn't spread by contagion alone. Buzz was accelerated through many activities the company undertook. For example, the marketers of the game sent samples to celebrities who were mentioned in questions. This helped to start buzz (and trivia parties) in Hollywood. For months more than a hundred radio stations broadcast trivia questions and gave away sample games to listeners. This helped to create buzz in *numerous* clusters all around the country, as winners of these games invited friends to play.

I call this type of acceleration leapfrogging. Instead of relying on Customer A to tell B, who will tell C, who will tell D (you start to sense how slow word of mouth can be), smart marketers know that

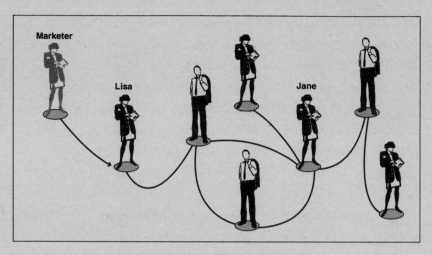

Lisa is reachable, but she's not best positioned to spread the word.

word of mouth almost always needs help. They do something to make word spread faster.

Let's look at a simple example of leapfrogging in action. In the illustration above a marketer wants to spread the word about a new product to seven customers. Assume that limited resources al-

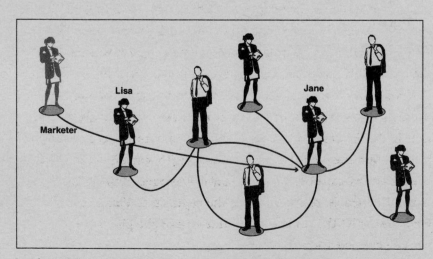

Jane is much better positioned to spread the message in this network.

low her to communicate with only one customer. A marketer who relies on the product to spread by itself would approach the closest person, someone with whom she already has a tie—in this case, Lisa—and expect her to pass on the message to others.

But notice that there are four steps from Lisa to the farthest individual in the network, and that only one person is one step away from her. The message is almost guaranteed to be blocked or distorted on its way to people in this group. Even if it doesn't get stuck, it will be very slow to spread.

A marketer who accelerates natural contagion, on the other hand, will try to locate and approach someone like Jane, who is more central in the group as a whole. Now *four* people are just one step away from Jane, and no one is more than two steps away from her. The message is more likely to reach its destination with minimum distortion and get there much faster.

## The Why of Leapfrogging

While our simple Lisa-Jane example illustrates the core idea behind leapfrogging, it only begins to suggest its power in helping a product to take off. Every new product starts with no one knowing about it except for a few insiders. The buzz at this point is zero. There's an enormous gap between the few people who know about the product within the company and the rest of the world. To spread the word, the creators of the product or service start reaching out and planting the news in other areas of the networks. This is a critical time in the life of a product. It is critical for a company at this stage to have at least one person who is obsessed with spreading the word. It sounds almost too obvious, but many new products fail because there is no obsessed person in place at the right time. This is the person who doesn't let the company be a tree—he or she plants the seeds of buzz all over the forest.

Let's look at an example from the very early days of FedEx.

On the night of March 12, 1973, employees of the young company gathered near the new sorting facility in Memphis, Tennessee, waiting for the company's Falcon airplanes to arrive from eleven cities, loaded with packages that needed to be sorted. A night that began with a lot of anticipation ended in bitter disappointment. When the airplanes arrived and the doors were opened, the employees found only six packages—including one sent by Fred Smith, founder of the company. "People hadn't heard of us," one employee told Robert A. Sigafoos, who described the scene in his book about FedEx, *Absolutely, Positively Overnight!* In the same way that only six packages traveled that night in the FedEx network, only a few comments about FedEx traveled around that time among potential customers. One lesson the company learned from this experience was that it needed to cover a wider network of cities to make its service more attractive. But another lesson was that it needed to get more aggressive in getting out the word about its service.

Ted Sartoian was one of those who made it happen. Previously a salesperson for UPS, he was hired by Federal Express in September 1973 as the head of their sales force. Business was still pretty bad when he joined—hardly the numbers needed to support a fleet of airplanes like the one FedEx was building. Sartoian remembered shipping about three hundred packages a night out of Chicago. Even today, more than twenty-five years later, he can't help but get indignant at this low number. "Three hundred packages out of Chicago— that's just sick!" he almost shouted over the phone.

Sartoian's approach was to lead a sales team of eight or nine people at a time into each city and stay there, conducting a sales blitz of a few weeks. "We'd get a bunch of people together and we'd take them to a city like Chicago," he remembers. "We'd sit down the night before or a day before and cut the city up into parts, and each person would have a territory, and you would go around and you would canvas. And you would canvas hard, get as many people as you could. And by canvassing I mean even door-to-door selling. It was very difficult." People of course didn't know what Federal Express was and had to be convinced of the concept. Sartoian and his people would sometimes take a sample package from a potential customer and ship it for free. They would come back the next day, with the name of the customer who signed for the package thousands of miles away. "That was a great selling tool," Sartoian says. This was the way that Federal Express leapfrogged into new cities, new industries, new networks. "We'd go in there and sales-blitz that city for four, five weeks with eight or nine guys, and all of a sudden now we're getting *thousands* of packages a day instead of three hundred." Sartoian wasn't the first to conduct a sales blitz. Originality is not the point here. The point is that you need to initiate these links somehow into a variety of networks to generate enough momentum for the word to spread. Without these links it is conceivable that, in time, almost every office in America would have received a FedEx letter and thus would have been exposed to the brand. But this is merely an academic hypothesis. In real life, with competitors and cash flow issues, companies need to get off the ground quickly. To get buzz going, a heroic push—*beyond natural contagion*—is usually called for.

### It's a way to enter new clusters

New products often spread in some networks but not in others. In a classic study in 1954, William H. Whyte, Jr., used aerial photos to analyze how the use of air conditioners spread within several neighborhoods in Philadelphia. As the locations of houses with new air conditioners were plotted on a map, the clusters became clear. One block might have eighteen air conditioners, while the next block over might have only three. These clusterings were the result of small word-of-mouth networks operating among neighbors. Whyte surveyed 4,948 houses. In the following diagram you can see just forty row houses. Any house where an air conditioner was spotted is

| | | X | X | X | X | X | X | | | X | | | | X | X | |
|---|---|---|---|---|---|---|---|---|---|---|---|---|---|---|---|---|
| | | | | | X | | | | | | | | | | | |

marked with an X. Clearly the product spread more successfully in the upper row, where nine neighbors have adopted it, than in the lower row, where only one neighbor has an air conditioner.

If you were an air conditioner dealer in Philadelphia back then, you could wait for the word to spread by itself. The alternative would be to leapfrog by knocking on a couple of doors in the least active area in row two, convincing the residents to be the first on their block to own an air conditioner. It would have accelerated the adoption process—and would have ensured that *you*, and not your competitors, were the dealer selling in these clusters.

At a macro level, leapfrogging can help a product break into

Row houses in the city of Philadelphia. The houses marked with an X are those with air conditioners. Notice the clusters. The photograph first appeared in an article by William H. Whyte, Jr., in *Fortune* magazine in 1954.

new social circles. Look at hamburgers. We take them for granted as an integral part of American life, but in the 1920s hamburgers were consumed mainly by working-class men; they weren't part of the American family diet. In fact, they were considered by many a health hazard. Billy Ingram, the founder of White Castle, one of the first fast-food chains, decided to change that. White Castle was founded in 1921 in Wichita, Kansas. During the twenties the chain expanded to additional cities. As the income of the working class dwindled during the Depression of the thirties, Ingram understood that growth required breaking into new social networks. To convince middle-class women to include hamburgers in their families' diets, Ingram hired Ella Louise Agniel as the official "White Castle hostess." Under the pseudonym of Julia Joyce (which sounded both sophisticated and trustworthy), she made frequent appearances at women's clubs and charity organizations in cities where White Castle had restaurants. She would inform her audiences about the company's high standards and the nutritional value of their hamburgers. And whenever she gave a presentation, Joyce would bring along sacks of hamburgers for tasting. She would also invite her audiences for a tour of a nearby White Castle's kitchen, so they could see for themselves how the food was actually being prepared. "The key to Joyce's success was her relentless determination and energy. She often spoke to several clubs in one day, in addition to hosting sessions at various Castle restaurants," according to David Hogan, who studied the history of White Castle. By changing a few women's attitudes about hamburgers during each meeting, Joyce/Agniel planted the seeds of change in the group. In following meetings the converted women would tell friends about their families' reactions to hamburgers. And they would spread the word about hamburgers in other social networks, legitimizing the food in wider circles. By about 1940 White Castle had reached its goal. "The fast-food hamburger had shed most of its negative connotations and was finally accepted by consumers from all classes," Hogan writes.

## The How of Leapfrogging

**Companies that accelerate** the process of natural contagion to speed up buzz go beyond formulas and beyond taking the obvious steps. They often bypass the obvious choice of formal networks. A traditional-thinking company might hear about "getting close to your customer" and think of their distribution channels—a familiar network. Certainly the channel is important, and as we saw in the case of *Cold Mountain,* it can help build buzz. But successful companies don't rely on it *alone,* because many potential customers are not directly connected to the channel. Customers may occasionally visit a retail outlet, but they may or may not get information about products from the retailer. Successful companies leapfrog into informal networks as well.

Suppose you were introducing a new game for adults called Pictionary. You would want to have the product on the shelves of stores so that people could find it. But to create buzz about a product such as Pictionary, you need to go beyond that. *You need to reach people where they hang out.* The makers of Pictionary, with the help of Linda Pezzano (who was also behind the launch of Trivial Pursuit), did just that. "We hired actors to dress up as artists and set them up with easels and flip charts in gathering places, and had them start engaging people in playing and giving out the sample packs at the same time," Pezzano recalled. Demos were held at parks, shopping centers, and other gathering places. As a result, in its biggest year, about 15 million Pictionary games were sold.

Companies that speed up buzz go beyond the most expected communication channels as well. Cisco Systems, for example, serves network administrators who virtually live on-line, so you'd expect Cisco to use on-line methods to spread the word about its products. They do. But Cisco doesn't limit itself to the on-line world. The company organizes more than one thousand seminars every year to meet potential customers face to face, they organize networking events for their current customers, and they attend dozens of trade shows. Relationships with many customers start via face-to-face communication. The Net is used to maintain the relationships. Bill Raduchel, chief strategy officer of another high-tech firm, Sun Microsystems, put it this way: "The most complementary technology to the Web is a 747." In other words, don't lock yourself to the latest electronic means of communications. Sometimes you need to get on a plane and meet people face to face.

## Other Ways to Accelerate Natural Contagion

In addition to actively leapfrogging, companies that accelerate buzz also work to create the *conditions* that make shortcuts more likely to happen. One way is to create environments where customers can meet people who are not customers from remote networks. Suppose, for example, that your company sells e-commerce solutions. Putting together a series of seminars on the topic for noncustomers, and then inviting champion users to tell how they use your product out in the field, creates perfect conditions for buzz to leap from cluster to cluster. The Internet offers significant opportunities to stimulate interaction between customers and noncustomers. Many companies have created forums on the Net where users and nonusers can meet, share experiences, and discuss ways the product can be used.

Another tactic is to hang out in the "dense areas" of the networks. There is a lot of randomness in the networks. Shortcuts often happen by chance, and you increase the chances of these shortcuts happening to *you* by being out there, especially in the densest areas of the networks, like trade shows and other industry events. Everyone is already there—you just need to make sure that they talk about *your* product. Experienced PR people know how to create shortcuts across a cocktail party. A good public relations professional can gracefully grab Person A and escort him all the way to the other end of the hall to meet Person B at an industry event, personally creating a shortcut.

## Misconceptions About Buzz

To create buzz and use it effectively, you should have a realistic view of the phenomenon, not glorify it. For example, some word-of-mouth enthusiasts argue that if you get good buzz, you don't need to do any marketing. This can be a major mistake. Distribution, advertising, promotions and other traditional marketing activities can translate the goodwill surrounding your product into sales. Good buzz is the best thing you could wish for, but it's just one component of your marketing mix. Here are three additional misconceptions that an overly enthusiastic view can lead to.

### "Buzz Spreads Like Wildfire"

It is true only in rare cases. Big news can travel fast, but most news about products is not earth-shattering and therefore can spread at a painfully slow rate. Several factors slow down buzz. First, there's always someone who wants to keep the word about your product from spreading. Buzz is about new things, and new things always threaten someone. Second, like NBC or CNN, the invisible networks are also starting to be crowded with messages, so while customers are still receptive to messages from their friends, they don't remember all these messages and certainly don't act on all.

Something else that slows down buzz is the fact that people live in clusters. Buzz can spread in circles within one cluster but is slow to leap outside these networks. Moreover, people within each cluster are selective about what they pass on to their friends. They act not only as network hubs but also as filters. People don't automatically press the "Forward" key in their e-mail program (although it sometimes seems that way). Yes, if every customer told two other customers about your product, you could reach more than a billion people in just thirty steps, but this is hypothetical. *Not* every customer tells two other customers. Some do. Many don't.

### "Buzz Is Truth"

To some people, buzz is the only real thing. The grassroots answer to corporate propaganda, free of any self-interest considerations. The reality is that some comments circling in the invisible networks are true and some are not. Just two examples: In 1999 rumors circled that the Miller Brewing Company was giving away free six-packs of beer to Internet users. In the early 1990s the makers of Tropical Fantasy had to deal with the rumor that their soft drink was secretly made by the Ku Klux Klan and was making African American men sterile. Both of these false rumors demonstrate that not all comments transmitted through the networks are true.

At the other end of the spectrum you find people who believe that just because something has been *heard* and not *read,* it's false. According to this view, word of mouth is inferior by definition. This is, of course, the mirror image of the same misconception. The fact is that buzz is just talk. Some of the comments that travel in the invisible networks are true and some are not.

## "All You Need Is a Good Product"

For buzz to spread, you need two things: a contagious product—one that has some inherent value that makes people talk—and someone behind the scenes who accelerates natural contagion. Yes, there are cases where having a great product or service alone is enough, but these typically occur when capacity is limited. A restaurant with thirty tables can rely on word of mouth alone if the talk is intense enough to keep these tables occupied. But this is not the case in markets where there's no such limit on capacity and where companies must act fast in order to turn their products into the de facto standard. Technology markets, for example, are almost like presidential election campaigns, where there's no prize for second place. Winner takes all. In these markets the natural spread of word of mouth *must* be accelerated. Having a good product is not enough.

Hiring practices can also be used to accelerate contagion in certain social networks. Companies that hire young employees have a better chance of linking into networks of youthful people. Companies that hire Hispanics help link into networks of Spanish-speaking individuals. It's part of the way Union Bank of California has grown. "Walk into a branch in a Latino area and you'll see lots of personnel who are Latino," vice chairman Rick Hartnack told *Fortune* magazine. Hiring people from diverse backgrounds—54 percent of Union Bank's employees are minorities—has given the bank an opportunity to spread its message into a *variety* of networks, a strategy that seems to have paid off in the stock market: The bank's stock "has appreciated at a 34% compound annual rate for the past five years," *Fortune* noted in 1999.

Leapfrogging is not easy, but to create buzz you almost always have to leapfrog to unfamiliar networks. Jim Callahan of The Dohring Company, a marketing research firm in the automotive industry, says, "There is a misconception that if a dealership gives good service it would automatically get good word of mouth. What we have found is that the dealerships that make a conscious effort to promote word of mouth are the ones that are most successful in getting word of mouth."

The third part of this book describes leapfrogging and some other strategies and tactics (such as viral marketing and publicity events) designed to accelerate the natural process. The techniques vary and will continue to change as new technologies evolve. But whatever the technique used, you can be sure that behind almost every good buzz there is someone who understands that success comes not only from having a contagious product but also from speeding the good word about that product to the far reaches of various networks, getting the attention of potential customers before competitors do.

# Stimulating

# Buzz

Part
Three

# Working

# with Network

# Hubs

**9.** **In the mid-1980s, Canadian** physicians were abuzz about the use of cesarean sections. It was clear that the surgical procedure was often used when it wasn't needed, causing unnecessary risks and expenses. The Society of Obstetricians and Gynecologists of Canada issued guidelines that unambiguously recommended a lower rate of cesarean births. The guideline stated that the fact that a woman had had the procedure before was not a reason to reach for the scalpel again. Most practitioners—94 percent of them to be exact—said that they knew of these guidelines, and 56 percent reported that they had discussed them with a colleague. But when researchers checked the monthly discharge data from hospitals to see whether there was a reduction in the number of cesarean sections as a result of the new guidelines, the answer was no.

It's not that the physicians disagreed with the guidelines—about 85 percent of practitioners said they agreed with them. In fact, many physicians claimed that they had changed their practices. "I think they truly were under the impression that they had changed their behavior," says Jonathan Lomas, a researcher who studied the case. "But in fact they hadn't."

Lomas and his colleagues were intrigued and decided to search for the most effective way to influence these physicians. They tried several methods and eventually found that the best way to change people's behavior in this case was to work with local opinion leaders.

The first step was to identify the network hubs. To do this, the researchers sent out questionnaires to physicians in each hospital asking them to nominate colleagues in the area who matched the "opinion leader" profile. When the opinion leaders were identified, they were invited to participate in a workshop that explained the rationale behind the guidelines. In the weeks that followed the workshop, the researchers asked the physicians to do a little "marketing." They asked each physician to mail a personal letter to his or her colleagues with some material from the workshop, to follow up with another letter, to host a meeting with an expert on the topic, and, in general, to talk with colleagues about the issue. The results were impressive: Seventy-four percent of the physicians in the hospitals with trained network hubs gave women the option of choosing regular labor, compared to 51 percent and 56 percent in groups where different strategies were tested. In one group the researchers simply mailed out the guidelines a second time. In the other group the reduction in cesarean sections was promoted in discussions at medical staff meetings and via an extensive audit procedure.

Whether you spread an idea, a product, or a service, you always have a choice. You can broadcast or you can connect. Broadcasting involves massive mailings or buying media time and packaging your message so that it can be transmitted simultaneously to all nodes in the network. Connecting involves starting a dialogue with *certain individuals* in the network that you are trying to influence. This chapter describes the latter: how to identify network hubs, how to connect, and how to get them to help you create change.

## Where to Find Network Hubs?

**When the concept** of opinion leaders was first introduced in the 1940s, marketers were excited. The idea that opinion leaders were out there, ready to transmit information to the rest of the public, was very appealing. "Now, if only we could identify these people," marketers thought. But they quickly realized that there was no simple way to pinpoint these influential individuals. For years now, researchers have struggled to discover the magic formula for finding such people, but with only limited success. Nonetheless, smart companies identify network hubs every day and benefit greatly from doing so. The practical approach to the issue is first to recognize that you will not be able to identify *all* network hubs. Once you accept this, there are four methods you can use to identify as many such influential people as you can:

1. Letting network hubs identify themselves

2. Identifying *categories* of network hubs

3. Spotting network hubs in the field

4. Identifying network hubs through surveys

Regardless of the method or methods you intend to use, always look for individuals who display the ACTIVE characteristics of network hubs: **A**head in adoption (at least slightly), **C**onnected, **T**ravelers, **I**nformation-hungry, **V**ocal, and **E**xposed to the media more than others.

### Letting Network Hubs Identify Themselves

One group of network hubs is easy to find—they're the ones who come to you. Your job here is to recognize them, and you may be surprised how many companies don't. These opinion leaders will come to you for something they like more than anything else: information. They may call to ask questions that go beyond what a regular customer would ask. They may spend extra time at your booth during a trade show to look at the new gadget you're announcing. They may e-mail again and again to see what's going on with that new feature the market is expecting. Some of your people may feel bothered by this excessive interest, but they need to understand that network hubs feed on information. Teach everyone in your organization how to spot them.

Of course, not all of those who seek extra information or claim to be influential are valuable network hubs. But often the best policy is to *assume* that they are. Many software companies, for example, err on the side of sending out too many when it comes to giving away review copies of their software. How generous you can be depends, of course, on the associated cost and benefits, but often all you have to invest to develop a good relationship with a potential network hub is some time and attention.

### Identifying *Categories* of Network Hubs

The previous method will help you find only *some* of the hubs—those that approach you. Yes, network hubs are information-hungry, but what if their hunger for information is fed by your competitors, or what if they're not *that* hungry? You need to use other methods, too. The most commonly used method to find network hubs is to identify a category of promising people—a group that might potentially include such network hubs. For example, readers of a fashion magazine are likely sources for information about the latest fashions. People who attend a conference on computer security are likely to be hubs in this area. This is an important method, and the only reason I don't expand on it here is that it is well documented and widely known: The use of trade magazines, conferences, and trade shows is a sure way to reach opinion leaders.

It's also relatively easy to identify people who are connected to other potential customers because of their profession. For instance, nurses often talk with young mothers about nutrition. As a result, companies that sell baby food try to influence these health care professionals. Similarly, in a virtual community, chat hosts are usually passionate about the topic they are hosting and serve as a central resource for information about it. The way to look for a category is to think of people who, by virtue of their *position*, have a higher than average number of ties with people in the networks you're trying to reach. If you sell books, you should know what books local spiritual leaders are talking about. "I keep an eye on what the pastors at the local churches are recommending from the pulpit," says Karen Pennington of Kepler's, a bookstore in Menlo Park, California.

## Spotting Network Hubs in the Field

**Identifying network hubs** by category usually allows us to find people with titles—teachers, nurses, physicians. Such people are important, but they aren't always the street-level network hubs we're looking for.

To find the grassroots network hub, you need to go out into the field. How do you see them through the crowd? "It's immediately obvious. You only need to be with someone like that five minutes, and that's true whether you meet them on-line or at a party," says Stacy

Horn, founder of Echo, an on-line community in New York City. When Horn started Echo, she used this method to locate network hubs who would liven up the on-line discussion. It's easy to find these hubs when you're part of a community. In fact, when you're part of a community, you don't really have to search. "We know who they are," says David Unowsky of Ruminator Books, a bookstore in St. Paul, Minnesota. Many of the network hubs he's in touch with either have book clubs or are associated with The Loft, a large writing center in town.

And what if you're not part of the community? You should ask established members of the community to help. Rochelle Newman, who was involved in promoting Crisco Oil in the Hispanic market in the early eighties, remembers using this technique to identify women who were known and admired in local communities. "You'd really just go into the community and start talking to people," she says. Often the owners of the corner store—the bodega—were used to help identify them. When you heard a woman's name mentioned by multiple people, you knew that you had a network hub. Once these network hubs were identified, they were engaged in product sampling, parties à la Tupperware, and special promotions.

The fact that they're vocal also makes it easy to spot them. "There are always a bunch of advanced users who enjoy acting as experts, and pretty soon they're listened to as 'influencers' on company strategy and product direction as well," says Jeff Tarter, editor and publisher of *Soft*letter*. "These opinion leaders aren't journalists or people with impressive titles—they're just ordinary folks who acquire a reputation on their own merits." In the K–12 software market these people are often the teachers who are willing to spend extra time to integrate technology into the classroom. "There's a champion in every building," says Dean Kephart, a high-tech marketing executive who's helped several publishers of educational software to create buzz among teachers. And how do you spot them? They are "the same people who go to the state and regional conferences." They speak; they write; they travel to conferences, trade shows, and Web sites; and they cause change.

Keep your eyes open for "connectors" as well—people who have the potential to transmit information across clusters. A physician who practices in two clinics may spread knowledge about a new medical device from one clinic to the other. A visiting professor at a lab can be invited to take demo versions of software back to his or her home university. Exchange students, part-time or temporary employees who work at more than one company, and service providers who interact with many different companies all can be possible connectors. Whenever you hear someone identify himself or herself as "wearing two hats," you may be dealing with a connector.

Another way to spot network hubs is to look for socially active individuals. As I discussed earlier, Roper Starch Worldwide selects their Influential Americans based on certain political and social activities. These people appear to talk more not only about local politics but also about commercial products. For example, 32 percent of these individuals report that they made recommendations about software (as opposed to 7 percent of the total public), and 24 percent of them report making recommendations about computer hardware (as opposed to 6 percent of the total public). Roper defines an Influential American as any person who within the last twelve months has done three things out of a long list of public, political, or social activities. Some examples of these activities are writing a letter to the editor, making a speech, and serving on a committee.

The practical implications of this are clear. If you come across people who are involved in social activities on a regular basis, that's a good indicator of their tendency to tell others about the products they use. Pay attention not only to the editor of your trade magazine but also to those who write letters to the editor. If you're entering a new geographical territory, look for those who serve on school boards, lead community groups, and voice their opinions in public forums.

## Identifying Hubs Through Surveys

**Some of the** informal concepts discussed above can be utilized in formal surveys. These methods have not been widely adopted in industry. But they could be. They can teach companies a great deal about how information spreads among their customers.

**1. Sociometric Methods.** Imagine having a map of various networks in front of you. You ask all members of a given network to name the people from whom they seek information about a specific topic. The network hubs will be those people who have the highest number of links. This is a reliable method, but it has limited applications. First, you would need to ask all (or most) members of a system in order to get an accurate map, so this method can't be applied on a very large scale. Second, people are reluctant to give out the names of their peers. Still, this method can be extremely useful on a smaller scale. Imagine being able to promote the habit of wearing seat belts among high school students this way. You'd survey the whole school and then influence those identified as network hubs. This method can be used to build a model of how purchase decisions are being made in such networks as well.

The pharmaceutical industry often uses physicians with certain specialties as local spokespersons in certain markets. In one particular city a drug company noticed that although they had a top expert as their spokesperson, sales of the company's drugs in that market were lower than expected. Comsort, a Baltimore-based consulting firm involved in the case, distributed surveys among specialists in that market and created a sociogram of the network. According to John W. Hawks, president of Comsort, the spokesperson was number one on the "technical-advice-seeking-network," but he did not appear on the "trust-and-friendship network" at all. After mapping the networks of specialists in that city, Comsort gave the pharmaceutical company the names of four physicians seen as leaders who were also key figures in the trust-and-friendship network. Having a map of the network allowed the company to target the right people.

**2. Informants' ratings.** In this method you ask people to tell you who the network hubs are. Sales reps use this method intuitively. When a rep for a software company who goes into a new school asks teachers for the name of the person to talk to, the teachers often refer the salesperson to the local software expert. Be attentive to clues that the people you talk to may give you. They may say, "Everybody here asks George" or "Jane is the person you ought to talk to if you want anything to happen."

A project that tried to promote safe sex among gay men used this method more formally. The researchers used the help of four bartenders in a gay bar to identify network hubs. For one week the bartenders were asked to observe who was being greeted positively most often at the bar. When the bartenders' recording sheets were cross-referenced, the names of 36 people emerged as opinion leaders. The researchers located about two-thirds of these people and asked them to name some additional influential people in the community. Based on that, the researchers put together a group of 43 individuals (39 men, 4 women), who then went through some basic training on safe sex. In the two weeks that followed the training, these individuals reported more than 350 conversations they had with other gay people in the community. Three months after this program began, the researchers again surveyed gay men in the city (and in two cities that served as control groups). In the city where the network hubs were identified and trained, there was a 16-percent increase in use of condoms among gay men, a change that was not found in the control cities. In a similar marketing effort, researchers asked villagers in Finland to tell them who the two most influential people in their village were on health care issues. The researchers then trained those who were identified as opinion leaders on ways to reduce heart disease risk factors. Once again the results were impressive, including a 28-percent reduction in smoking in these villages.

**3. Self-designating method.** There are a number of methods that measure the degree to which individuals perceive themselves as central and influential in a certain product category. Because such methods are based on self-perception, they are not as reliable as other methods. Nonetheless, such methods are practical and relatively widely used. For example, here are some of the questions included in a study by Rogers among Ohio farmers:

1.  During the past six months have you told anyone about some new farming practice?

2.  Compared with your circle of friends are you

    (a) more likely to be asked for advice about new farming practices?
    (b) less likely to be asked for advice about new farming practices?

3.  Thinking back to your last discussion about some new farming practice,

    (a) were you asked for your opinion of the new practice?
    (b) did you ask someone else?

4.  When you and your friends discuss new ideas about farm practices, what part do you play?

    (a) Mainly listen
    (b) Try to convince them of your ideas

5.  Do you have the feeling that you are generally regarded by your neighbors as a good source of advice about new farm practices?

Another method, the "Strength of Personality" test, was developed when managers at *Der Spiegel* magazine in Germany were trying to understand the active consumers who set standards in their community. A group of German researchers, led by Professor Elisabeth Noelle-Neumann, developed a questionnaire that asked a series of yes/no questions. Sample questions included "I like to assume responsibility" or "I am good at getting what I want." Follow-up research has shown that people with central positions in their social networks are those who score high on the "Strength of Personality" scale.

## How to Work with Network Hubs?

**The first step** in working with network hubs is to keep track of them. Building a system to record information about hubs is mostly a matter of making everyone at your organization aware of them. The database you build should have telephone numbers, e-mail addresses, regular mailing addresses, as well as information about the scope and source of their influence and the nature of the networks they belong to.

Timing in reaching out to them is important. In each network there are a given number of network hubs and mega-hubs, and with a new product or service it is critical to capture their hearts and minds before your competitors do. Often you can try to accomplish this by seeding, a technique I describe in the next chapter. It may be worth seeding network hubs in a particular segment before you target that particular segment, to get the network hubs hooked in. (Of course, this is true only if you won't turn them off with a half-baked solution). Once they do respond positively to a product, remember that adoption is just the beginning. There's a lot more to do. Network hubs are not as loyal as you might hope, and if something better comes along, they can jump ship.

### Target Hubs First

Network hubs at all levels love to be the first to know something new. The software industry has had a long tradition of giving advance copies to hubs and mega-hubs. Regis McKenna, in describing the introduction of Lotus 1-2-3, says, "Lots of people had early prototypes. I had one. Many magazine editors had them. We talked to each other about it, and the excitement grew. We could hardly wait for the final product to hit the market. By the time of introduction, 1-2-3 was the industry's worst-kept secret, but also its most surefire success."

The same type of excitement was created when the PalmPilot was first presented at Demo, an invitation-only event for the high-tech industry. "Every time they showed a feature, the audience would kind of gasp," Rafe Needleman, a journalist who attended the event, remembers. The young company combined the sneak preview with a seeding tactic, offering the device to attendees at 50-percent discount. Ed Colligan took between four-hundred and five-hundred orders. "Those people were the first to get them when we shipped," Colligan says. "It was pretty much the Who's Who of the industry."

While expert hubs are important, it's also important not to overlook the power of social hubs. Record companies routinely give sneak previews to DJs, record stores, radio stations, and other recognized expert hubs in order to promote new records. In a classic marketing experiment, however, researchers obtained the names of *social* leaders in high schools in several cities. Class presidents, sports captains, and cheerleaders were invited to join a select "expert panel" that would evaluate rock and roll records. (The researchers found later that most of these students owned very few records, which means that they would have not been classified as expert network hubs as far as the music industry was concerned.) The participants received free records in the mail and were asked to identify potential hits. They were then encouraged to discuss their choices with friends.

Joseph Mancuso, describing the experiment in the *Journal of Marketing,* says, "The total cost of the experiment was less than five thousand dollars. In turn, several records reached the top ten charts in the trial cities. These hit records did not make the top ten selections in any other cities. Thus, without contacting any radio stations or any record stores, a rock and roll record was pulled through the channels of distributors and made into a hit." The buzz created by letting these social network hubs discover these songs made them hits before they became hits anywhere else.

### Give Them Something to Talk About

Buzz needs ammunition. How many times can you tell your friends that you now drive a Jeep? But if you come back from a two-day, action-packed Jeep Jamboree, you'll have *a lot* to talk about. What's a Jeep Jamboree? This is an off-road weekend trip designed for Jeep owners only. Although this activity is not designed exclusively for network hubs, it is very likely to attract them. The Jeep Jamboree tradition goes all the way back to 1953, when the first fifty-five Jeep vehicles took on the Rubicon Trail—driving from Georgetown, California to Lake Tahoe. The 155 passengers and drivers who participated had something to tell everyone back home—the nine-mile trail took about nine hours to complete! Since then, thousands of Jeep owners have crossed the Rubicon and many other trails established by Mark A. Smith, who acts as a consultant to the Jeep division of DaimlerChrysler. "A Jamboree makes for good cocktail talk. That just reinforces the Jeep name," Ed Brust, a DaimlerChrysler executive, told *Brandweek.*

### Stimulate Them to Teach Others

Are network hubs buzzing about your product as you read this? Some of them may be, but how many? Network hubs, like everyone else, are extremely busy, and they have their own priorities.

Jeep Jamborees provide participants with experiences they are likely to
share with others.

They may love your product, but talking about it may not be the first
thing on their mind. Bringing them to forums where they can talk is
a way to stimulate discussion.

Once you succeed in gaining the support of network hubs,
you may be surprised at how much they are capable of doing. The
hubs who assume the role of advice-givers in their cliques may gain
even more respect for your product or idea as they start to spread the
information to others. This happens as they process (and sometimes
slightly modify) your message. Network hubs tailor the message to
the language of their cliques. "Give them the information and they
will translate it for you," says Ivan Juzang, president of MEE Produc-
tions, a Philadelphia-based communications company that specializes
in spreading the word among inner-city kids. MEE produces antidrug
videos, for example, but the company doesn't do it on their own. "You
need to identify and recruit the peer-group leaders," says Juzang. Together with these young people, MEE creates tools that use the language employed by urban youth. For these kids the government's

standard message, "Just say No" to drugs, is meaningless. They are much more likely to be influenced by a message that comes from their network hubs.

## Give Them the Facts

Don't be concerned about boring expert hubs. Dell Computer Corporation came to realize that network hubs are willing to spend twenty minutes with an ad and go through the specs and the features. That's why Dell's ads look like catalogs. These hubs may be less influenced by brand names, and some marketers believe that they are therefore less brand-loyal. "Those people by their very nature are brand-agnostic," says Joe Gillespie of Ziff-Davis. "They are not to be fooled. They will not pay a 15-percent premium because there's a name on the product, and that's exactly how Dell made all its money." Brand-agnostic or not, network hubs put a lot of weight on facts. They are not to be fooled because they have acquired a great deal of knowledge. Give them more facts.

Never assume that network hubs already know about your latest product review. They may have missed it, or they may have noticed the one bad review you got in a different publication. Although many hubs consider themselves independent thinkers, they are influenced, like all of us, by others. Make sure that any endorsements or positive reviews that might add to their confidence in a product do not escape their attention. Although some of them may not be as impressed by popularity as other people, network hubs understand that ubiquity is important. Keep them up to date as the product passes certain benchmarks ("more than a million copies sold") or wins awards.

## Don't Abuse the Relationships

Heidi Roizen, one of the best-connected people in Silicon Valley, asked Walt Mossberg, the influential columnist from *The Wall*

*Street Journal,* to meet with an entrepreneur she works with. Mossberg agreed to meet him the next day. When the two met, the business-man expressed his astonishment at Roizen's power. "I do everything she tells me to do," Mossberg told him. The reason? Because she doesn't ask him to do much. Roizen has a good relationship with Mossberg but is careful not to abuse it. "I'm on the board of six com-panies, and I've only called Walt once," she says. It's pointless to nag someone like Mossberg about a product that wouldn't interest him. "In order to use my network wisely, I don't call someone unless I'm absolutely certain that the product is ready and the idea is good." The same respectful attitude should be used with regular network hubs. Keep in touch with them, but don't overdo it. In fact, you should be even more sensitive about this issue in dealing with people who are regular hubs. Mega-hubs—the media, politicians, celebrities—are used to receiving press kits, phone calls, and e-mails and understand that it comes with the territory. Regular hubs are not always comfort-able with this and may be turned off by *too* much attention.

## Make Sure People See Hubs Using Your Product

Network hubs may be using your product, but this has only limited value if the world doesn't know about it. PowerBar imple-mented a special program to take care of that, enrolling thousands of leading athletes to be part of the company's "PowerBar Team Elite" program. Team members earn money when their picture appears in the media eating PowerBars or wearing the PowerBar gear. "Through that program you see PowerBar everywhere," says Alyssa Berman of the company's marketing team.

Luxottica Group uses this concept by placing its sunglasses with mega-hubs in the entertainment industry. In 1988, when Luxot-tica introduced its Armani line, most glasses in the market were housed in large plastic frames. The Armani glasses were compact and made out of metal. "People thought they were weird-looking," says

Steve Hollander, vice president of marketing for the company. Luxottica used a Hollywood placement agency to have celebrities like John Travolta, Billy Crystal, and Robin Williams wear the glasses in numerous movies. "They wear them in their personal life as well, so you get the publicity of the movie, but they're also in *People* magazine and *Variety* and seen on the street," Hollander says.

## The Bias Toward Mega-Hubs

Clearly, a successful marketing campaign should target both regular hubs and mega-hubs. Yet often only the mega-hubs are addressed. Why is this? First, because they are visible. It's easy to identify top analysts and press people in a certain market; simply read the trade publications and see who writes for them and who's being quoted. The second reason is that there are fewer mega-hubs. By covering several dozen individuals who follow an industry—sometimes even fewer than that—you're pretty much done. Look at the computer industry: "It really is a small group. When you really look at the industry and who people quote and which writers get the widest audience, it's a handful. It's fifteen to twenty people," says Heidi Roizen. The third reason is our bias toward hitting a home run. "Get on the cover of a major trade journal, and you've got it made," most people think.

Mega-hubs *can* be extremely influential, and their support can radically change the life of a product. Look at Oprah Winfrey and her book club. Oprah took a title like *The Book of Ruth* by Jane Hamilton, which sold fewer than 50,000 copies in its first seven years and turned it into a mega-bestseller, with more than 1 million copies in print. It's no wonder that marketers are trying for a home run. They should. But they also need to work at the grassroots level. First, because there's a limit to how many products mega-hubs can endorse—Oprah chooses only so many books a year. Second, regular hubs, cumulatively, can be as important as mega-hubs. Look at a book like *Cold Mountain,* which became a bestseller with no help from Oprah or any other mega-hub. It's all because thousands of network hubs recommended it in reading groups, on the Web, and over the counter.

The problem is that grassroots campaigns are much more tedious. "It's hard to get most companies excited about talking to their own users," says Jeff Tarter, editor and publisher of *Soft\*letter.* "And the PR community reinforces bad habits by insisting that 'the press' is tremendously influential for building a company's reputation. Maybe for a few giants like Microsoft and IBM, but if the end result of the PR campaign is six little news stories scattered throughout the trade press . . . Well, I think a much more productive effort would be to talk directly to users. Of course, that's not as good for the CEO's ego as getting quoted in an obscure trade magazine," says Tarter.

In the short term, targeting mega-hubs may seem to produce more results than focusing on regular hubs. It's much easier to quantify the effects of mega-hubs by tallying up "hits" in the media. And indeed, the backing of an Oprah Winfrey, a Rosie O'Donnell, or a Walt Mossberg could send sales of your product through the roof. But the untapped, neglected regular hubs ultimately may have as much or even more power. Since regular hubs engage in frequent *two-way* exchanges with their contacts, members of the networks are potentially more likely to hear and remember what these hubs say. This is the true source of strength that you can tap into by using word-of-mouth marketing and the invisible networks.

# Why Reach Hubs Early

Approaching network hubs at an early stage can help your product reach critical mass earlier than it would have otherwise. Why is that important? Because when a product reaches critical mass, adoption gains enough momentum to become self-sustaining.

Reaching that point is, of course, every marketer's dream. What do you do about it? You can just sit there and wait for hubs to hear about your product. The danger in that approach is that you might run out of energy or money before they decide to try your product. This is especially important for products associated with a high psychological or monetary risk, because network hubs are reluctant to be the first to adopt these products.

Remember that although network hubs are usually slightly ahead of the rest of their network in adopting new things, they are often not *the first* to adopt new ideas or products. "They will oftentimes wait to see whether or not the community is going to support their adoption behavior," explains Tom Valente of the University of Southern California. "They are not going to adopt it until they're sure it's the right thing for them to do."

Many innovations are first adopted at the *margins*, by people who aren't as central as network hubs. Either they have less of a reputation to maintain In their communities or they associate with groups of people who value risky choices. These people are usually imitated by only a few other people. When they are the only adopters, adoption spreads slowly.

That's why you want network hubs to adopt as early as possible. Bring the product to their attention. Address their concerns. Give them the facts. Assure them that it's safe. Show them hubs in other networks who have already adopted. Let them talk to these hubs. Do anything possible to make them adopt sooner rather than later. Once they do adopt, they'll give your product their seal of approval, making it okay for their followers not only to adopt but also to recommend it to all of *their* friends. That, in turn, increases the chance of a person hearing about the innovation from multiple acquaintances.

"Once the opinion leaders adopt, you're much more likely to reach critical mass, and then the process becomes self-sustaining," explains Valente.

# Active

# Seeding

**10.** **My favorite game as a** six-year-old was a special form of hide-and-seek called "Clutch." Maybe I liked it because I hated counting. When you played Clutch, you didn't have to count: One kid would jump on the edge of the "clutch"—a two-foot-long stick that was placed against the curb—causing seven smaller sticks to fly like rockets all over the street. The kid who was "it" had to collect the seven sticks while the rest of us would run frantically to find a hiding place. During first grade we spent long afternoons playing Clutch, and we would stop only when our mothers' threats not to serve dinner began to sound serious.

During the summer following first grade I was sent to camp. I was the only kid from our neighborhood at summer camp, and on the first evening I found myself at the dinner table with five other kids, all as nervous as I was. I thought that exchanging some Clutch tips might break the ice, so I mentioned a couple of my better ones. The other kids moved uncomfortably in their chairs as they tried to figure out what I was talking about. I poured a lot of salt on my french fries before understanding that no one, not even the kid who lived thirty minutes away from my house, had ever heard of Clutch. That was my first encounter (not truly appreciated at the age of six) with an important principle outlined in previous chapters: Information spreads easily *within* a cluster, but not as smoothly—and sometimes not at all—between different clusters. Clutch spread well in our immediate neighborhood, but for some reason the game had not reached other communities.

What does all this mean to marketers? What happened to Clutch can happen to your product. While the word about your product may spread effectively in some clusters, it may leap over to other clusters very slowly—if at all. Very few products spread like wildfire. Most products need help, and that's where seeding enters the picture.

## What Is Seeding?

To accelerate the rate at which the word about a product spreads, smart companies seed their products at strategic points in many different clusters with seed units. A seed unit is an actual product or a representative sampling from the product that you are trying to promote (a book, a computer, a software package), which you place in the hands of seed customers. The logistics vary: The seed unit can be offered at full price, at a discount, on a loan basis, or for free. You can use sampling programs, touring programs, or demo programs, but the principle is always the same: You give people in multiple clusters direct experience with the product. By doing so you plant a seed to stimulate discussion *simultaneously* in multiple networks. By seeding the networks you are accelerating the regular adoption process. Instead of waiting for the natural (but sometimes painfully slow) transfer of information from one cluster to the next, you take the initiative and ensure that this transfer occurs.

As I mentioned earlier, when the makers of Trivial Pursuit introduced the game back in the early eighties, they promoted it through radio stations around the country. "In New York there was a guy on the radio who loved to ask trivia questions," recalled Linda Pezzano, the PR manager behind the introduction of the game. "So I thought he was a natural guy to do a promotion with. And then I thought; 'Well, there must be guys like that in every market.'" Pezzano had a student intern call radio stations around the country to find their local "trivia maven." It didn't take long before radio stations started to broadcast trivia questions from the game. More than a hundred stations were running the promotion, and each one of them was giving away copies of the game to listeners who answered trivia questions correctly. This simple tactic created a double effect: The radio personalities broadcast information to thousands of people, *and* people who won the game began bombarding those around them with questions like "What woman was *Time*'s Man of the Year for 1952?" "What was World War I known as before World War II?" or "What does the J&B stand for on the scotch?" (Queen Elizabeth II. The Great War. Justerini & Brooks.)

To seed the product in additional networks, the makers of the game distributed sample cards in popular spring-break hangouts, organized Trivial Pursuit parties in bars, and, as I mentioned earlier, mailed games to celebrities mentioned in the questions. "The celebrity mailing turned on a lot of opinion leaders to the game, and they loved it," says Pezzano. The campaign generated unprecedented buzz in the invisible networks. During 1984, 20 million games were sold with almost no advertising.

Notice the two levels that the seeding campaign targeted: the media (radio personalities and celebrities), and the grassroots (radio station *listeners*, students on spring break, people in bars). Both of these levels are very important, but it's the grassroots level that has been generally underutilized. Almost all companies have done some seeding at one point or another, but the vast majority of seeding programs are PR campaigns that target the media.

## Seeding at the Grassroots Level

**A good seeding** campaign goes beyond mailing sample products to a small group of press contacts and "the industry elite." For example, seeding a book should consist of more than sending proofs to a few dozen key buyers. I am talking about a different scale here. *Cold Mountain,* for example, was sent to more than 4,000 buyers, readers, authors, reviewers, and other influential people. *In Search of Excellence,* one of the biggest business books of the 1980s, was sent to 15,000. A proper seeding campaign lets individuals in *numerous* networks experience the product firsthand. When Steve Jobs donated an Apple computer to every school in California in the early eighties, he did just that—he seeded multiple networks. Suddenly every school had this box in some classroom, generating interest, discussion, and excitement among all kinds of students and teachers. Sun Microsystems used a similar approach in its early days. Marleen McDaniel, who was responsible for Sun's academic market at the time, explained how they seeded the market. "I went to the most influential engineering campuses first: Stanford, Berkeley, MIT, Carnegie Mellon, Caltech," says McDaniel. At each campus McDaniel and her staff identified a seed customer, usually a professor in the computer science department. Allowing the professor to use one of the company's workstations helped create discussion about Sun's hardware, first within one department, then in other departments, and ultimately in the whole school. One day in the mid-1980s Sun got an order for a thousand workstations from UC Berkeley. At the time that was the largest single order the company had ever received. "But you started with one professor," says McDaniel.

The ideal seed customer shouldn't be shy. People who called radio stations to win a free Trivial Pursuit game weren't shy almost by definition. Sun chose influential professors on each campus. This is important, because you need your seed customers to do one thing: talk. When Chrysler came out with its LH models back in 1992, the company targeted accountants, engineers, and other professionals whose opinions carry weight with car buyers. The new models—Dodge Intrepid, Eagle Vision, and Chrysler Concorde—got great reviews in industry magazines such as *Car & Driver, AutoWeek,* and *Motor Trend,* which praised the models in terms like "worldclass" and "Hallelujah!" To spread the word further, Chrysler offered to lend its new models for a weekend to over 6,000 influential individuals in neighborhoods all over America. Through these network hubs the company was able to insert itself into people's daily lives and break through the noise barrier. People may not notice a commercial for yet another new model, but they all notice when *their neighbor* drives a new car.

Seeding works only in categories that people talk about: cars, books, computers, fashion, and so on—what we call "conversation products." It doesn't work with paper clips. The idea of seeding is to get selected people from different networks *more involved* with these products so that they talk about them with others. Sometimes this is achieved by giving away products for free, but it can also be achieved by letting potential customers use your product for a period of time or by having them participate in some event associated with your brand. This type of seeding is limited only by your imagination.

I wrote the above at the Exploratorium, a science museum in San Francisco. The day I visited the Exploratorium, there were children with Polaroid cameras all over the place. People from Polaroid were handing out cameras outside the museum. You left some sort of ID and got a camera with film for ten instant pictures. In the museum's cafeteria a boy at the table next to me took a picture of a girl's behind. The boy and the three girls at the table then watched the picture develop, giggling the entire time.

Throw a Polaroid camera into any social network and you're guaranteed to get conversations started. The people at Polaroid understand that. When Polaroid decided to renew interest in instant photography among younger people, the company took its cameras on a road tour. The campaign vehicle parked outside the Exploratorium is a conversation piece in itself—a long motor home, completely wrapped in a colorful original design created especially for the tour. The vehicle parks in towns en route, and people who stop by are lent a Polaroid camera for a few hours. The first year Polaroid attempted this, in 1996, people were asked to bring back a picture that showed their town; they were told their picture might eventually be selected as part of an art piece entitled "America: An Instant Self-Portrait." More than 30,000 instant photographs were collected from people around the country, and the event became part of tens of thousands of conversations. In 1997 the company used the promotion to reach college students during spring break. As you might expect, the camera became the center of thousands of social interactions on the street, at parties, and on the beach. The focus of the 1998 and 1999

How Polaroid spreads the word about its new cameras among young people.

tours was on preparing a time capsule with pictures that would describe life at the end of the millennium to future generations.

Polaroid found ways to get people involved, and involvement leads to buzz. "Did the buzz lead to sales?" I asked Arlene Henry, marketing communications manager at Polaroid. "That's always difficult to track with any PR effort," she says. "There are so many other things out in the marketplace, ads and promotions. There's no way to isolate the data to say that this particular promotion has moved sales by X percent." The company *does* track some other relevant numbers, though: The 1996 campaign generated 40 million media impressions and had 120,000 customers participate in the experience. In the 1998 tour these numbers went up to 50 million and 250,000 respectively. We can only guess how many conversations were generated by participants. People tend to share pictures with their relatives and friends, and each participant got to keep half of the pictures for him- or herself.

I saw dozens of groups taking pictures that morning at the Exploratorium. "Say 'cheese,'" one girl commanded her five friends. Click. Then all six of them crowded around staring at the picture as it emerged. When these kids got home, they were likely to show the pictures to their parents and perhaps mention the new cameras that were sneak-previewed—the Barbie and Tasmanian Devil cameras and the small I-Zone pocket camera (which is really neat!).

## Numbers Make a Difference

**Tom Peters attributes** part of the success of his first book to an extensive seeding campaign. In 1980 Peters and his coauthor Bob Waterman put together a 125-page summary of what later became the classic management book *In Search of Excellence*. They gave it to just a few executives they knew, but very quickly these individuals started discussing with others what they had read. As word about the coming book started to spread, demand soared, and the authors decided to seed the market with 15,000 copies of this preliminary report. Their publisher was worried that Peters and Waterman were giving away too many. Edward Burlingame, who commissioned the book for Harper & Row, said that the company expected to sell around 60,000 copies in the first year, meaning that the 15,000 copies represented 25 percent of that amount. But Peters believes that these copies were important in generating word of mouth and sales. "Within days of the book's launching, supportive reviews appeared, and the network of 15,000 (plus at least an equal number of photocopied knockoffs) hurried to buy the real thing, often in bulk for their subordinates," Peter recalls in *Thriving on Chaos*. *In Search of Excellence* sold 1.5 million copies in hardcover alone.

Because information can get stuck in clusters, seeding in *numerous* clusters is key. One of the most talked-about products in the mid-1990s was Windows 95, and seeding played an important role in that buzz. Microsoft had 450,000 advance copies out before the product was actually released. Seeding wasn't the main reason these copies were sent out. Fifty thousand copies were distributed as part of the beta testing program to ensure that the product was put through its paces by a large number of users. The other 400,000 copies were distributed as part of the Windows 95 Preview Program, which allowed information technology professionals to plan their move to the new operating system.

Regardless of the motivation, Microsoft placed a copy of its new software at just one or two degrees of separation from any PC user. With 85 million PC owners around the world at the time and 450,000 advance copies of Windows 95 out, it is safe to assume that if a PC user didn't know someone directly who had an advance copy, at least he or she knew *of* someone who did. One out of every 189 PC users had an early version of Windows 95.

In searching for beta testers, software companies look for people from a variety of backgrounds who use their computers in a variety of configurations, and this is exactly what made these programs into such effective seeding efforts. To compile the list of participants, Microsoft used a variety of mailing lists, input from their sales teams, resellers, etc. This breadth is what made it into such a good seeding program. Rob Bennet, product manager for Windows 95, commented that "The number-one goal with the beta program was to ensure the product was put through its paces by a large number of users representing a broad range of use scenarios, so having the beta testers in a number of industries and business sizes, for example, was key to this goal. The fact that this resulted in a broader set of beta testers to work with from a marketing perspective was just a nice by-product."

Not all comments that spread in the networks about Windows 95 were positive ones. That's the risk you take when you send your product out there. But overall, Microsoft created real excitement, especially among end users. As part of what *BusinessWeek* called "a marketing and advertising blitz that could make Revlon blush," Microsoft also invited 70,000 people to product launch parties around the country, and of course employed its efficient PR machine to generate coverage in the media. Microsoft released the software at the stroke of midnight on August 24, 1995. Long lines and instant sellouts stimulated even more discussion when they were reported through the media on the following day.

One million copies of Windows 95 were sold within the first four days it was available in retail stores. MS-DOS 6.0 was the previous record holder for the fastest-selling software product, and it took forty days to sell its millionth copy.

## How Much Seeding Is Enough?

**The seeding that** took place in Microsoft's case was intense; most companies find it difficult to create that kind of interest in their product. Still, seeding is an incredible tool even if it's not executed on a grand scale. How much seeding is enough? There is no simple formula for finding the optimal number of seed customers that will allow information to spread as fast as possible while keeping your costs down. This is a challenge each company has to face individually, based on its cost structure and its market. If you give just one copy of your product to a Fortune 500 company, your cost will be minimal, but the information about the product is likely to spread at a very slow rate. On the other hand, if you give the product away for free to everyone at the company, the speed will be maximized, but so will your cost.

One smaller company that has been growing significantly through seeding efforts is Wizards of the Coast, the company behind trading-card games such as Magic and Pokémon, and role-playing games such as Dungeons & Dragons. A lot of their efforts in the United States focus on touring, sampling, and demo programs. "While they are more time-intensive and they are more expensive, we have found that those programs work about 100 percent better than traditional marketing like print ads or TV ads," says Charlotte Stuyvenberg, VP of marketing at the company. The company's Internet presence accelerates diffusion, but letting seed users personally try out its games is key. "Reading about something on the Internet is not enough," says Stuyvenberg. "They have to be able to experience it themselves, because what gets the buzz going on the Internet is [direct experience]." The company focuses its seeding efforts on fifteen markets in the United States working closely with specialty stores as well as bookstores and other retailers. The company also flies its employees to different parts of the country to manage game tournaments.

The biggest potential pitfall in seeding is redundancy. Seeding twenty units of your product in a large organization can mean different things, depending on the distribution of those units. If the twenty units are scattered in twenty different departments, you are probably making good use of these seed units. If all twenty units are clustered in one department, then you've spent a lot of money that could have been used more effectively. (Of course, if the visibility of that particular department is especially high, it may justify such concentrated seeding.)

## Protect the People You Seed

**As any gardener** will tell you, seeds are fragile. Birds and rodents eat them, and they need just the right amount of water and other nutrients to grow and flourish. The seed customers who use your product in companies or neighborhoods are also fragile. They need care and support. Nowhere is this more evident than with new technologies, although the concept applies to any new idea that is being adopted in a large organization.

Technologies are not always willingly adopted by companies. They often invade organizations against the will of information technology (IT) managers who are desperately trying to set standards that will be easier to support. Individuals in companies adopt a wide variety of new technologies because they believe the products will help them do a better job. Marketers should help these early customers in any way possible. McAfee, a company in the antivirus software business, did just that. Their strategy was simple: Every time they wrote a new version of their antivirus software, they posted it on electronic bulletin boards for free. Within seventy-two hours after launching a new release, the software would be on thousands of electronic bulletin boards around the world and in turn on desktops of millions of people. Bill McKiernan, former president of McAfee, says, "We would support the hell out of our user base, knowing that they were going to become our salespeople, our evangelists." McAfee provided free technical support to people who were using its free software. How did they make any money out of this? Initially they didn't. But eventually the support paid off, and companies adopted the seeded technology by licensing the software. In fact, the companies didn't have much choice. They had hundreds or thousands of employees who were already using the product. Dedicated support of these initial seed users turned them into loyal customers, as McKiernan had predicted.

It's also important, of course, with new technology to try to get the IT managers to adopt the technology themselves. After all, why swim against the current if you don't need to? As Palm organizers continue to invade companies all around the world, 3COM tries to build support within the IT departments. At the Gartner Symposium, for example, an annual conference that attracts thousands of information technology managers, the people from 3COM preloaded Palm devices with the conference agenda. When attendees walked in to register, they were offered a Palm that had all the conference information loaded on it. That gave IT managers the opportunity to actually use the technology. At the end of the meeting each of these people had the option to buy the unit he or she had used. Ed Colligan, the former VP of marketing at the company, estimates that about five thousand people used Palm handhelds at the conference and about fifteen hundred actually bought them—the latter group returning to their networks as supporters of the device.

## Pay Attention to "Dead" Networks

**Seeding should be** an ongoing effort. No matter how much care you provide, some seeds won't germinate, and as a result their corresponding networks will be inactive. I call those networks "dead networks." A dead network may indicate low activity, or it can suggest that a competing brand is successfully spreading in that network. To identify dead networks, you should use all the traditional sources of information used in marketing intelligence: sales data, marketing research, and your own observations. But instead of focusing on traditional measurements such as brand awareness or media exposure, focus on answering a single question: To what extent are people *talking* about my brand in a particular network?

Anecdotal data is very important in identifying dead networks. A sales rep can come back from a sporting event and report that biking fans in Seattle don't know about the new helmet you introduced to the market. Dead network. You come across a discussion on the Net that suggests that Ph.D. students prefer a product from a competitor of yours and don't even mention your product. Dead network. The Internet can in fact be very helpful in this respect, since the activities of different on-line communities are usually more visible and more easily accessible to outsiders. At one point, for example, our company noticed that medical librarians hardly ever discussed EndNote in their on-line discussion groups. There were lively discussions about EndNote among medical researchers, biology students, and in other newsgroups, but the network of medical librarians was dead as far as EndNote was concerned. This was especially alarming, since each one of these librarians was part of a local network that influenced what students and researchers were buying. We decided to distribute hundreds of seed units to medical libraries around the country. As a result, medical librarians started teaching courses on how to use EndNote, recommending the software enthusiastically to library patrons.

Sales data can offer another good indicator of inactive networks. If you're a book publisher, for instance, you know exactly how well a title is doing in each market. When Simon & Schuster published *The Road Less Traveled* by psychiatrist M. Scott Peck, poor sales in most markets were an indication that most networks were flat dead. However, there were two markets in which the book sold exceptionally well: Washington, D.C. (where it got a great review in the

*Washington Post*), and Buffalo, New York, where the networks were working overtime. The wife of one of Peck's college roommates had sent the book to her friend Cornelia Dopkins, a teacher in Buffalo. Dopkins gave the book to the rectors of two local churches, who in turn invited Peck to talk. People in Buffalo proceeded to buy hundreds of copies.

Both Simon & Schuster and Peck himself understood that the excitement wouldn't spread easily from Buffalo to, say, Seattle. But dead networks can be brought to life with some help. Peck hired a Connecticut schoolteacher to send copies of the *Washington Post* review to newspaper editors around the country, and Simon & Schuster paid for a two-week, ten-city promotional tour. As a result of this effort, individuals who were introduced to the book spread the word in *additional* networks. This was really more of a PR effort in its scope, but it illustrates the main point: Using your own sales figures, you can identify the dead networks and seed them. From 1980 through 1984, sales doubled annually, with more than 600,000 copies selling in 1986. The book was on the *New York Times* bestseller list for over ten years. Sure, other factors played a role in the success of *The Road Less Traveled*, but the impact of these actions taken during the early days shouldn't be underestimated. Seeding accelerated the buzz.

This is a good place to remind ourselves of the busy network paradox. As I discussed in Chapter 5, our natural tendency as marketers is to pay attention to the networks that are "happening" and ignore those that are dead. In fact, as I pointed out, the more successful a company is, the more likely it is to be flooded by messages from its existing networks, and therefore fail to notice and seed the inactive ones. We pay attention to the networks that stimulate us, and it's hard to look beyond them. But you can expand your audience and your products sales far more rapidly by seeding inactive networks than by focusing all your efforts on existing active ones.

# The Four Rules of a Successful Seeding Campaign

Successful seeding is an *active* process. It goes well beyond the *Field of Dreams* cliché "If you build it, they will come." Rather than waiting passively for people to come to you, you go out and plant seeds all around the forest. Here are a few guidelines:

1. *Look Beyond the Usual Suspects.* Although seeding traditional channels is important, successful seeding efforts go beyond your normal channels, be these the media, the bookstore, the car dealership, or the department store. Think broadly. In the same way that you identify ZIP codes in which you don't have enough customers, you should be able to identify social circles, industry segments, or academic disciplines in which people don't talk about your company, product, or service. Seek them out for seeding.

2. *Put the Product in Their Hands.* Most often the "seed" has to be the product itself. In some cases, such as the sneak preview of *In Search of Excellence*, people may get excited just by getting a sample, but in general, people need the experience of the whole product to get involved. The seed product has to be placed directly in their hands. Remember, there is a big difference between making a product available for free on the Web and actually going out to hand that product to individual people. Seventeen years after the introduction of Trivial Pursuit, Parker Brothers is now using the Web to make the game available. Anyone can come and play at www.trivialpursuit.com. Great! It's another way to reach out to people about the game. But to generate even half of the buzz the game got in the early 1980s, a proactive seeding campaign is needed.

3. *Reduce the Price Barrier.* In some cases your analysis will show that you can afford to distribute seed units for free; at other times a discount is the best you can do. But don't underestimate the price barrier for an unknown product: Make the product free to a seed customer if possible, or at least as low in price as feasible.

4. *Listen for Silence.* When you hear silence from dead networks, your natural tendency will be to ignore them. Successful seeding requires *paying attention* to dead networks and doing further seeding.

Seeding is more than just a technique; it's a state of mind. Suppose you start a band with three of your friends. You're good, and you find a club willing to let you perform. Several cliques hang out at the club, and your products—your songs—start spreading in these cliques. Before long another club owner on the other side of town is interested. Now you perform on a regular basis in two clubs, and you start to develop a group of followers. A few months later you borrow some money from your cousin and press three hundred CDs that sell pretty well in the clubs. The local fans love you! After a while a third club is interested, and some high school kids ask you to listen to their band on Thursday evening, and you perform almost every night, and teenagers call you at home and— Hey, you're busy. So busy, in fact, that you can't even think of going anywhere else. So how do you turn your band into a national success?

Successful bands know that in order to build a real fan base, they need to get out. In the music world, seeding is done through tours. A band can be the hottest thing in one network, but it doesn't mean a thing to networks just thirty minutes away. If you have a band, you need to get a van, an old school bus, anything with wheels, and start touring. It isn't easy. You can drive for five hours to appear in front of fewer than a dozen people. But as musician Stephen Carpenter, a guitarist for Deftones, says, "If ten people see a killer show and tell their friends, you've succeeded." This is the seeding idea in a nutshell. You go from network to network and hook the first few people, who then proceed to spread the word.

At the same time, you seed the media. In fact, an important part of touring in the music industry these days is to stop at radio stations in each town to get radio programmers' attention, a routine practiced not only by new bands but successful bands as well. You don't stop there, though. You don't want to limit yourself to grassroots support alone. The importance of MTV or VH-1 in creating buzz in the music world cannot be overemphasized. You go after both—mega-media and grassroots networks.

So now your band is on MTV (you've come a long way in just a few paragraphs). But even bands that appear on national media keep touring. Once a band is successful, the seeding efforts and the media exposure start to feed on one another and can amplify earlier efforts enormously. Bands continue to tour not just to seed dead networks but to keep people talking in the active networks. As difficult as tours are, successful bands realize that very few stars can maintain their momentum through exposure on MTV alone. Most stars and bands keep touring. People from all over the networks come to their concerts to hear the songs they love. And at the concerts new songs are planted in their minds ("This one's from our new album"), to be carried back to the networks. It's a thrill to fans to be among the first to hear a song that was created just days or weeks earlier. They tell others about it and eagerly await the opportunity to buy the new CD upon its release. This "sneak preview" then generates even more buzz for future products.

# The Elements

# of a Good Story

**11.** **The children emerging from the** first screening of the movie *The Wizard* on a winter night in 1989 had just come out of a time machine. They had journeyed somewhere none of their friends had been—four months into the future. Four months doesn't sound like much when it comes to time travel, but for these kids this trip was more meaningful than a trip to the year 3000.

It wasn't the movie itself that excited them so much. I've certainly seen more exciting films. *The Wizard* tells the story of a boy named Corey who takes his younger brother Jimmy on a cross-country trip to California to enter a video game championship. What excited the audience so much was what was shown toward the end of the movie. With only three contestants left in the championship (little Jimmy among them), the announcer let the contestants—and the audience—know that for the final, tie-breaking match, they would have to play a video game no one had ever played before.

For months, rumors about the next version of Nintendo's Super Mario Brothers were circling the playgrounds. And now the children in the movie theater had a sneak preview of it right there on the screen. "Ladies and gentlemen, we have three contestants . . . one . . . two . . . three," the master of ceremonies announced dramatically. "So I give you Super Mario Brothers Threeee!"

"The excitement in the theaters was far greater for Super Mario Brothers 3 than for the movie itself," David Sheff, who studied the history of Nintendo, wrote in his book *Game Over*. For about five minutes, kids were able to see the upcoming game in action. New challenges. New tricks. It's not difficult to imagine what these children did first thing after they got home. They did what any reasonable person would do after being in a time machine—they called all their friends and told them what they knew. "Mario can fly now, and they have these whistles that take you to any level you want!" In the following days each one of them tried to tell as many other kids about it as he or she could. As more and more children went to see the movie, kids were increasingly geared up for the release. When Super Mario Brothers 3 hit the stores, it outsold any video game in history up to that point and grossed more than $500 million. The special arrangement between Nintendo and Universal Studios resulted in this sneak preview, which was one of the factors that generated phenomenal buzz for the game.

The anticipation for the game was already there, but the people at Nintendo understood that buzz needs to be fueled. Without new information, comments about a product in the networks become empty and dull, and customers eventually move on to other, more exciting topics. The company, in fact, used the sneak preview concept routinely in other ways to keep interest up. Nintendo employed hundreds of game counselors, assigned to help players who called with questions and problems. Once the counselor resolved the issue, he or she used the opportunity to get the customer excited about the next version ("Oh, by the way, wait till you see what we're working on now"). "In a sense they made kids feel that they were part of this insider club," says Sheff. "They were getting inside information about something that was incredibly relevant to them and their friends."

Creating buzz is similar in some ways to good storytelling. You build suspense by withholding information and releasing it gradually. You deliver the punch line at the right point in the story. You create characters that grab the audience's imagination. In this chapter I'll look at the elements that help buzz reproduce itself rapidly in the invisible networks, similar to the way an urban legend or a folk story can. It isn't a coincidence that the techniques described in this chapter are being used extensively in the film industry—sneak previews, taking the audience behind the scenes, creating publicity stunts, and using celebrities to announce or advertise a product. Whatever your feelings about Hollywood, the people there know how to tell a story, and they know buzz.

## Tantalize with Scarcity and Mystery

In his book *Influence: The Psychology of Persuasion*, psychologist Robert Cialdini tells how he never had any desire to visit a Mormon temple in the city of Mesa, Arizona, where he lives, until one day he read about a special inner sanctum of the temple that only faithful members of the church can enter. The article said that this section would be open to non-Mormons for a few days. His instinctive reaction was to want to go, and to call a friend to ask if he wanted to join him.

We value anything that is scarce: rare baseball cards, places with restricted access, and information that is not widely available.

This is an important concept to keep in mind when trying to create buzz. It has to do with not only spreading the word but withholding information and releasing it gradually over time.

Companies that secretively protect information about their products can use this to their advantage to fuel buzz. There has to be an underlying interest in these products, of course, to begin with. No matter how mysterious you are about the new clothes hanger your company is designing, you're not likely to make many customers curious. Also, there's a limit to how much you can play this game, because customers can tire of it.

But as a rule, when we don't have access to information, we want it—badly.

Part of the initial buzz around *The Blair Witch Project,* a low-budget film that became the hit of the summer of 1999, stemmed from the mystery surrounding the movie. "The biggest part of the buzz was that we wouldn't let anyone see it," Kevin Foxe, the film's executive producer, told Reuters. He refused to show the movie to the press prior to the Sundance Film Festival, and that made them talk. Buzz among viewers, especially at the early stages, was further stimulated by the mystery surrounding the production of the film. Was this a documentary?

Remember the movie *The Crying Game*? A lot of what fired the buzz about that movie was the mystery associated with the twist in the story. I remember a conversation I had with someone at work about it.

"You *have* to see this movie, *The Crying Game,*" he said.

"What's it about?" I asked.

"It's about this soldier . . . I can't really tell you. You just have to see it."

"What soldier?"

"It's in Ireland, this soldier . . . I can't tell you what happens. They ask people not to give away the plot."

"But why?" Now I was intrigued.

"It's a surprise twist. Just go and see the movie."

I didn't. Other things came up, and I wasn't *that* intrigued. A few weeks later I was with a group of friends, and someone mentioned *The Crying Game*. The room was suddenly divided into those who had seen it and knew and those who had not. I went to see the movie the next day.

The sense of mystery about your product can be incorporated into your message. When Sony introduced its PlayStation, its campaign revolved around a little mystery message that consisted of the letter U, the letter R, the letters NOT, and then a red E. "We stuck that out there, and we never told anybody what it meant or what it stood for," says Charlotte Stuyvenberg, who was director of public relations and promotions for Sony Computer Entertainment at the time. "And it was really cool to watch kids figure it out. Once they did, they started talking about it all over the place," she says. Stuyvenberg knew that the message had become a household phrase when she walked into a store one day wearing her PlayStation jacket, which didn't have the slogan on it, just the PlayStation logo. A little kid, maybe four years old, came running up to her and grabbed her by the sleeve. "You are not ready! You are not ready!" he said, demonstrating that he too, had solved the puzzle: URNOT + a red E added up to "You Are Not Ready." The message challenged young people even after they had deciphered it, asking, "Are you ready for the Sony PlayStation?" Created by ad agency TBWA Chiat/Day, the mystery symbol was distributed through brochures, T-shirts, stickers, and so on handed out from an eighteen-wheel truck that appeared at festivals and sporting events across the country.

Mystery is routinely drawn upon in Silicon Valley to create interest. One technology company that used this principle was General Magic. "The company was very deliberate about promoting itself, keeping an aura of secrecy around the substance of what it was doing, and that created a certain mystique that caused people to talk, to wonder, to speculate," says Chris Moore, who worked for General

Magic "I got chased through hotels by executives from ten-billion-dollar corporations who wanted to do deals with us. They didn't know why, but they had heard about it, they knew their friends were doing it. They knew they needed to do it," Moore says. In this particular case, the network technology that the company developed didn't make it. Competition, technology issues, and bad timing contributed to this. The extensive mystery probably didn't help either as it raised expectations to levels that were hard to meet. This is an effect one should be aware of when creating an aura of mystique. Use this principle with caution. But it's clear that the mystery made people talk. It built interest.

## Build Anticipation

**Withholding too much** information won't get you very far. To get people talking, you need to whet their appetite. A good story always contains a strong element of anticipation. A good buzz campaign creates anticipation as well. The launch campaign of the BMW Z3 Roadster is one such example in recent years. Through a series of nontraditional marketing efforts, the campaign created incredible anticipation for the car. "We knew that if we brought it to market in a traditional launch, it would do very well," says Jim McDowell, VP of marketing for the company. But the people at BMW saw this as an opportunity to position the Z3 as the icon of roadsters and to draw attention to the BMW brand. Managers at BMW were talking about this as "leveraging the buzz." And about getting the car on "people's conversational agenda."

The first—and probably the most memorable—element in the campaign was placing the car in the James Bond movie *GoldenEye*. The movie, which was going to be released a few months before the car, provided a perfect sneak preview. Because this was a truly special-looking vehicle, they didn't have to point it out too aggressively. In fact, the Z3 was shown only very briefly in the movie. The character Q, the head of R&D who develops all the neat gadgets for Bond, presents the new car to him early on in the movie; later Bond is shown driving it out in the country. That's it.

Once *GoldenEye* was ready, but *before* it was released to the public, BMW ran private screenings of the movie. Dealers sent invitations for the events to between 200 and 400 of their best customers, and some combined it with receptions before or after the show. A dealership in Concord, California, for example, had a party at the Blackhawk Automobile Museum, where the new roadster was displayed next to one of Bond's older cars. Overall, about 40,000 customers participated in these prescreenings. The following day at the office, on the golf course, or over lunch, these people were likely to tell their friends about what they had seen—the new James Bond movie *and* the new BMW.

The psychological principle behind the sneak preview idea is simple. When we tell others something new, we feel that we're "in the know," and we're typically rewarded by their reaction. The people at BMW understood that showing *GoldenEye* to a select group of 40,000 customers before the movie was available to the rest of the world would generate a great many comments in the networks. And because the car was so appealing, they were confident the comment would be enthusiastic.

It is the uneven distribution of information that ensures the continuing spread of buzz in the networks. For example, months before the release of *Star Wars: Episode I, The Phantom Menace*, fans were speculating about when the *trailer* would be released. The official debut date was finally set as November 20, 1998. The excitement among fans was at its peak when, three days prior to the official date, Lucasfilm and Twentieth Century Fox released the trailer in seventy-five theaters, a relatively small number of screens. Kind of a sneak preview of a sneak preview. For three days only part of the population had access to the trailer; the rest could just hear about it from friends who lived near one of these theaters or read about it on the Internet.

On Friday the trailer was released on thousands of additional screens. Timing the sequence of how you release the information is more an art than a science, and the rules that applied to the highly anticipated *Star Wars*—some fans paid full admission just to see the trailer—don't necessarily apply to other movies or products. But the main idea is still valid: Releasing information gradually can heighten the buzz about your product.

### Sneak Preview to Mega-Hubs

In the case of the BMW roadster, mega-hubs were simultaneously treated to a special sneak preview of the car in New York's Central Park. More than two hundred media representatives showed up. A huge box that looked as if it came from a scene in the movie was set onstage. Supporting characters from the movie also appeared onstage and explained how the car worked, but nobody was able to open the box, not even Q. Finally Helmut Panke, chairman and CEO of BMW Holding Corporation, came to the rescue by entering the secret code that exploded the crate and unveiled the car. Simultaneously, in drove Bond himself (played by actor Pierce Brosnan) in another Z3. There was true excitement there. People rushed to take pictures of the car onstage, and of Brosnan. "Photographers were trampling on top of each other," Jeff Salmon, executive vice president of Dick Clark Communications, which organized the event, remembers. After the initial excitement the journalists got the chance to interview the actors and the BMW management team, as well as drive the Z3 around Central Park.

When the movie was released to the public, the car drew a lot of attention, so much so that one cartoon showed Bond leaning against the car while three paparazzi taking pictures are trying to figure out who's the star: the new 007 or the new Z3. For old Bond fans there was an additional "news" element here: The BMW replaced Bond's signature car, the Aston Martin he'd driven in many of the previous movies.

## Go Beyond the Obvious

Good stories go beyond the obvious, and the best scenes are often the unexpected ones. "What we were trying to do in that non-traditional launch," says McDowell, "was appear in what we hoped would be surprising places." One of these places was the Neiman Marcus catalog. BMW offered a limited edition of the car—twenty cars to be exact—through the prestigious outlet.

Offering a car through a catalog? And not just "a car," but the car that 007 drove in the movie *GoldenEye*, with a commemorative "Specially Equipped 007" dash plaque? It got people talking. The car was featured as one of Neiman Marcus's top Christmas gifts, right next to a $900,000 necklace. BMW generated even more buzz this way.

"What we had completely *not* anticipated was what the demand would be," says McDowell. He remembers attending the Neiman Marcus press conference and getting on a flight to the Frankfurt Auto Show in Germany right after it. "By the time I got off the airplane in Frankfurt and checked my messages, we had a crisis on our hands," he remembers. In the first few hours, about a hundred people tried to purchase the car, and nobody could tell for sure who were the first twenty to order it. Some people called the 800 number, others came to the store. At the request of the catalog company, BMW increased the number of cars to a hundred. By Christmas the catalog had about six thousand (!) names on a waiting list. One can only imagine how many comments were exchanged around water coolers and over dinner tables about that special edition of the Z3 ("Mommy, does it come with guided missiles?"). It was a surprising and memorable way to get buzz going.

In another unexpected appearance, even before the movie premiere, the roadster was incorporated into a skit on Jay Leno's *Tonight Show*. This brings me to the issue of control. If you want to go beyond the obvious, if you want surprising elements that people will talk about, you often have to work with people who are not under your control. There is a great deal of uncertainty that comes with this territory. For example, the people at BMW did not know up to the last minute how Leno was going to include the car and what he was going to say. In the end it worked out fine. In the skit Bond was trying to get around security guards to penetrate the NBC studio. When the Z3 finally drove onstage, the car door opened and out came . . . comedian Steven Wright. Bond himself had already made it inside the studio by another route.

The same kind of uncertainty was present with the Z3 DJ program. When you buy regular advertising, you determine every single word, but your message is not likely to be repeated in the networks— it's advertising. If you're willing to take some risks and let third parties spread the word for you, you'll have more impact, but you may need an extra supply of Pepto-Bismol. BMW wanted hosts of morning-drive programs around the country to talk about the car. But what if the hosts made fun of the car or the movie? The team at Dick Clark Communications used the reputation of company founder Dick Clark, a well-respected figure in the radio business, to make sure DJs took it seriously. "Dick wrote to every program manager and called every DJ," Jeff Salmon remembers. As it turned out, the DJs appreciated the freedom they were given and responded to the car with enthusiasm. "They really liked the fact that somebody was trusting them to come up with their own promotion to help launch this car, and that we didn't want jingles on the radio, and that there was no required text that somehow had to be woven into whatever they said," says McDowell.

Radio stations came up with lots of interesting ideas on how to promote the car. In Atlanta, a DJ dressed up as Santa drove a Z3 onto the Atlanta Falcons' playing field at halftime. In Los Angeles, Mark and Brian, the two popular morning-drive DJs, drove the car around L.A. for four hours, doing a live broadcast from the roadster, drawing everyone's attention to the car with a megaphone. They even drove to the KTLA television station and got the morning news team to come out to the parking lot to look at the car on a live newscast. Then they drove across the street to the Disney Studios and got Tim Allen behind the wheel to race around the Disney parking lot. That made it on the air, too.

Not every customer who bought the car was swayed by these marketing activities and the extensive media coverage that followed. It is also a special car. Some customers I talked to saw the James Bond movie after they already owned the car. Still, in an informal survey among six BMW dealers around the country, the most influential marketing efforts were the sneak preview and the car's placement in the Bond movie. "It was one of the most successful product launches I've been involved in in twenty-five years in the car business," one dealer said. Another emphasized that the movie launch helped the car hold its full sticker price (of around $30,000) for a very long time. More than nine thousand orders for the roadster were prebooked, about four thousand more than the company projected.

## Take People Behind the Scenes

We humans are curious creatures. We love to know how things work and why they are done in a certain way, and we love to feel—even when we know it's not real—that we're backstage. Having "inside information" and feeling engaged in a new adventure prompts us to share our knowledge and excitement with others. "I went to a lot of concerts growing up, and I don't ever remember going backstage," says Kevin Conroy, senior VP of worldwide marketing at BMG Entertainment. Now, through five Web sites—each dedicated to a different genre of music—Conroy and his staff try to give their audience this "backstage" feeling. For example, when Australian-born singer Natalie Imbruglia visited New York, BMG Entertainment's Web site invited people to join her on a virtual horse-and-buggy ride in Central Park. The experience also included exclusive interviews with the artist and a chance to win autographed merchandise. The cost to BMG was minimal—buy tickets for the horse-and-buggy ride. But the buzz it created was significant. "What is absolutely amazing is to see how fast word travels. We didn't promote the Natalie event on BugJuice [their alternative music site], and yet it took no time at all for tens of thousands of people to find out that it was there and to come and participate." As a result, BMG accumulated thousands of e-mail addresses of current and potential Natalie Imbruglia fans.

Present-day Hollywood may understand this better than any other industry, although that wasn't always the case. In its early days the movie industry was very controlled and protected. "You didn't have film crews shooting behind the scenes on *Gone With the Wind*," says Steve Rubin, a movie publicist who's written several books about the subject. "Nobody wanted journalists buzzing around the set, especially with cameras." But with the rise of TV, both as a competitor to the movies and as a medium to transfer information about films, the industry opened up. A lot of it has to do with the invention of the video and the TV show *Entertainment Tonight*, according to Rubin. "*Entertainment Tonight* came on the air in 1981. That certainly popularized the 'behind-the-scenes story.' People had done documentaries before on those movies, but video all of a sudden gave you the ability to just go and get the story done. *Entertainment Tonight* had a behind-the-scenes story on movies every night, and then even regular news stations would do stories about moviemaking," he says.

The studios fuel the public interest by providing access to the press and by initiating behind-the-scenes documentaries. Short programs on the making of *Beauty and the Beast* started airing on cable TV more than a year before the release of the movie. Documentaries like *The Making of Star Wars* or *E.T.* are always great hits among movie buffs, who then discuss anecdotes, techniques, and scenes with people around them.

People love behind-the-scenes stories, whatever their nature. In the world of business, think of how many times you've heard of how Fred Smith, the founder of FedEx, got a C in college for a paper that described the concept of the company. Or how many times you've heard the story behind Post-it notes—that the inventor struggled for years to convince others within 3M to turn his idea into a commercial product. These stories spread very well in the invisible networks, but someone has to start them.

## Be a Little Outrageous

**The noise level** in the networks is astonishingly high. As a result, outrageous messages have a better chance of being heard than quiet ones. Here, too, there's a lot we can learn from Hollywood publicists, who aren't shy about trying out risky publicity stunts. My favorite stunt was the one done in 1974 for Mel Brooks's *Blazing Saddles,* a spoof of Westerns. For the premiere of the comedy, Warner Brothers invited some very special guests. "Any picture by Mel Brooks calls for something outrageous, so for his picture *Blazing Saddles* I invited horses to a special showing of the picture," the late Marty Weiser said in an interview taped in 1987, a year before he died. Weiser, who worked for Warner Brothers for over fifty years, was the man behind many ideas that generated a lot of talk over the years. Weiser and his staff at Warner Brothers rented a drive-in theater in Los Angeles, placed a small ad in the *Los Angeles Times,* and put up flyers near stables in the area advertising a free showing of the movie to horses and their owners. Then they waited and prayed that someone would show up. The media loved the idea; at the designated time the parking lot was full of TV crews and journalists. But no horses. Just when Weiser was beginning to lose hope, a police motorcycle drove in, escorting a parade of horses. About 250 of them—and their owners—showed up to watch the comedy and have some oats and "Horse d'Oeuvres" at the "Horsepitality Bar."

This kind of stunt certainly passes the "What will they think

To make people talk about his 1972 movie *Frenzy*, director Alfred Hitchcock had a dummy of himself float down the Thames River.

of next?" test. If your audience's reaction includes that thought, you know buzz is being generated.

Imagine that you walk along the Thames River in London one morning and see a body floating. When you get a little closer, you realize that the body is that of Alfred Hitchcock himself! Hitchcock understood the value of shock. He certainly used it in his movies, but also to create buzz about them. When he was shooting the movie *Frenzy* in the early 1970s, he created a dummy of himself and had it float down the Thames. Clearly everyone who saw the "corpse" and many who saw a picture of it in newspapers made a comment about it to a friend or a family member, which was exactly what Hitchcock wanted them to do.

Outrageous stimuli create buzz. When Tina Brown put a picture of Demi Moore nude and pregnant on the cover of *Vanity Fair*, a lot of people talked. But it's the uniqueness that creates buzz. If you simply repeat what *Vanity Fair* did with another actress, don't expect much. Part of the game of buzz is always to top your last stunt. (Put a pregnant *actor* on the cover, and now we're talking buzz . . . )

## Give Them a Hero

**An essential element** in a good story is a main character. Similarly, buzz spreads faster when the focal point is *a person*. Why was there so much buzz about the movie *Titanic* among teenage girls in 1998? Was it the great cinematography? The compelling story? No— they were all talking about Leonardo DiCaprio. Most conversations people have are focused on people and not on abstract ideas. Connect a person to a product—be it a movie, a car, whatever—and you jump-start buzz.

Here we can learn from the launch of another car—the Mustang. On the week the car was launched in 1964, it appeared on the front covers of both *Newsweek* and *Time*. But it wasn't only the car itself. Prominently featured next to it was a picture of "the explosive young general manager of the Ford Division," Lee Iacocca ("rhymes with try-a-Coke-ah," *Time* noted to its readers). In fact, Iacocca's picture on the *Time* cover is about five times larger than that of the car.

Iacocca wasn't shy about personally associating himself with the brand. The article in *Newsweek* took readers behind the scenes, telling them his annual salary ($250,000 with bonus), what he did on Friday nights (played nickel-dime poker with friends), and what his grades in college were (an A average—except for a D in machine design).

This was just one part of a highly intensive buzz campaign that included seeding (disc jockeys, college newspaper editors, and others got Mustangs on a loan basis), a series of sneak previews that started two years before the car was launched, and a very successful PR effort. "This week it is the Mustang," *Newsweek* wrote. "Americans will have to be deaf, dumb, and blind to avoid the name." But the other name they couldn't avoid was Lee Iacocca's.

Iacocca is one of several businesspeople who have understood that attaching their face to the product can help generate buzz. Others include Steve Jobs, Bill Gates, Ted Turner, and Michael Eisner. Two more recent examples are Amazon.com's Jeff Bezos and Yahoo's Jerry Yang. By increasing the visibility of an executive, a company can turn him or her into a mega-hub, someone with special access and credibility with millions of other people. Such people become part of our own network. This has significant value in a world where thousands of brands compete for customers' mindshare. If one company is represented in customers' minds by its brand name alone and another is represented by its brand name *as well as* by a mega-hub, which do you think most people will remember better?

By *closely* associating your product or company with a person, you have a better chance of occupying space in the consumer's mind.

Lee Iacocca on the cover of *Time* the week the Ford Mustang was launched.

I italicized the word "closely" because the effect of a basketball player who advertises several brands is very different from that of an executive who is always identified in people's minds with a particular brand. You're most likely to remember Michael Jordan in your brain independent of the brands he's associated with. He's Michael Jordan. On the other hand, Michael Eisner is probably equated instantly with Disney. Executives who take extra steps to associate themselves with their companies are usually doing a great service to the brands they are promoting.

An important part of the celebrity concept is the story that develops around the person. "There's sort of a mythology that develops about an author, and that is another thing that spreads by word of mouth," one reader explained to me when I asked her to recall the buzz she'd helped to spread about *Cold Mountain*. She remembered telling others the story of how Charles Frazier came to write the book—how he was intrigued by a snippet of family history that he'd

## How Events Create Buzz

In an earlier chapter I mentioned the creation of the Jeep Jamboree—the weekend off-road trip organized exclusively for Jeep owners. Why do these trips generate buzz? For two days participants eat, drink, sleep, dream, and think Jeep. When they get back to the office on Monday, Jeep is pretty much the only thing they can talk about.

Several car companies now engage in similar activities. I visited two such events. One was The BMW Ultimate Driving Experience, a two-hour driving event that took place near Berkeley, California. The other was the Saturn Homecoming in Spring Hill, Tennessee, a two-day "customer enthusiasm" happening.

How do these events stimulate word of mouth? First, there's a very simple effect. When I watch a commercial or read a piece of direct mail, I usually don't announce it to the world. However, before I went to Tennessee for the Saturn Homecoming, I told everyone I met about it. When I came back, I told some more people about it. The man sitting behind me on the plane told the person who sat next to him that he was going to the Saturn event, too. People are constantly reporting to each other about what they do, and activities that are unique get a higher chance of being mentioned. When you think that 30,000 people attended the Saturn event and assume that each of them mentioned their plans to just 8 acquaintances, you realize that some 240,000 comments were made about Saturn. Add to that comments made by 150,000 additional customers celebrating Homecoming at Saturn dealerships around the country. That's some buzz.

You can't, however, count on this effect alone to create the buzz you want. In order to prompt customers to spread comments, your event should provide some memorable moments that participants can take back to their networks with them and converse about. When I came back from the BMW event, for example, I told everyone about their traction-stability presentation.

You could not re-create this demonstration in an ad. The BMW, the staff explained, has a special traction-stability system that allows the car to stay stable on a slippery road. The BMW staff laid a huge piece of plastic on the ground and poured buckets of water on it to create the effect of a puddle on the road. They asked for a volunteer and instructed him to sit in the driver's seat of a BMW. A driving instructor sat next to him to make sure events wouldn't get out of control. The volunteer was told to drive on the dry ground to develop some speed, then cross the sheet of plastic. In order for us to appreciate the usefulness of the system, they were going to first demonstrate what happens when the system is turned *off*. "Everyone take three steps back," the instructor said, and the crowd laughed nervously.

"Put the pedal to the metal!" the instructor shouted. "Ready, set, Go!" And the guy floored it. The car spun twice on the sheet before he was able to drive off of it. No one there will ever forget that sight. Then they asked him to do the same thing again, but with the traction-stability system *on*. Deep inside, I suspect everyone wanted to see the awesome spinning again, but instead the car slowed down automatically and passed the slippery area without even varying in direction. "Did you press the accelerator the second time the same way you did the first time?" the instructor asked the volunteer when he got out of the car. "Yup—all the way," he said. This is the type of demonstration people tell their friends about.

Of course, what's memorable to one customer may not leave much of an impression on another. To me, the plant tour at the Saturn Homecoming, for example, wasn't that impressive. It was interesting, but not something I would tell my friends about. On the other hand, other people around me found it fascinating. What left the biggest impression on me was a dance called "The Spirit of Saturn." A group of dancers used actual Saturn parts as musical instruments and told the story of how a car is built. It was almost magical. At one point each one of these dancers put a car panel on each foot, as if they were snowshoes, and tap-danced. The rhythm of the panels hitting the wooden floor, combined with percussion, lights, and video-screen displays, created a memorable moment. Then suddenly all the dancers formed a circle and flipped onto their backs with their feet high up in the air so that we could see that there wasn't even a scratch on the panels (that's one of the selling points of the car). With their feet still up, a drummer banged on the panels with the fervor of Ringo Starr. Again, an original and memorable moment that customers were likely to pass on.

heard from his father, quit his job as an English professor, and worked for years to develop it into a novel. Another aspect of generating buzz has to do with personal contact with the mega-hub. That's why readings by someone like Frazier are so important. "I told everybody about going to hear him at the bookstore," my reader recalled. Meeting the celebrity personally creates an alliance between the mega-hub and the other person. Often this "other person" is a network hub himself or herself, who then can go back to her network or cluster and share the experience with others.

Hollywood's movies may not always live up to viewers' expectations, but we can certainly learn from the way Hollywood builds excitement about some of its products. Sneak previews, behind-the-scenes footage, publicity stunts, and the use of celebrity are all part of a complex buzz machine run by the studios. It's worth repeating here, however, that it is best to underpromise and overdeliver, even when whetting the networks' appetites with these techniques. Sometimes the excitement surrounding a movie or other product may lead nowhere. When audiences and reviewers pan a movie, it becomes known as a product that failed to live up to the expectations of Hollywood buzzmakers and network members alike. The negative impression that results can cause an explosion of negative buzz, killing products faster than can be believed.

# Viral

# Marketing

**12.** **George picked up a new** golf magazine at the newsstand. At first he was turned off—too many ads. But then he found a great article about Pinehurst, a resort in North Carolina he'd always wanted to visit. There was also an article that addressed an argument he'd once had with his younger brother Jim about what happens when holes are played in the wrong sequence. At the family barbecue that weekend, he showed Jim the article, proving to him once and for all that George was right. At the golf course later that week, he told his friends Brad and Joe about the magazine and about the number-two course at Pinehurst.

Again, this is the basic force behind buzz. People tell others about a product or service because they are impressed by it and because it somehow relates to their lives. Can this be stimulated "artificially"? Can the magazine publisher successfully encourage George to pass the word about the new magazine to *more* friends or do it more frequently? If George likes the product—and this is essential—the answer is yes. Many publishers push their magazines through tell-a-friend promotions that prompt readers like George to think of other people in their lives who might enjoy the magazine. These programs range from pass-it-on cards to more elaborate gift programs, all of which involve tools designed to make spreading the word easy and rewarding. Although such promotions have been around forever, "they have not been part of the pantheon of major direct marketing concepts," as one marketing executive put it. As a result, they have been ignored by many marketers. But they shouldn't be.

While traditional pass-it-on paper coupons get little notice or respect, their "virtual" siblings on the Internet are getting more and more attention. Because each customer who receives information from a friend on the Net can reproduce it instantly and spread it to dozens, hundreds, or thousands of others, this form of Internet marketing is called "viral marketing." In the same way that the common cold spreads through sneezes, coughs, and handshakes, your offer now spreads through e-cards, electronic coupons, and invite-a-friend e-mails. The case of Hotmail, which I discussed in Chapter 2, demonstrates the impressive growth rate that can be associated with viral marketing.

To examine the effectiveness of electronic tell-a-friend promotions, let's turn from an imaginary golf magazine to a real Web site devoted to the sport. The on-line community GolfWeb was founded in 1995 as an information source for golfers. If George, for example, likes this Web site, all he has to do is type his friend's e-mail address in a designated box on this site and push a button. The text that invites his friend to join is already written up for him, and he can e-mail it as easily not only to Jim, Brad, and Joe but to everyone in his e-mail address book. If they like the site as much as he does, they can spread the word just as easily.

George is also more *motivated* to tell others about GolfWeb than he would be to tell them about a paper magazine, because George's self-interest comes into play. The more people he recruits, the better the service will be. How so? "Every member is adding value," explains GolfWeb cofounder Cynthia Typaldos. Golfers want to know everything about golf courses, so GolfWeb created a world-wide database of golf courses that allows members to input course reviews and rate these facilities. "There are thirty thousand golf courses in the world," says Typaldos. "There's just no way that we can know what's going on at all these golf courses." They also let users find playing partners on-line, enter their own member profiles, and form groups with other players. The more people participate in these activities, the more ratings of golf courses will be available on-line, and the easier it will be for George to find partners to play with. The *structure* of the service now stimulates him to talk.

How can you build buzz accelerators like these into your marketing plan? We'll start by looking at some *paper* tools that can be used to stimulate talk. Although these methods are viewed today as the primitive ancestors of viral marketing, they can be quite effective and should not be ignored. Following that, we'll move on to the on-line world.

## Paper Pass-It-On Tools

**Such ideas are** embarrassingly simple, but if you're not giving your customers the tools that make it easy for them to spread the word, you're missing out on opportunities to increase buzz. It doesn't need to be a complicated incentive program. "I just sold another copy of EndNote the other day," professors often told us. "A student came to my office, and I gave him one of the coupons that I had lying around on my desk. He went straight to the bookstore and got it." Over the years, loyal EndNote customers passed out those coupons enthusiastically all the time. Our job was to make sure they had enough of these coupons available. To keep it simple, and since many of the coupons were given to students by their professors, we kept incentives out of it. Still, even though our customers didn't benefit from them financially, we sold a constant flow of copies through these tell-a-friend programs.

Such promotions are very easy to test. Next time you mail something to your customers, slip in a tell-a-friend offer and monitor its impact. I asked Barry Berkov, former executive vice president at CompuServe, how well these campaigns worked for his company. "They were reasonably successful. They always produced a higher total response rate than a standard direct mail," he said. Since these promotions are hardly ever done independently—usually they piggyback on another mailing to customers—they can be quite cost-effective. In fact, says Berkov, "they're such low incremental cost that you can hardly *not* do them."

You can also use these paper tools to locate people who share your current customers' interests. "It's a very cost-effective way to find people," says George McMillan, president and CEO of BMG Direct, another company that has been using these promotions for years. Finding specific types of customers by renting other companies' lists can be expensive. Asking for friends' referrals can give you these names for a much lower investment. Lovers of classical music tend to know people who love classical music. People who are into country music hang out with others who love country. BMG Music Services usually offers customers free CDs when they bring a friend into the club, and has found this to be an effective way to reach new customers.

Beyond the obvious advantages—prompting your customers to tell their friends and making it easy for them to do so—these programs provide a hidden benefit to network-conscious marketers. Suppose that Jennifer is the most popular girl in her high school class—she's friends with virtually all the boys and girls in tenth grade. Now suppose that you are a maker of bicycle helmets and you mail discount coupons to tenth-graders in Jennifer's neighborhood. Obviously, you don't know Jennifer, nor do you know anything about her social ties. The chance that she'll get one of your mailings is equal to the chance that any other kid will get them. Now, if you include *two* discount coupons and encourage recipients to pass on one of them to a friend, something interesting happens to Jennifer's chances of getting a coupon—they skyrocket. The more central a person is in her social network, the more likely she will be exposed to these pass-on promos. Referral programs, therefore, are another way to locate and reach network hubs who are more influential in their networks.

Pass-it-on tools may have a variety of objectives. Unilever used them to accelerate sampling efforts of Dove soap. The sooner customers open a sample package and try it, the sooner some of them will go back to the store, coupon in hand, to buy the actual product. But sometimes customers don't open samples as fast as you would hope. The solution? Brand promotion agency Einson Freeman created an original promotion for Dove called "Share A Secret." A freestanding insert was run in Sunday newspapers offering two free bars of Dove soap to customers who recommended the names of three friends, and each of these friends would receive a gift-wrapped bar of soap as well. The campaign, aimed at women between the ages of twenty-two and forty-four, even allowed the customer to write a personal note to her friends. When the friends received the gift-wrapped sample at their homes, the initiator's name was prominently printed on the outside sleeve of the mailer. Suddenly it wasn't a sample from a soap company but a gift from a friend. Something you open immediately. Dove's market share increased more than 10 percent over the base period, according to Jeff McElnea, chairman and CEO of Einson Freeman.

## The Next Level

**In 1991 MCI** took this concept to its next level. If you were an MCI customer back then, you may remember receiving a letter that announced their "Friends & Family" program. It offered a 20-percent discount on calls made to a number of preselected locations. "All you have to do is tell us the friends and family members whom you'd like to include in your Calling Circle," the letter read. "We'll check to see if they're already MCI customers. If so, they'll automatically become part of your Calling Circle and your savings will begin soon. If not, we'll invite them to become MCI customers and to start their own Friends & Family Calling Circle so they can get their own 20% bonus discount." The letter asked the customer to make a list of up to twelve people they would like to call at a discount (MCI later increased the circle limit to twenty).

The invisible networks started working for MCI right away. People signed up their mothers, uncles, friends, and cousins. A few weeks later the customers who responded received a confirming letter (in the shape of a family tree) that listed the people whom they could call at a 20-percent discount. In addition, the letter listed those friends who "needed encouragement"—those who had chosen not to join. The company suggested that customers make a (free) call to invite these into their Calling Circle. While some customers were not enthusiastic about having to give a company the names of their relatives and friends, raising concerns over privacy issues, overall the campaign was a tremendous success and is believed to have caused 10 million residential customers to switch to MCI is less than two years.

Rather than focusing on a stimulant that would cause a comment to pass from Customer A to Customer B, the effort in the MCI program was on locking *whole cliques or clusters*. Len Short, former president of Ross Roy Direct, the agency that produced this promotion, points out how this helped in customer retention. One of the problems faced by both MCI and AT&T with other promotions was constant switching between discount programs. Now when a customer got an offer from AT&T, she would say to herself, "Well, yeah, that's very nice, but what about my calls to my mother? I'm not going to switch to AT&T because we've got this Friends & Family program," Short explains.

Arthur Hughes, vice president at M\S Database Marketing in Los Angeles, says, "That is certainly considered to be the most outstanding example of a referral program that there is." Hughes, who wasn't an MCI customer at the time, remembers receiving a letter from the company saying that his son-in-law had mentioned him as a potential MCI customer. "That is very personal, very direct, and very powerful," he says.

If you're not a marketing executive at a telephone company, you may think, "Okay, but what can *I* do about this?" Before the Internet explosion of the mid-1990s, the answer would have been "Not much." When people used to connect mostly through the telephone, promotions like Friends & Family could be implemented mainly by the MCIs of the world. But with the Net, this type of promotion is no longer limited to telephone companies.

## Viral Marketing on the Internet

**The case of** GolfWeb I mentioned earlier offers an example of how effective viral marketing on the Net can be. They created a structure that motivated each customer to bring in more customers. They also provided an easy way for customers to invite friends to join. As a result, the site has experienced tremendous growth, reaching over 8 million monthly page views in January 1998, when it was acquired by Sportsline.

One reason it worked so well for GolfWeb is that golf is a social activity. "Remember, golfers get together a lot," says Cynthia Typaldos. They love to play, and they love to talk about the equipment they use, the courses they've visited, and so on. Viral marketing techniques lend themselves to products that allow people to interact somehow. They are more natural for a telephone service—which is *all* about interaction—than for, say, selling wigs for men—which is not. "If at some point your customer isn't touching another potential customer in the use of the product, then there may not be any viral marketing happening at all," says Steve Jurvetson, a venture capitalist who is considered by many the guru of viral marketing.

The specific techniques will vary, and in the fast-moving Internet environment, new techniques keep popping up. But here are three principles that you should keep in mind if you want to use viral marketing on the Net.

## 1. Make Your Product Part of the Communication Process

Viral marketing still has the strongest effect if your product can be somehow incorporated into the communication between two people. This includes phone systems (MCI), electronic postcards (Blue Mountain), free e-mail (Hotmail), and the communications tool that someone is inventing in his or her garage as you're reading this chapter.

Look at what happened with ICQ, the service that tells you when your friends are on-line. Once a friend who's on-line is detected, ICQ allows you to chat with him in real time. This instant-messaging service is not that useful to you if your friends don't have it, too, so you're likely to start telling all your friends about it, encouraging them to download the ICQ software.

An interesting thing about ICQ is their marketing—or the lack thereof. When journalist Ami Ginsburg came to interview the young Israeli founders, all the "marketing" they could show was a brochure they had once produced but that was hardly ever used. They simply didn't do marketing as we know it. All their efforts are directed at motivating *the user* to spread the word. They seemed to understand that as much as people liked the service, they wouldn't necessarily go out of their way to promote it. So they tried to make it very easy to spread the word. For example, they use the standard e-mail that will invite your friend to join, but the software can also be instructed to scan your address book and send all your friends invitation letters. Telemarketers from ICQ will never call you up during dinner the way MCI did. Their idea is to build a tool that includes an inherent mechanism for spreading the word and then letting it grow. When a structure like this works, there is no need to nag customers. "The less you do, the more it grows," Ted Leonsis of AOL, the company that now owns ICQ, told *Newsweek*.

### 2. Have Your Customers Interact

Many companies that started selling on the Web first adopted a conventional selling model. "We thought of ourselves as more of a store," Cliff Sharples, cofounder of Garden.com told *BusinessWeek*. Very quickly, however, Sharples and other vendors realized that one excellent way to make customers spend more time on commercial Web sites is to let them interact with other customers. "We underestimated how important community would be," he said. Once Garden.com added chat rooms, people started spending more time at the site and coming back more often. Now you can chat with other gardeners twenty-four hours a day (in case you need to discuss your thoughts about growing garlic at 3 A.M.), you can chat with an expert gardener, you can post a picture of your beautiful sunflowers for everyone else to see. All these activities do two things: They link you to the site, and they make you talk about it. The fact is that people talk about what they do. And the more they do that is related to your company, the more likely they are to talk about you and draw others to your store, product, or Web site.

A good example of customer-to-customer interaction creating buzz can be seen with eBay, the Internet auction site. I first heard about eBay from a friend who sold four *Star Wars* coasters in an on-line auction for $12.50. He was amazed to receive so much money for something he got for free as part of some promotion. He offered them initially for .99 cents, but several bidders kept driving the price up. You can just hear the guy who bought them telling *his* friends; "You won't believe it. I paid just $12.50 for these mint-condition *Star Wars* coasters!" It seems that almost every transaction on eBay gets a buzz residue from sellers who tell their friends how much money they're making and buyers who tell their friends what great deals they're finding.

The point is that if almost every transaction stimulates comments to spread, the best marketing eBay can do is to make sure that there are lots of transactions on their site. And this is exactly what they have been doing. "The bulk of our business today still comes from word of mouth," Brian Swette, COO of eBay, told *Marketing Computers* magazine in 1999. "So our No. 1 priority is to get people talking to other people about eBay."

First they created a structure that makes buying and selling on-line really easy. It's straightforward and even fun. As I write this chapter, I've placed a bid on a BMW Z3—the James Bond movie model I described in Chapter 11. And the price is only $29! (Okay, it's only one-eighteenth scale.) One morning I got an e-mail from eBay informing me that another user had offered $35.99 for the car. I topped that and got the car for $36.99 (plus shipping). Don't ask me why, but I'm now the proud owner of a (very small) BMW Z3. I must have told at least ten people about my car, and always mentioned eBay in the process.

By understanding how social networks operate, the people at eBay make sure that transactions occur in many different social circles. A thousand transactions among collectors of Barbie dolls do not spread the word nearly as well as a thousand transactions spread across four different circles: say, collectors of coins, gemstones, sports memorabilia, *and* collectors of Barbie dolls. That's why eBay employees go to dozens of collectors' trade shows every year—to generate activities and thus buzz in multiple circles. "People see each other after a show and they talk about eBay," George Koster of eBay told *Marketing Computers*.

The bottom line: If you can create a structure that will allow your customers to interact, you may increase buzz. What you end up creating may not be as elaborate as eBay's structure. In fact, it could be totally different. The important thing is to focus on ways to motivate your customers to talk to each other and spend time at your site. Your site should be more of a café than a subway station, as Jurvetson and Draper put it in their now famous article in which they coined the term "viral marketing." People rush through subway stations, but they love to mingle in cafés.

How to create an on-line community is beyond the scope of this book. There are books on the subject and software that will help you from companies such as PeopleLink and Tribal Voice. Cynthia Typaldos, cofounder of GolfWeb, is now CEO of RealCommunities, a company that develops community infrastructure software precisely for that purpose. She emphasizes that in order for a community to work, it must have a purpose. "In the GolfWeb Players' Club, the community is built around people improving their golf game," she says. If every member of the community feels that adding more members will help the community achieve its purpose and will help the member achieve his or hers, you get real buzz going.

In the long run, the more your customers interact with each other, the more likely it is they will stick around. Why? Think of the Boy Scouts or Girl Scouts. Who is more likely to stay a member, the kid who has five other friends in the troop or a kid who has only one friend who's a member and four who are not? Of course, the boy or girl who has links to five other kids *within* the organization is more likely to stay on board. By linking customers to each other and by providing a welcoming place for them to socialize, you're decreasing the likelihood of your customers switching to another brand. So although customer groups on the Net seem scary at times to marketers, they are good news.

### 3. Prompt Your Customer to Spread the Word

You may want to offer tools for your customers to spread the word. In their simplest form, these are prewritten e-mail messages that a customer can forward to his or her friends, as in the case of GolfWeb. In the case of Hotmail, which I discussed in Chapter 2, the prompting was done automatically through the line at the bottom of every e-mail message: "Get your free e-mail at Hotmail.com." With multimedia capabilities, the tools can be much more creative. Many sites use colorful electronic postcards. "Send a personalized on-line postcard to your friends and family, on us," reads a banner on www.parentsoup.com, a popular Web site for parents. To create a postcard, the user is asked to click on an image, select the card message (or write his or her own), and send. The person on the other end receives the e-mail postcard along with a little promo for Parentsoup. "These postcards have been very effective in spreading the message," says Hillary Graves, VP of marketing for iVillage, the company behind Parentsoup. Like many other Web sites, iVillage also encourages visitors to e-mail content to their friends, which is "a really nice way to get your members to market for you," as Graves explains.

One company that has experienced tremendous growth as a result of their interactive tools is Blue Mountain Arts. I first found out about Blue Mountain when I received an e-mail from my daughter that exclaimed, "Guess what! You have just received an animated greeting card for Father's Day." Although I'm sure I'd seen the name before, it never got past the perceptual screens that filter out most of the new brands I'm exposed to. But now the company had my full attention. I was sitting in front of that screen watching a cat dancing to a goofy tune as he was covered with hugs and kisses until you could only see his head.

This is how everyone finds out about Blue Mountain. Daughters, sons, fathers, and friends send each other cards. Blue Mountain has never advertised, even on the Web. "The viral marketing inherent in the concept of an electronic greeting card allowed the experience of sending our cards to spread like wildfire," says Jared Schutz, CFO for the company. "In a given month over one-quarter of all Internet users visit the bluemountain.com site, according to Mediametrix," he reports. Does it help sales of the regular paper postcards that the company retails? Yes, according to Schutz.

I do want to make a couple of points about these promotions. Remember, the customer doesn't owe you anything. She will pass the word on to her friends if she feels that they may benefit from your product, not because you nag her. Use a friendly voice to remind the customer that her friends may also be interested. Pay special attention to the tone you use if you suggest a text that your customer may pass on to others. I often receive e-mail messages from friends who point out new Web services to me. These messages are frequently written by the creators of the Web service itself. One message I received recently is an example of how *not* to do it. The message started by complaining to me that I didn't already have the service. That if I had the service, it would make life so much simpler for both of us. "So do us both a favor and please get [the service] NOW." Talk about making a potential customer feel uncomfortable.

We can expect it to get worse. As with other tools, there will always be those marketing people who will use a new concept ad nauseam. Viral marketing is a hot concept as I'm typing these words, but I won't be surprised if by the time you read this, a backlash is being felt. As customers, and as friends of other customers, we can fight the avalanche of these tell-a-friend e-mails, e-cards, and coupons by using our judgment about what to forward and what not to. There are some viruses you'd rather not catch.

To use these tools successfully as a marketer, don't be intrusive. The moment you start making your customers feel that they're *supposed* to advertise you, they'll be turned off. Good viral marketing is humble. The companies that use it creatively without being intrusive are the ones that will win.

# Should I Give Incentives for Referrals?

One decision you may face once you decide to launch a tell-a-friend promotion is whether or not to include an incentive in your offer. Here are some guidelines that may help you make a good decision.

## The Incentive Should Not Be the Main Motivation

These promotions typically work best on a foundation of existing goodwill. Whatever incentive tactic you use, it should always rest on the foundation of a quality product—one that people *want* to recommend. When people feel that they're "supposed to be excited" about a mediocre product, they tend not to be. And keep the reward reasonable. Felipe Korzenny, principal and cofounder of Cheskin Research, offers the following advice: The reward should never be so great that people feel that this is the only reason they're recommending a product. They have to feel that they're advocating a product because they believe in it. People need to maintain their self-respect and their credibility among their friends.

## Ask Your Customers What *They* Think

Tell-a-friend campaigns are not without problems. Here's how Scott Cook, founder and chairman of Intuit, describes the experience his company has had with these types of promotions: "We've tried various artificial stimulants to word of mouth, like financial incentives to recommenders. None have worked. Some produced isolated, but surprising, negative reaction: 'I don't sell my friends for a bit of cash . . .'"

Before you start any such tell-a-friend promotion, it's worth checking how your customers feel about it. This can be done through focus groups, interviews, or informal conversations. Intuit found that users of Quicken (the company's personal finance software) did not like the idea of giving names and addresses of interested friends to the company—it made them feel guilty or cheap. Most also didn't like the idea of receiving a gift for recommending the product. "Our customers told us that they would gladly spread the word about our products," says Tanya Roberts, former vice president of direct marketing and sales at Intuit, "but that they would do it because of the product quality and not because we give them any incentives."

In some situations you can ask each customer individually how he or she feels about an incentive. "What we tell our dealers is that they should have a menu of items that they can offer," says Jim Callahan of The Dohring Company. "We'd like to thank you for referring someone. Which of the following items can I offer you?" Callahan suggests offering a menu of items, such as credit in the service department, cookies, cash, movie tickets, and so on. Another way to help customers overcome the uncomfortable feeling of getting an incentive for a referral is to take the sting out of the situation through a game. If you refer somebody, you get a game card. From the card you may win one of several prizes. "It's a little bit lighter," says Callahan. Of course, all promotions and incentive programs should be reviewed by your legal department.

### Minimize Loopholes, But Keep It Simple

There's always some potential for abuse of these promotions. Some people may try to get a reward without giving anything in return, or find a way through which they can get some cash out of your company. You should try to minimize these loopholes. In a "member get a member" promotion for a frequent-flier program, people get bonus miles only after the person they recruited has actually made his or her first trip. That's reasonable. Otherwise, someone could fly to China and back for free after he or she signed up a whole network of acquaintances who will never fly with that airline. As George McMillan, president and CEO of BMG Direct, says, "Make sure if there's any kind of value being exchanged that you're a little bit careful you don't get scammed." McMillan's main concern is the high-volume scammer, not the college kid who puts his roommate's name on the form and pays him back.

At the same time, if you make incentives too complicated, you may be left with a very secure promotion—but no participation. "You need to have a balance between keeping the thieves out and not making it too difficult for people to participate in the program," says Barry Berkov, a former member of the executive team at CompuServe. The most thorough way to stop shoplifting in a supermarket is strip-search everybody, but you won't have too many customers if you do.

## Multilevel Marketing—the Ultimate Buzz?

"If the invisible networks are so powerful in spreading the word about products, why not use them to *sell* the product itself?" many people ask once they're familiar with word-of-mouth marketing. In recent years we've witnessed an explosion of multi-level marketing (MLM) and other programs on the Net that try to do just that. Even before the rise of the Internet, some companies were very successful in creating distribution channels in the invisible networks, companies such as Tupperware, Avon, Amway, and Mary Kay.

While these programs work for certain companies, it's important to note that the phenomenon they're based upon is not exactly buzz. There is a key difference between buzz and a marketing scheme in which friends are supposed to sell something to their friends or recruit them as distributors: While buzz may be stimulated with an occasional incentive, it is usually free from any monetary transaction. A customer recommends a product because she truly believes in this product. Part of her credibility comes from the fact that she has nothing to gain by recommending the product, which is not the case when she's selling it.

Advocates of MLM love to point out the potential for exponential growth that comes with this method. ("If your friend tells two friends, and these two friends tell two friends, you reach a huge audience very fast.") But in real life this exponential growth is hardly ever reached. Why not? Because many people don't want to get involved in this type of business and don't feel comfortable selling to their friends. Most people want to talk with their friends without having to sell them anything. When they meet a relative, they want to hear about the family, without thinking of how they could enroll him as part of their "downline" (the industry term for the chain of distributors one recruits).

Multilevel marketing is probably far from gone, however. The very same trends that cause customers to rely on their friends in making purchasing decisions—information overload, customer skepticism, and customer connectivity—could help MLM organizations to expand, especially in product categories such as skin care, personal services, and food supplements. There is also evidence that this marketing method is more effective in certain social circles and countries than in others. But as MLM grows, it's important not to confuse it with buzz. Don't expect an MLM organization to grow at the rate of an ICQ or a Hotmail. It's a different phenomenon.

# Does Madison Avenue Still Matter?

**13.** **So who needs advertising?** As this book should have demonstrated by now, creating buzz is a powerful approach to getting out the word about a product, generating interest, and getting sales. In preceding chapters I've raved about products that did well with little or no traditional advertising—Trivial Pursuit, *Cold Mountain*, and Hotmail, to name a few. So it might seem that Madison Avenue's traditional approach to advertising no longer matters.

The truth is that very few products can rely on buzz alone. When used correctly, advertising can help buzz. However, it's also worth noting that ads can sometimes hurt genuine word of mouth. So in this chapter I want to focus on answering three questions:

- **Can advertising *stimulate* buzz?**
- **Can advertising *simulate* buzz?**
- **Can advertising kill buzz?**

## Can Advertising *Stimulate* Buzz?

**Absolutely. A good** ad can help get people talking. An ad that is well conceived, well placed, and well timed can contribute to buzz in several ways.

### Jump-start the Process

Information in the networks has to come from somewhere. The day your new product is released, very few people know about it. What is the likelihood that someone will tell his friend about your product? Very low. Once you've accumulated some customers, there are more people out there capable of using their experience to talk about the product. How do you get these first customers?

In some cases your product is so contagious that you don't need to advertise. In other cases you get enough buzz from seeding, sneak previews, and other buzz tactics. But often you're not that lucky, and you find that while there's good buzz in some clusters, other clusters need encouragement.

One of the first things we did when we released EndNote was to send a press release to various scientific publications. *Science*, the largest scientific journal in the United States, published a short article about the product. This announcement started buzz in certain networks, but only in rare cases does such buzz grow exponentially. That's why we followed up with small ads in *Science* and additional publications to recruit first users in additional networks. These ads generated only one-tenth the leads of the original product announcement. Still, since the editors of *Science* weren't going to repeat the editorial for us every week, we needed some way to follow up our efforts. We did it with paid advertisements. Hotmail used advertising for exactly the same purpose. The cash-hungry start-up placed ads in campus newspapers around the country to help create the initial core group of users in each school. "We would try to start 'little fires' all over the place," says Steve Douty, former VP of marketing for the company.

### Reach Hubs

Advertising is also a fairly effective way to reach network hubs. Many studies confirm that opinion leaders are more exposed to print advertising than are "average" people. That makes sense: Because they're hungry for information, they read more. By advertising in a magazine like *Car & Driver* you reach hubs who recommend cars and related products to others. A study conducted for the magazine by Market Probe International found that 68 percent of the subscribers had given others advice related to cars in the past year. For example, those readers who spoke with their friends about auto sound equipment advised 14.7 other people on average.

The mirror image of the last point is that an ad in a daily newspaper or on TV can also stimulate members of the network to seek more information about the product from network hubs. "I saw an ad for the new Jeep recently. Is it worth checking out?" a neighbor may ask the local "car expert."

### Reassure Buyers

Another important way in which advertising can stimulate buzz is by assuring customers that they are not alone. Once we sold more than 100,000 copies of EndNote, we always mentioned this fact prominently in our ads. This common tactic is based on the assumption that people are more comfortable sharing information with their friends about a popular product. Studies have found that people are more likely to express their opinions about public issues when they think that there is sufficient public support for their opinion. Although these studies focused on public affairs, it's reasonable to assume that many people feel this way about commercial products. Advertising also gives your customers the facts they need to justify their purchase decision. Your existing customers are very likely to read your ad, even though they already own the product (this is true especially for big-ticket items). They will use these facts when talking with others about the product.

If you market a product associated with a taboo, advertising can reassure consumers that they can talk about the subject. Viagra got a lot of buzz from day one, but jokes on late-night shows won't necessarily help get people to talk. "The joke-a-day monologues on TV run the risk of trivializing erectile dysfunction and having a reverse effect of not bringing people out of the closet for the condition," David Brinkley of Pfizer told *Advertising Age*. Advertising the drug in a positive context made it easier for men to talk about the issue with their physicians.

## Get the Facts Straight

Finally, advertising can affect the content of buzz. Messages that spread in the invisible networks are constantly distorted, twisted, and diluted. Remember the old "telephone" game we used to play as kids? Several children sit in a circle and one of them picks a phrase and whispers it to his neighbor. The neighbor passes the word on to her neighbor and so on until the last person announces what he heard. Do you remember how a phrase like "fish in the water" was transformed into "dishes in the dishwasher"? The invisible networks can distort your message in a similar way. By broadcasting *accurate* information your ads can at least partially take care of that. In 1989, when the apple industry had to deal with public panic that Alar-treated apples could cause cancer, they published ads stating that a person would have to eat 28,000 pounds of Alar-treated apples *every day* for 70 years to reach dangerous exposure.

## Advertising as Buzz

Sometimes ads generate buzz because people talk about the advertising itself. "Got milk?" and "Where's the beef?" and *"Yo quiero* Taco Bell" are some examples of ads that got people talking. It's not a coincidence that all these campaigns are humorous. Nothing spreads faster than a really good joke. I remember being dragged to the TV by my children, who insisted that I see that talking chihuahua—and one that speaks Spanish! The dog created waves of buzz as *"Yo quiero* Taco Bell" became a catchphrase. According to Taco Bell's tracking study, advertising awareness after the campaign was over 50 percent higher than the pre-chihuahua level of awareness for the same season in the previous year. The campaign's objective was to stop the fast-food company's decline in sales. Indeed, not only did the ads help stop the decline, but Taco Bell was able to report an increase in sales as a result of the campaign. Chihuahua T-shirts and other novelty items accelerated the visual buzz on the street, as did the dogs themselves as they popped up in neighborhoods all over the country—the American Kennel Club reported a 72-percent increase in chihuahua sales in 1998.

    The practical implications? Sure, if your ad agency can create such a commercial, by all means go ahead. But saying that is a little bit like advising writers to write with the Nobel Prize in mind—"It will be good for your career." Everyone in the advertising industry would *love* to create an ad that gets that kind of buzz, but very few become such mega-hits. Remember that for every chihuahua or Energizer Bunny, there are thousands of commercials that try to make people talk but fail. In the process of creating these commercials, some ad agencies forget what ads are originally meant to do—sell a product.

## Can Advertising *Simulate* Buzz?

**What about ads** that masquerade as word of mouth? This is a tricky topic. You have to understand that an ad can hardly ever enjoy the credibility of buzz. But an ad can gain some credibility when advertisers either successfully mimic a tone used among friends or bring the friends themselves into the advertisements to give testimonials.

### The "Friendly" Tone

Back in 1966, Ernest Dichter, a psychologist who specialized in consumer motivation, noted, "When the consumer feels that the advertiser speaks to him as a friend or as an unbiased authority, creating the atmosphere of word of mouth, the consumer will relax and tend to accept the recommendation."

Dichter's idea still has validity, but the way friends talk to each other has changed since 1966. People are more skeptical and cautious today, and this is reflected in the tone of their comments. Irony, sarcasm, and cynicism are common in conversations about commercial products. Companies that try to sound friendly by using a chatty, confidential tone often fail to create an authentic atmosphere. On the other hand, those who manage to create ads with a wink and a nod often have a better chance of producing the desired effect.

One campaign that played on customers' sense of irony was ABC's 1997 promotion. The advertisers based the content of their ads on common put-downs about TV-viewing. Self-deprecation and humorous exaggeration both played roles. With headlines such as "Don't worry, you've got billions of brain cells," the creators of this campaign recognized what's bad about the product, the way a friend would. Measuring the effectiveness of this campaign is tricky, because response to individual programs—not the ad campaign—ultimately determined whether the network's ratings would go up. But in terms of its tone, the campaign is an example of one that was accepted with a smile by many customers. You can't resist smiling when you see a statement such as "If TV's so bad for you, why is there one in every hospital room?" Good point!

I'm not suggesting that you make fun of your product in your ads. But if you want to create an effect that simulates word of mouth, you shouldn't use phrases like "Perhaps, like true love, we were meant to last forever" or "We believe we have the management teams, the strategies, and the market position to achieve success well into the next century." Both of these sentences appeared in ads in the summer of 1999, and neither one comes close to imitating the way real people talk to one another.

## Testimonial Advertising

An ad, again, will never enjoy the credibility of buzz, but it can get closer by simulating buzz through testimonial advertising. The execution is challenging, however. Many ads are so bad that you wonder if they were meant as parody.

Creating buzz successfully is all about authenticity. Think of ads that are supposed to show, for example, the broad range of "ordinary folks" who use that product. Often these types of commercials are victims of the advertisers' endless pursuit of political correctness. The ads feature conspicuously diverse people it's hard to believe were chosen at random: a black man, a white woman, a Latino man, and an Asian woman. Customers see through that. These commercials may still build awareness and even sales, but don't expect them to have nearly the impact of an ad that rings true.

Compare this to Budweiser's "Whassup?!" commercials that began airing at the end of 1999. Nothing fancy. Just some guys who greet each other repeatedly with that goofy expression: "Whassup?!" But the commercials struck a chord. Sixteen years earlier director Charles Stone III had used the greeting with his buddies. When Stone and Budweiser's ad agency, DDB Chicago, decided to turn this male bonding ritual into a beer commercial, they looked for people who'd be able to re-create the warm brotherhood atmosphere in an ad. After a long but unsuccessful search, they all agreed to have Stone's real-life friends and himself play in the commercials. The result? It felt right. Authentic. The greeting is being heard all around the United States. "You just can't fake the dialogue they have going on," Kent Kwaitt of DDB Chicago said.

Another company that has been effective in bringing real people into its advertising in a credible way is Saturn. John Yost, who managed Hal Riney, the agency that created the Saturn ad campaign, explains why he thinks it worked: "The testimonials were highly credible because they were customers. And not just customers, but customers that actually acted and behaved like real people, so there was this tremendous empathy and credibility that came from them."

Bringing real customers into an ad is very different from using celebrities. Famous people draw our attention, and we sometimes imitate their behavior. But since we all know that they're being paid for doing an ad, many of us don't believe that their use of the product is authentic. A survey by Wirthlin Worldwide in 1999 asked adults in the United States to rate different sources in terms of how believable they are. Only 3 percent considered celebrity endorsements very believable, 49 percent said they were somewhat believable, and 47 percent said they were not at all believable. "Anytime you're using a borrowed interest, whether it's from a celebrity or from an idea that is not intrinsic to your product or your company, then you have to be aware there's a good chance that the consumer is going to see this as an overt attempt to sell him something," Yost points out.

The people at GolfWeb found similar attitudes among their golf-enthusiast customers. They conducted a survey using two versions of the survey form. In one, Jack Nicklaus was featured as the spokesperson. The second version, which was sent to a different set of customers, featured an average-looking golfer (actually it was a picture of cofounder Ed Pattermann, but nobody knew him). People preferred the average user. "Golf is not fandom," explains Cynthia Typaldos, cofounder of GolfWeb. "Golf is a participants' sport." People want to see what others like themselves are doing. They care less about Jack Nicklaus's endorsements partly because he is in such a different league. "But if someone similar to you in ways that matter in golf—same sex, around 20 handicap, playing for the same number of years, goes to the same kinds of courses—if they say, 'Now, I bought this putter and my putting is 10-percent better,' *that's* interesting."

I don't argue that companies should avoid using celebrities. In fact, Jack Nicklaus's picture is now featured on GolfWeb's Players Club Web site, and he serves as chairman of the Players Club Advisory Board. The effect, however, is different than word of mouth. Celebrities definitely draw our attention and can prompt us to imitate their behavior. But their appearance usually doesn't simulate word of mouth the way an authentic testimonial ad from average folks can do.

## Can Advertising Kill Buzz?

Although there are many good reasons to advertise, advertising is a tool that should be used very cautiously if you want to promote buzz. Because advertising can also kill buzz when people feel that someone is shoving the message down their throats. A customer tells her friends about new products she discovers because it reflects on her as an innovative and forward-thinking person. She doesn't want to sound like someone who's repeating a company's propaganda. Nobody does.

So what do you do to be sure your ad doesn't end up killing

rather than building buzz? One word that comes to mind is "honesty." Your ad must be honest, not only factually but also in the sense of being true to the product. "I can't think of an example of a product or a service that really generated a firestorm of positive word of mouth that didn't market from a platform of truth and honesty and directness in its relationships with its consumers," says John Yost, who now does the advertising for Yahoo! "As a generation, we've been so overly marketed to and we've been so exposed to hype, that at this point we're pretty savvy customers and don't fall easily to some of these traditional pitches anymore."

Consider the following two ads in a magazine: One is for a car. It talks about the car company as representing a separate school of design, one that considers the emotional needs of people. Can you imagine customers repeating this to their friends? I don't think so. In fact, this kind of ad can kill genuine enthusiasm, because it's pretentious. The other ad shows a big picture of V8. The headline reads, "It can't actually replace working out, but if you shake really, really well, you might get your heart rate up a little." Now, *this* ad adopts the right tone. It doesn't make any claims that aren't 100-percent supported by facts, and it has a chance of being repeated because it's funny.

Timing is important, too. Momenta's big advertising splash created high awareness but didn't leave room for grassroots support to grow. My sense is that people don't like to feel everything is too organized. They talk more about something they *discover* than about something everybody can see in a spread in *The Wall Street Journal*.

# The Six Rules About Ads and Buzz

## 1. Keep It Simple

The message needs to be simple in order for people to pass it on. Short, straightforward messages based on current beliefs have a better chance of replicating themselves in the networks.

Use simple language. This sounds obvious, but very often companies use jargon and acronyms that prevent comments from spreading at the rate they might otherwise. From ancient fortified cities to current gated communities, people have always put walls and other barriers around themselves to keep intruders away and to differentiate themselves from others. Networks have their own walls and fences, but instead of wire or bricks, people use dialect, jargon, and acronyms to keep strangers out. There's nothing inherently wrong with that—in fact, it's the most efficient use of language *within* a subset of the network. However, when communicating *across* clusters, comments get stuck because they cannot be understood. When your advertising is trying to appeal to several areas in the networks, make sure all areas can understand your message.

## 2. Tell Us What's New

Fluff doesn't travel well in the networks. A typical customer will not recommend a company because "they offer a tradition of excellence, the best value for your money, and a set of powerful features." For your ads' messages to be passed on, they need to be relevant and have news value. Nobody comes back from a lunch break and says, "Guess what I had at McDonald's? A hamburger!" But I have heard people talk about a new offering they tried at McDonald's (like a hamburger with cheese, bacon, and mushrooms). Considering their extremely boring core product (ground beef), the people at McDonald's have an amazing talent for adding news value to their message. Of course, a big part of it is because they *don't* see their product as only a hamburger. McDonald's *creates* news about all its products—walk inside and you'll discover something new: from the latest Disney movie tie-in to a new size of french fries.

This is true not only for advertising but for all of your company's communications. People have a good ability to distinguish between empty and meaningful comments. No one is going to pass along the comment from a bank's vice president who says that the bank truly cares about its customers. Conversely, a useful comment like "Bank X opens its branches on Saturday morning" has a much greater potential to spread from person to person.

### 3. Don't Make Claims You Can't Support

Don't tell customers that you care about them unless you really mean it and can *consistently* demonstrate superb customer service. I recently called a company that boasted about "great customer service" in their catalog. They also talked about three easy ways to order. I sent them an e-mail, which they ignored. When I called them on the phone, I was put on hold for twelve minutes. The fact that they bragged about their customer service made me twice as furious and more likely to spread negative word of mouth about that company.

### 4. Ask Your Customers to Articulate What's Special About Your Product or Service

You may be very proud of the quality of your product or the level of service you provide, but your pride won't help buzz spread. Your *customers* need to feel the difference. A very simple way to find out if they do is to talk to them. If they can't tell you what's unique about your product, they won't be able to explain it to their friends. Car dealerships that offer one-price shopping view it as a great advantage and expect customers to pass on their impression. In conducting surveys for some one-price dealerships, however, it was found that 30 percent to 35 percent of the people who bought cars from these dealerships didn't realize that they were at a one-price dealership (incidentally, these surveys did not involve Saturn dealerships).

### 5. Start Measuring Buzz

How much attention do advertising agencies pay to word of mouth? "Very few agencies pretest advertising for its conversational impact, which is just not commonly recognized as an advertising objective, though it should be," Thomas Robertson wrote in

1971. Robertson, now dean of the Goizueta Business School at Emory University, doesn't think that this has changed. In evaluating advertising, it can be very useful to ask two questions: Will the ad help network hubs answer questions they may get from other people in the networks? Will the ad stimulate members of the network to seek information from network hubs? Perhaps the only industry that pays attention to measuring word of mouth is the movie industry. Prior to the release of every major motion picture these days, the studios run test screenings to predict audience reaction. Survey questions, known in the movie industry as "the cards," can vary based on the genre and what the producers want to find out, but the first two questions are almost always the same. How would you rate this movie? Would you recommend this movie to a friend? In post-screening focus groups, participants often are asked to expand on what they would tell friends about the movie.

A good way to begin making your organization aware of the power of the invisible networks is to measure word of mouth. When you conduct customer satisfaction surveys, ask your customers whether they have recommended the product recently. If so, to how many people? Once you have data over a period of time, you'll be able to tell which of your strategies created the most positive buzz.

## 6. Listen to the Buzz

Another point Robertson makes is that monitoring what people say about products can help companies design better advertising. By listening to the networks, marketers can get answers to questions such as these: How is the product being used out in the field? What problems are encountered by users? What are the product attributes being discussed? This, of course, is somewhat facilitated today by the large volume of communication being done on-line. Keep in mind, however, that on-line discussions may or may not represent the opinions of *all* your customers. Good old face-to-face interaction with customers (and noncustomers) is equally important.

# Buzz in

# Distribution

# Channels

**14.** **I don't recall having any** conversations with my friends about model trains before I bought one. Growing up in Israel, I also don't remember ever seeing an ad for model railroads. So how did I first learn about the Märklin? It all goes back to a toy store on Dizengoff Street in Tel Aviv. A little engine was circling in the window pulling six cars behind. I stood there, pressing my nose against the window, following the black engine with my eyes. When I finally got the courage to walk in to take a closer look, the store owner told me all about it. It was a Märklin, and the way he said the word made me understand that this was a good thing. He also said it could pull ten cars or even more if he wanted it to. It could go backward as well. All he had to do was turn a switch. The store owner was my only source of information about trains and, as it turned out, a good one—I own that Märklin engine to this day.

In the simple world of my childhood (Israel didn't even have a single TV channel at the time), buzz often spread through the same channels as the physical goods did—from manufacturer to reseller to end user. In that world, distribution channels were the only sources of information about certain products.

Obviously we live in a different world today. Now a kid who considers buying a model train can consult with experienced users on a newsgroup such as rec.models.railroad. He can visit Web sites dedicated to model trains and is likely to have been exposed to advertising for several brands. Does the channel still have a role in creating buzz? Can today's reseller provide the same personal interaction and trusted advice I remember from my childhood? Can resellers be part of this word-of-mouth experience?

In answering these questions, I will look at both traditional distribution channels and on-line channels. Customers clearly get information through both channels. This happens through point-of-purchase displays at a traditional store or through product listings in the case of an e-retailer. To create a word-of-mouth experience, however, two factors need to be present. First, interactivity. At the toy store of my childhood I could ask any question about the train and get an answer. Moreover, that answer was tailored to my needs and interests. The second factor is trust. As far as I was concerned, there was no difference between that salesman at the toy store and any of my friends. I fully trusted him. Let's examine whether these two elements—interactivity and trust—exist in channels today.

## Can Brick and Mortar Channels Spread Buzz?

**Traditional channels have** all it takes to foster interaction with customers and to develop trust. How effective are they in spreading the word in practice? That depends.

First, the channel's ability to spread buzz differs from one industry to another. Moviegoers, for example, don't usually ask the guy at the box office to recommend a movie, but customers at bookstores *do* ask store personnel for their recommendations. Bicycle shops tend to employ racers who know a lot about biking and therefore have high credibility with their customers. The same goes for surf shops, where the store clerks (if you can call a guy at a surf shop "a clerk") are often part of the same social networks as the store's customer base.

Even within each industry some stores are more effective in spreading the word than others. In some bookstores you'll have to look hard for someone to talk to, let alone trust. In others, salespeople enjoy tremendous credibility with their customers. They also know how to ask the right questions to identify the type of book the reader would enjoy. These booksellers are no different from any other network hub. When they recommend a book, it becomes a local hit. A similar situation exists in the sporting goods industry. In some stores, especially heavy discounters, you're on your own. On the other end of the spectrum you find stores that specialize in running shoes or mountaineering equipment. "The clerks or the owners in those specialty retail stores are known as enthusiasts for certain sports, and their recommendations are taken very, very highly," says Helen Rockey, a former executive at Nike and Brooks Sports.

To create buzz about a product through the channel, you need to work with those salespeople who interact with customers and are trusted by them. Keep in mind, though, that the ability of a particular channel or an individual store to spread buzz can change over time.

Store personnel in the PC industry, for example, used to be very knowledgeable—and some of them still are. But higher salaries in corporations lure knowledgeable salespeople away from retailing, leaving some stores with less qualified staff to interact with customers.

## Can On-line Channels Spread Buzz?

Amazon.com makes finding information about books extremely easy, but can the on-line reseller create buzz about a particular title? In their present state, on-line channels involve very little person-to-person interaction and therefore have a limited ability to push a particular product through "hand selling," to borrow a term from the brick and mortar world.

Where on-line retailers can help tremendously in spreading the word about products is by bringing customers together. Reviews are one form of this. On February 20, 2000, there were 2,244 reviews of J. K. Rowling's *Harry Potter and the Sorcerer's Stone* available on Amazon.com. The average rating given was five stars. Now, that's some buzz.

Another way that Amazon simulates word of mouth is through a technique called "collaborative filtering." A customer who buys the book *Relationship Marketing* by Regis McKenna may see that customers who bought this book also bought *The One to One Future* by Don Peppers and Martha Rogers. The bookseller in this case doesn't recommend anything. It just tells you, "Look at what customers who are interested in the same topic you are have bought."

Other on-line retailers allow for even more active interaction. On eHobbies, a portal for hobbyists, customers who are interested in model railroads can chat with others live or post questions and answers on a bulletin board. Here again, the retailer doesn't do the actual recommendation but offers the forum for buzz.

There are also on-line resellers who do a good job spreading buzz the old-fashioned way—giving advice, help, and useful information. One example is Kenny West, president of PalmGear H.Q., a Web portal and e-commerce site for Palm OS users. Post a question on a newsgroup that is related to the Palm and if nobody else responds, Kenny West is likely to step in and give you the answer. "Kenny is always in the newsgroup," says Jim Thompson, who's a regular customer. "His presence does a lot for making [PalmGear H.Q.] look like a personable place where you want to go buy stuff, like the corner store where you know the people."

More and more on-line retailers are starting to realize that customers often want and need to interact with a live person in the way they did at the corner store. So now shoppers on certain sites can look at the merchandise and talk to a sales rep simultaneously. Once a human touch is introduced, buzz channels are open again. Whether or not these channels really work depends, again, on whether or not trust and true interactivity are actually there. A sales rep who is required to read a trite script will be less effective in generating buzz than a sales rep who can be spontaneous, open, and friendly.

It's reasonable to believe that we will see all types of resellers in the on-line world, as we do in the physical world. Some will emphasize price and will provide very little extra service. Some will emphasize service, and that's where you'll see more interaction with reps. If you are a manufacturer, these are the channels you should nurture to generate buzz.

## What to Do with the Channel?

**Most of the** ways to create buzz among customers described earlier can be used to create buzz in the channel. Here are some examples of how these methods apply to distribution channels.

## Seed the Channel

A key strategy for creating buzz through the channel is to seed resellers who are trusted in their networks. In early 1991 about five thousand managers, clerks, and buyers at bookstores all across America received a package from the publishing company Knopf. When they took off the gift wrap, they found a special hardcover edition of Josephine Hart's first novel, *Damage*. Enclosed was a note from Sonny Mehta, president and editor in chief of the publishing house. Knopf picked the right title for this promotion. Hart's dark and passionate novel is the story of a successful British doctor and politician who lives a staid life until he meets Anna, his son's fiancée. Outrageous stimuli, as we know, get more buzz. It's the type of book that leaves you with the feeling you get after witnessing an accident or seeing a person collapse on the street—you have to tell someone about it. Many of the booksellers who received the book in 1991 did just that. One bookstore owner whose store got three copies told *Publishers Weekly*, "Everyone read it in one sitting and loved it. We'll sell ten times as many because of that." The book became a *New York Times* bestseller.

As always, execution counts. Knopf didn't send a hundred books in brown envelopes. They sent *five thousand* books, all elegantly gift-wrapped. "It was an attention grabber," remembers one bookseller, David Unowsky of Ruminator Books in St. Paul, Minnesota, almost ten years later. As in the case of *Cold Mountain*, the credibility of the publisher played a role here, too. "Sonny would not write more than a letter a year, so when Sonny wrote, you knew it was powerful stuff," says Carl Lennertz, former marketing director at Knopf.

## Use the Channel as a Springboard

You should consider not only seeding the channel but also using it as a springboard for seeding. In a campaign to promote the

EV1, General Motors' electric vehicle, the company started test drives in two markets: Southern California and Phoenix, Arizona. GM invited car buffs for a thirty-minute drive in one of these new cars, but they realized that in order to help people spread the word, they should give them ammunition. Each customer received fifty baseball cards with the picture of the car on one side and performance stats on the other. The cards, imprinted with unique tracking numbers, all had phone numbers for scheduling test drives. GM found that a typical customer gave a card to ten to twelve other people.

Another company that uses the channel as a springboard for seeding is Kiehl's Since 1851 (that's the company's name), a maker of skin- and hair-care products. The company insists that its resellers hand out samples aggressively. Kiehl's even sends staff to department stores to monitor how much sampling they do, and they've been known to cancel an account if the salespeople don't hand out enough freebies. When I visited Neiman Marcus at the Stanford Shopping Center, the woman behind the Kiehl's counter handed me *four* small tubes with different creams for my wife. In effect, she made sure that I would tell my wife about Kiehl's. The company doesn't advertise. It turns store visitors into carriers of the Kiehl's message.

## Consider Limited Distribution

Another strategy used by Kiehl's to build buzz is selective distribution. This is not a strategy that will make you into the next Procter & Gamble, but it is something to consider, especially for marketers of high-end products who want to drive sales by word of mouth. Scarcity stimulates interest, which in turn stimulates buzz. Kiehl's strategy illustrates this point. Originally you could buy Kiehl's products only at the company's single retail store. Aaron Morse, who managed the company until 1988, refused to sell to department stores, and the word about his shop in Manhattan's East Village was passed from person to person. Over the years the company expanded to a few prestigious stores such as Saks Fifth Avenue, Neiman Marcus, and Fred Segal, but to this day you can't find the product line at most retail outlets. *The Wall Street Journal* describes the buzz that Kiehl's get as "deafening." Selective distribution and aggressive seeding are two of the reasons behind that buzz.

## Use Public Areas in Shopping Malls

When you think about the channel, think not only about the stores that currently carry your product but also of the places where customers go to shop. When Procter & Gamble introduced Dryel, the company conducted demonstrations not in supermarkets where this cleaning product eventually will be sold but near department stores in the 275 largest shopping malls around the country. By locating the demos where people buy fashion, the marketers also put Dryel in the right context—the product is designed to clean and freshen "dry-clean only" fabrics.

The introduction of Pokémon cards to the United States also included a major mall tour. It's a way to reach a wide variety of customers from different groups and segments. "Everybody goes to the mall at some point in their life," says Charlotte Stuyvenberg, VP of marketing at Wizards of the Coast, the company that makes the Pokémon cards.

The effectiveness of mall demos depends to a large extent on staffing. If the people who are giving the demo are friendly, reliable, and knowledgeable, the effect can be very similar to word of mouth. This was the case at a recent demo for Dryel that I attended. There was nothing for sale at the booth, so it was immediately clear that the only purpose of the booth was to tell you about the product. The friendly demonstrators asked me to try to remove a stain from a shirt, showing me how to put the clothing in the dryer and letting me smell it when it came out. The only thing that detracted from the experience was the fact that they obviously had memorized their scripts. Authenticity and spontaneity are crucial to create a word-of-mouth experience.

## Talk to the People Who Talk to Customers

I cannot emphasize this enough. You need to get right to the people who are in *direct* contact with customers to make sure the excitement doesn't get stuck somewhere in the distribution pipes (buzz doesn't store well in warehouses).

One of the first people in the publishing business to understand that was Jacqueline Susann, author of *Valley of the Dolls*, whose promotional campaigns became a legend in the industry. She wasn't the first writer to go out and meet booksellers, but she was probably the first bestselling author who made a sustained nationwide effort to work with resellers. Edward Burlingame, former editor in chief and publisher at HarperCollins, remembers that "what Jackie Susann appreciated was that people who were standing around in bookstores were an army [that] could be recruited on her side." And she did. Susann made it her business not only to go and meet them but to find out who they were ahead of time so that she could talk to them as a friend. She also distributed free autographed copies to store clerks and explained, "I tell them 'be my guest,' and then they can honestly recommend it to their customers. A clerk won't really push a book if he hasn't read it himself."

At the American Booksellers Association meetings, she would pose for photographs with hundreds of booksellers who stopped by her publisher's booth. Each one of these pictures was then sent to the bookseller's hometown newspaper, and it's not hard to imagine that many of these newspaper clips were shown to friends or displayed at the store. Again, notice the level of execution: It's not about only the *Washington Post* or the *New York Times*. It's about hundreds of small newspapers all around the country.

## Use a Little Mystery

Mystery gets people talking, and this applies to resellers as well as customers. Linda Pezzano used mystery to create buzz about Trivial Pursuit before the product launch at Toy Fair 1983. "We wanted to get the buyers' attention before they even came to New York," she recalled. To do this, Pezzano and her staff created a series of teaser mailings that were sent to several hundred key buyers in the toy industry a few weeks before the trade show. The first mailing came in a small envelope, hand-addressed, with a real stamp and no return address. It contained a little card with the Trivial Pursuit logo and a random card from the game.

Now, imagine that you're a buyer at a toy store and you receive a card with questions such as "What's the largest city between Ireland and Canada?" or "What sport did John Wayne play at the University of Southern California?" (Reykjavik, Iceland; football). It's likely to get your attention, and you may even mention it to your co-workers. Three or four days later a second random card arrives: "What was Elvis Presley's middle name?" "How many sides does a nonagon have?" "What was Al Capone's nickname?" (Aaron; nine; Scarface). Now you're really curious as to what all this is about, especially since you still have no clue who's sending you these cards. When the third card comes (finally identifying the sender), I can see you getting up from your chair and stopping the first person you see: "Hey, Joe, guess what word was intentionally omitted from the screenplay of The Godfather" or "Who invented peanut butter?" (Mafia; George Washington Carver.)

"Buyers started calling up Selchow & Righter [the makers of the game] before Toy Fair, and some people even complained that other buyers got cards and they didn't," Pezzano recalled. A very simple and inexpensive idea created significant buzz in the channel. Selchow & Righter's showroom at the Toy Fair was mobbed, and they wrote up an unusually high number of orders for Trivial Pursuit.

## In Search of Validation

Often, before you can create buzz through distribution channels, you need to get over the initial resistance and indifference. More often than not you will encounter rejection, especially if your product comes from a small company. Resellers want to see evidence of consumer demand. Until they do, they'll be skeptical of your product.

When Margot Fraser decided to market German-made Birkenstock sandals in this country, she first went to the most natural channel: shoe stores. She found, however, that this channel was unwilling to sell the shoes. Shoe store owners didn't believe that the product would be accepted by Americans. When Fraser displayed Birkenstocks at a shoe trade show, the reaction was so bad that she decided to leave early, despite the fact that the show organizers were going to penalize her for leaving the booth before closing time. "I picked up my stuff and escaped through the fire exit," she recalls, laughing.

So shoe stores were out. Who else would be willing to champion such a strange-looking product? A friend told Fraser about a convention of health food stores that was taking place in San Francisco. Fraser rented a table at the show. "I just talked to people going by: 'You know, you ought to try this.' And that's how it started." Owners of health food stores were somehow more receptive to the unconventional sandals, and many of them bought Birkenstocks for their own use. When they got back to their networks, they buzzed to their customers about the magic of these sandals. The word about Birkenstocks initially spread through the networks of health food enthusiasts.

Another alternative channel emerged from among the customer base. Some students who saw this as a way to sell a useful product and make a living approached Fraser, who jumped at the opportunity. Melanie Grimes, for example, got to know the shoes when she was living in Vermont. "They were just unlike anything I'd ever seen. They were so incredibly comfortable," she says, remembering her first pair. Grimes became a walking ad for the sandals. When she moved to Seattle to attend school, people would ask her about her Birkenstocks, but there was no place in town to buy the shoes. So she wrote to her friend in the Vermont health food store where she'd purchased them and asked where she had found them. The friend sent her Fraser's phone number, and soon Grimes had started a little business out of her bedroom closet selling Birkenstocks. After about a year she decided to open a store.

After a while the demand created in these alternative channels started to get the attention of shoe stores. "I see people coming out of the health food store with shoe boxes under their arm," one shoe store owner told Fraser when he called to inquire about the shoes. The few stores that started to carry the product gradually gave it the validation it needed in the traditional channel. It took the brand many years to gain the status it enjoys today. Acceptance by traditional shoe stores was the first step that allowed Birkenstocks to spread beyond the networks of health food customers and into mainstream America.

# Putting It Together

**15.** **Up to this point I've** talked about the isolated factors that create buzz. Now let's look at how these factors work together. This chapter features studies of three companies from three different industries—consumer products, high tech, and toys—showing how each has spread the word about its products. In all three cases success wasn't the result of a single factor. It was a combination of a contagious product and extensive efforts to accelerate natural contagion. Success didn't come quickly either. A lot of hard work and patience went into creating buzz.

## Consumer Products: PowerBar

**The idea for** PowerBar originated in 1983. Marathon runner Brian Maxwell had been leading in a race by over a minute at the twenty-mile mark when stomach problems caused him to fall back; he ended up finishing seventh. The disappointment of that race was also the beginning of a long search for a new food for athletes that would be easy to digest, low in fat, tasty, and nutritious. In their Berkeley kitchen, Maxwell and his girlfriend, Jennifer Biddulph (they have since married), started cooking. With the help of a third friend, and after some initial trial runs that Maxwell once described as "horrible glop," they came up with something pretty close to what we know today as PowerBar.

Fourteen years later, in 1997, the company's sales passed the $100 million mark. But when the first PowerBars came off the production line, they didn't immediately become the talk of the town. Spreading the word took a tremendous effort. How did a small company from Berkeley convince the world to start eating energy bars?

### How the Product Creates Buzz

It definitely wasn't the taste that made people recommend PowerBar product to their friends. "It was like brussels sprouts or spinach," one athlete described the early bars. You don't like it, but you know it's good for you. The initial buzz among serious athletes can be traced to that: Endurance athletes are always on the lookout for anything that will give them that extra edge. When one of their fellow athletes—Maxwell is a world-class marathon runner—came up with a solution, they started buzzing about it.

An energy bar is also a highly visible product. PowerBars are usually consumed in public and thus advertise themselves. The first person on a team to pull a bar out of his or her pocket, tear off the

Because information doesn't flow easily from one sport to another, PowerBar plants
separate seeds in each sport. PowerBar staff handing out samples to skiers.

shiny wrapper, and eat the strange-looking thing inside immediately found himself or herself answering questions from his or her
teammates: "What's that?" "How does it taste?" "Does it really
work?"

## What They Did to Stimulate Buzz

The single most important factor that launched buzz about
PowerBar was the company's grassroots seeding efforts. When the
product was first being formulated, Maxwell and Biddulph went
out to San Francisco Bay Area running, cycling, and triathlon
events and bombarded athletes with questions. How much did
they exercise? What did they eat before they exercised and before

they competed? How did people feel their food affected them? Maxwell estimates that they talked with about twelve hundred people during the development stage. Then, when the product was ready, they sent these athletes a little box containing five bars and a follow-up survey. The hundreds of people who responded and ordered started telling their teammates and friends about the new product. Buzz blossomed, first in the San Francisco Bay Area. The buzz grew as Maxwell and Biddulph set up their table and started handing out bars at different sporting events in an ever-expanding geographic area.

Although they didn't call it "viral marketing," their next move could be best described this way. To stimulate word of mouth in other parts of the country, the company sent a letter to its existing customers offering to send five PowerBars on their behalf to anyone in the United States for just three dollars to cover shipping costs. "We would even put a note in, [such as] 'To Charlie from Amy in San Francisco,'" Maxwell says. When Charlie in Boston got that package, he would usually call Amy in San Francisco to find out more about the bars. Again—excellent response resulted with additional word of mouth in new clusters.

Working with network hubs was another key element of PowerBar's marketing. Maxwell and Biddulph put a tremendous emphasis on their relationships with regular hubs—coaches and leading athletes. We're not talking Michael Jordan here, and that's part of why this program is so powerful. Currently around twenty-five hundred athletes are part of the "PowerBar Team Elite" program. Most of them approach the company to seek sponsorship. Once accepted, an athlete or a team gets an allotment of gear and product. A built-in incentive encourages participants to broadcast their affiliation with PowerBar: Athletes earn money when their picture appears in the media, with the amount of compensation depending on the amount of exposure the athlete gets.

## How Traditional Marketing Tools Have Helped Buzz

Public relations jump-started buzz early on. Maxwell got a call one day from the captain of the 7-Eleven cycling team that was about to leave for the Tour de France. The team needed about a thousand bars. Giving so many bars away wasn't a trivial thing—the young company was selling only about eight hundred bars a month at the time—but Maxwell agreed. In return, the captain of the team promised to try to get some publicity. On a Saturday afternoon a few weeks later, when everyone in America who was interested in cycling was watching the Tour de France on CBS, the PowerBar founders got their payoff in the form of a three-minute television segment. While French riders were shown eating ham and cheese sandwiches, the American team could be seen munching on a new fuel: PowerBar. This broadcast was the fountain that fed thousands of additional streams of buzz. "Have you tried it?" "How does it taste?" "Does it really work?"

Distribution channels were key to spreading the word early on. At first PowerBar sold mostly direct and through only one store in Berkeley. Shortly after the CBS broadcast, an independent bicycle rep called and offered to add the product to his line. Teaming up with another well-connected individual took the company to the next level. "Within about two or three months he had us in about three hundred bicycle shops," Maxwell recalls. Since bicycle shops often employ biking enthusiasts who have their own networks, this accelerated adoption among cyclists even further. The independent representative also helped them expand to other parts of the country. "And again it was sort of a networking thing there, because the guy we had in Northern California knew his counterparts in Southern California and people in other parts of the country," Maxwell says.

As competitors emerged and the product category started to become mainstream, distribution has become even more important, as it is for any consumer product. Today you can find PowerBars everywhere.

This switch to mainstream required some changes. The first was in product formulation. In the early 1990s PowerBar responded to pressure to improve the taste and consistency of the product. Serious athletes would eat almost anything to improve their performance, but to appeal to health buffs, kids, seniors, and busy people, the product would need to taste better and have a better texture.

Another change was the need for more attention to brand-name recognition. Although PowerBar had the support of thousands of network hubs in different sport niches, the people at the company felt that to appeal to wider circles they needed a big name to endorse the product. This was a challenge "The American public is very sophisticated," says Maxwell. "We all know that top athletes are paid to endorse products. We all see the athletes wearing Reebok one year and Nike the next year, and we know that they got paid more." In 1995 the company chose San Francisco 49er quarterback Steve Young as a spokesman. Young is known as someone who endorses only products he uses, and he seems to be in this for the long run. Young has appeared in the company's ads since 1995, and in 1999 he joined PowerBar's board of directors.

The company still pays a lot of attention to its grassroots seeding efforts, sponsoring hundreds of events every year. Seeding is still key. A few years ago I attended a talk that Maxwell gave in San Francisco. It had nothing to do with sports, but a table with sample products was set up at the entrance. It seems that the guy can't go anywhere without leaving a trail of seeds behind.

## High Tech: Women.com Networks

Women.com was founded by Ellen Pack and Nancy Rhine in 1992 as Women's Wire. At the time, only 10 percent of on-line users were women, and as a result there wasn't much content available online that was geared toward women. Pack and Rhine's goal was to change that. The service was launched in January 1994 as a direct-dial bulletin board service. Through a simple user interface, you could post questions, send e-mail, look for information, and make friends. Georgia Jones, an early member, recalls telling eight friends about it. "It spread very much by personal contact," she says. But despite the early buzz, the service grew at a modest rate. In mid-1994 the service had only about 1,300 members.

Jump a few years later. In January 2000, Women.com Networks had 4.3 million unique visitors. Women on the Net now number around 50 percent. Nobody claims that Women.com did that by itself—major changes contributed to the rise of the Internet—but here we will focus on what one company did to help the word about the Net spread among women.

## How the Service Creates Buzz

As I've pointed out several times already, an on-line community becomes more useful to each member as more people join. A community with five people is warm and cozy, but it's limited in the services it can provide to its members. Early users of Women's Wire told their friends about it because of the novelty, but also because by bringing more people on board, the service would become more valuable—there'd be more people to interact with.

Another factor that drives buzz is content. When Jane finds a useful article about children's vitamins, a topic she just discussed at length with her sister, she's likely to mention Women.com to her sister next time they talk on the phone, or simply e-mail the article to her. From its early days Women.com offered a variety of information channels that cover topics such as business, career, art, health, and relationships, to name just a few.

These channels, however, weren't enough for the product to

propagate itself. The early business model of Women's Wire required each new member to obtain a disk with access software from the company, and to make a commitment of $15 a month ($180 a year). While this may have made perfect sense from a monetary perspective, the price and the extra step worked against the company as far as buzz was concerned. America Online, a company that used a similar business model, chose to flood the market with start-up disks to simplify the delivery of its services.

In 1995, with the rise of the Web, Women.com changed its business model and removed the cost and delivery constraints. As a result, word spread much more easily. Now if you wanted to tell a friend about the service, all you had to do was point her to www.women.com.

## What They Did to Stimulate Buzz

With friction removed and with network effects working for the company, the word of the company just spread by itself, right? Not really. With only 10 percent of women on-line, somebody had to bring the word to the 90 percent who weren't. To make this happen, the Women.com team started to leapfrog into women's networks, and not only to on-line networks. Marleen McDaniel, a high-tech industry executive who joined the company as president and CEO around that time, described their activities in this way: "The first year or two we spent an inordinate amount of time talking to women's groups, evangelizing the Internet." They took a directory of women's organizations and, going down the list, made phone calls, wrote letters, and arranged numerous speaking engagements. The American Association of University Women, the National Association of Women Business Owners, the National Organization for Women— the list goes on and on. "Creating buzz is an enormously hard job, and it has to be done both on-line and off-line," McDaniel explains.

Women, of course, heard about the Internet from other

sources as well. The media and competitors such as iVillage or Cy-bergrrl all put the Internet on people's conversational agenda. America Online and thousands of smaller access providers were selling their service to both men and women. The rise of the Net at the workplace also stimulated discussion. Women.com knew both how to ride the wave and further enhance it, an important characteristic of companies that get buzz.

Over time it became easier to have people try the service. But it's one thing to get people to visit a Web site and a totally different thing to make them tell their friends about it. This goes back to content. People are more apt to pass the word about specifics that they find on a site like Women.com than just to spread general praise to all their acquaintances. The people at Women.com try to provide content that's worth talking about. Then they make it as easy as possible for members to spread the word. On almost every page of the site, there's a button that reads, "Send this page to a friend"—not an original tactic on the Web, but one that can stimulate existing customers to tell others.

Encouraging members to link to each other is another way to create buzz. Services such as chat rooms or message boards strengthen ties among members, which makes them spend more time on the site. How does that affect buzz? People talk about what they do, and the more they do on Women.com, the more they're likely to mention it to others who don't use the service. On the Entrepreneurs message board two women from Australia ask for marketing tips on how to get more traffic on their Web site. On the Horoscope message board some members try to find their AstroTwins—people who were born on the same day ("August 15, 1962—Anybody?"). Connections that result from this contact have a better chance of staying within the Women.com community.

What else does the company do to stimulate buzz? Customers can get a free e-mail account à la Hotmail on Women.com. When your friend gets a message from mary@women.com, she can't ignore the brand. The site also has postcards that users are encouraged to pass on to friends. Users can also create their own personal Web sites. The company devotes staff to monitoring on-line discussion groups and forums. "We have full-time people who go out on the Net and get into discussion groups of related subjects and talk about stuff they might find on Women.com," says McDaniel. The exact percentage of customers who learn about Women.com through word of mouth is hard to track. McDaniel estimates it at up to 30 percent.

## How Traditional Marketing Tools Have Helped Buzz

Although she acknowledges the importance of word of mouth, McDaniel argues that buzz is not enough. "Word of mouth will get you here," she says, raising her hand to about her shoulder level. "And to get *here*"—now she raises her hand way above her head—"you need to do more. You need to do real-money marketing."

What are these "real-money" marketing activities? The company advertises on sites such as Yahoo!, Lycos, and Go Network, as well as on TV programs such as *Friends, Oprah,* and *Martha Stewart Living*. A 1999 article in *Advertising Age* estimates the TV, radio, print, and outdoor branding campaign at $15 million.

Another important venue for growth is strategic alliances. Women.com has been engaged in partnerships with Microsoft, Yahoo!, GeoCities, and other companies. In 1998 the company acquired the Stork Site, a popular site for expectant mothers, and entered into a joint venture with the Hearst Corporation. These types of strategic moves can accelerate buzz dramatically as they expose millions of additional people to the brand. The acquisition of the Stork Site, for example, can be seen as a mega-shortcut into the social networks that formed around that site. Does this guarantee good buzz? Of course not. But it is an opportunity to impress many new people and eventually encourage them to tell their friends.

## Toys: Yomega

Yomega started in the mid-1980s in the basement of Alan Amaral in Massachusetts. "My parents and my aunt and uncle and one cousin were the first assembly workers," remembers Joyce Amaral, his sister and cofounder. Their product was a high-performance yo-yo, one that, unlike the traditional yo-yo, returns to your hand automatically. The business boomed in the fifteen years that followed. As a privately held company, Yomega doesn't release sales data. But in 1999 Yomega yo-yos were believed to be the number-two-selling toy in the United States (second only to Beanie Babies), and worldwide annual sales of yo-yos in 1999 were estimated to reach $1 billion.

### How the Product Itself Creates Buzz

A large part of the buzz about Yomega can be traced to the product's contagious nature. Remember the example of the Kodak camera in 1888? The Yomega yo-yo exploded similarly. Because its special clutch system made the yo-yo automatically return to the child's hand, it made his or her first experience with the toy successful. Regular yo-yos are difficult to master. "The Yomega yo-yo removed a lot of the frustration," says Alan Amaral, now company president. "Kids were able to see progress much faster than with the traditional slip-string yo-yo." This had a double impact on buzz. First, the moment children succeed in something, they *must* show it to others. Second, their initial success encourages them to try additional tricks and become *long-term* participants in the sport.

The special clutch system wasn't the only innovation that made Yomega a highly contagious product. Another innovation that appeared around that time was the transaxle. This is a sleeve around the yo-yo axle that reduces the friction significantly, letting novice users "sleep" the yo-yo. Sleeping the yo-yo means that it spins at the bottom of the string for a long time. Before, players could sleep a reg-

The clutch mechanism in the Yomega yo-yo made a child's first experience with the toy successful, and children *have* to show others when they succeed.

ular yo-yo for five to ten seconds. With the transaxle, players can sleep the yo-yo for thirty to sixty seconds, so they're able to perform more tricks and create more visual buzz. "When one child understood how to play with it, how to make it sleep, he became a walking advertisement," says Joyce Amaral.

### What They Did to Stimulate Buzz

Despite these enhancements, it took a while before a real craze took shape. In the early days Yomega focused on finding sales reps who would push the product to dealers. That got some products on the shelf but not beyond it. The yo-yo is a classic contagious product that advertises itself, and the technological enhancements made it even more so. But its contagion is worthless if it just sits on the shelf at the toy store. Word about yo-yos spreads only when people are seen playing with them.

Sales began to take off when Yomega and its distributors demonstrated the yo-yos at schools and other gathering places. The craze began for real in Hawaii. Dr. Lucky J. Meisenheimer, who has studied the history of the toy, believes that behind every yo-yo craze is one individual who champions the product. In the case of Hawaii, that person was Alan Nagao, who owns several kite stores in the state and started to push Yomega aggressively. Nagao and his staff at Team High Performance went to schools, taught kids old and new yo-yo tricks, and organized championships. Relatively few people actually participate in these sorts of contests, but they create a core group of enthusiasts, boys and girls extremely skilled with yo-yos. As these kids practice, other kids see them and want to get yo-yos, too.

Yomega also took off in Israel. This happened partially through an accidental seeding campaign. The local Yomega distributor, Pini Gamzo, bought about 150 units but couldn't sell any. Store owners felt that they were too expensive. After about a year Gamzo was so discouraged that he started giving the yo-yos to his friends for free. It didn't take long before word began to get out about the Yomegas. "People were asking my friends how they could get these yo-yos," he recalls. Encouraged, Gamzo started driving around neighborhoods. When he saw kids playing on street corners, he'd stop, pull out some yo-yos, and teach them fancy tricks. The following week he would see a spike in demand in that neighborhood. Gamzo started to make emergency calls to Yomega to ship him more product. "All of a sudden we couldn't build enough yo-yos to ship to Israel," Joyce Amaral remembers. What happened in Israel and in Hawaii started to happen in other locations. "We would call these 'hot pockets of activities,'" says Joyce Amaral. "All of a sudden we'd just have orders like crazy from a certain community." Sometimes it was due to activities initiated by Yomega or a local dealer. In other cases competitors or independent demonstrators ignited the craze by going out to schools and other gathering places. All the retailers in the area would stock their stores as the buzz about yo-yos spread in their town. "We bought every kind of yo-yo we could find," remembers Beth Reynolds of Pick Up Your Toys, in Albuquerque, New Mexico. This attracted network hubs—kids who were especially good with yo-yos—to her store. "We had a couple of kids I call 'my yo-yo homies' who really spread the word in the schools, and before you know it we're considered 'Yo-Yo Central,'" she says. To further support their customers, dealers started holding yo-yo workshops. "We just had a yo-yo work-shop Saturday," Reynolds told me when I talked to her. "We had fifty kids come out, and we basically just did maintenance and taught them tricks and gave them strings, and they loved it. And now those fifty kids are going to tell another fifty kids."

One interesting thing about these yo-yo homies is their use of the Internet. In previous yo-yo crazes in the 1930s or the 1960s, kids were not as well connected. Today kids still learn tricks mostly from other kids they see, but the Internet offers an easy way to tell others and pass on new tricks. Chat rooms, newsgroups, Web sites— all serve as channels to spread tips and tricks across geographical

Yo-yo crazes in the 1930s and 1960s were also started through yo-yo demonstrations and contests. Here a flyer announcing a contest organized by Duncan.

areas. In the spring of 1999 Yomega's Web site was getting 12 million hits a month.

Schools are hotbeds of information on yo-yos. "School would end in June, and the summer would be very quiet," Joyce Amaral says of yo-yo sales. John Stangle, president of the American Yo-Yo Association, has observed the same phenomenon: "During the summertime nobody sells any yo-yos," he says. "The kids don't have a large enough group of other kids that are yo-yoing with them." Think about this in terms of network hubs. Assume that at a school of 500 there are 50 yo-yo hubs—kids who know the latest tricks and have the latest models. During the school year *every* child has a chance to see these kids in the schoolyard. Now, during the summer, the 500 children break into small groups of, say, 3 each. Now we have 166 groups with 3 friends in each. Fifty of these groups have a yo-yo expert in them, but 116 don't. So yo-yoing doesn't spread as easily. When school is back in session, the network hubs are again exposed to hundreds of children, including a new entering class of young students.

## How Traditional Marketing Tools Have Helped Buzz

In Japan, Yomega had an opportunity to see how grassroots efforts can be accelerated with traditional marketing tools. To market their product in Japan, Yomega signed a distribution agreement with Bandai, the company responsible for such successes as Power Rangers and Tamagotchi. Bandai was able to put significant resources behind the Yomega brand. To manage the grassroots efforts, Bandai brought Alan Nagao from Hawaii. He conducted yo-yo contests and promotions for thousands of people in arenas around the country. In addition, Bandai ran an intensive advertising campaign on TV and promoted the toy in local comic books. "All of that working together made a huge national craze," Joyce Amaral notes. "It certainly wasn't a grassroots, slow-to-start-and-then-build-up effort. It was all choreographed," she says.

Yomega uses TV advertising in the United States as well, which lets them build the brand and introduce their yo-yos to a wider audience. "TV is an important element in the marketing mix, but I don't think it is the most important element," Alan Amaral notes, adding that the real interest in yo-yos comes as the result of a child's being inspired to pick one up, and then from the enthusiasm that follows his or her early success. As that child starts to master the game, there will always be another child who will want to learn how to yo-yo.

# How to Keep Buzz Alive

Buzz is about newness, and when newness fades, buzz will decline. Athletes who've been eating PowerBar for years now treat it almost like bread—something you eat, not talk about. Some women who were excited by the novelty of the Internet just two years ago don't talk about it as much anymore, and some children who've mastered all the yo-yo tricks move on to the next thing.

Is there a way to keep buzz going over time? It's hard, but the answer lies in three areas: customer involvement, new customers, and innovation.

## Customer Involvement

The first element that will determine how much long-term buzz your company gets has to do with the degree of involvement your customers feel over time. The more they *think* about your product, the more they'll *talk* about it.

Yomega, like other yo-yo manufacturers, tries to get its customers involved by cultivating and supporting yo-yo clubs, contests, and events. Turning the yo-yo into a collectible item also helps maintain interest in the industry. Collectors interact with each other and spread the word about their hobby to others. The more collectors out there, the more long-term buzz will there be about yo-yos. At Women.com, new content is supposed to create involvement and make people talk. As with any other media company, this is a never-ending challenge. You have to engage your readers, members, or viewers every day.

## New Customers

The second way to keep buzz going is to find new people who have not been exposed to the product yet. When Women.com promotes its service in Japan, or when Power-Bar goes after golf players, that's essentially what they are doing—moving on to the next network where buzz and new sales can be generated. It is also important to realize that younger generations who haven't been exposed to your product are a fertile ground for new buzz. Yo-yo manufacturers need to make sure to come back to a market every few years, in order to train the kids who were too young to hold a yo-yo during the previous craze. It's not an automatic transfer, though, as younger generations have their own preferences and tastes. When Brian Maxwell looks at some of the emerging Gen X sports—roller blading, skateboarding, snowboarding—he understands this. "It's a challenge to determine how do you have legitimacy and become part of those [sports]," he says.

## Innovation

"We spare no expense nor effort in trying to make our yo-yos do more by way of spin-time and performance features," says Alan Amaral of Yomega. Amaral realizes that the way to keep kids talking is to come up with new and exciting improvements. This, of course, presents a huge challenge to companies. Usually, after a breakthrough development that gets significant buzz, companies are able to come up with only incremental improvements. The companies that consistently introduce creative improvements that are worth talking about—and find creative ways to market them—are those that get most of the buzz. "Creativity is probably the most important factor in keeping it alive," says Amaral.

# Buzz

# Workshop

**16.** **My hope is that** *The Anatomy of Buzz* has helped you to develop a different approach to marketing. In the end, though, what I'm sure you most want to know is how these concepts and techniques can be put to work for you. I've created this chapter as a workshop, in the sense that it leads you through a series of questions you can pose in thinking about whatever product or service you're trying to market.

## Do You Have the Right Product?

**People will pass** on positive comments—the kind of buzz you want—only if the product or service really does impress them. There is no point in stimulating the networks to create buzz unless your product meets the test.

**Am I offering a quality product or service?** In order to generate positive buzz, your product needs to exceed the expectations of the people you're trying to reach. Not all products that get positive buzz are of the very highest standard, but they all do outstrip consumers' expectations. The product has to work from day one and offer everything that was promised, if not more. Do you underpromise and overdeliver?

**Does my product enhance the lives of people who use it?** Is it compatible with what people do, fitting readily into their current belief systems or lifestyle? Does it make their lives better by "doing the rest"?

**Is my product visible—and can I help make it more so?** Contagious products are often visible—they draw attention to themselves. Can you do something to make your product, or its users, more noticeable in a positive way?

**Am I offering something new?** Buzz reflects excitement. Excitement doesn't build around old ideas, familiar approaches, or "me too" products. Something about your offering must be fresh and different.

**Is my product ready?** If buzz begins now, is it too early?

# Do You Have the Right Approach?

**Generating buzz calls** for a different attitude, a different approach to the promotion of your product than is typical.

**Am I operating in a spirit of truth, honesty, and directness?** Openness and candor are key to developing strong, long-term, grassroots support.

**Am I thinking in terms of networks?** Thinking of markets, segments, and categories can be useful. So can thinking of your relationship with every individual customer. But when you think of buzz, think of customers as part of a network. Your objective is to maximize the number of positive comments about your product that flow among nodes in this network.

**Am I willing to work to accelerate contagion in the network?** Without stimulation, word of mouth can spread at a very slow rate—often too slowly for success in today's highly competitive markets. Intense personal effort may be required to push the word and to leapfrog directly to the most productive hubs or into untapped clusters.

## Personal Effort: Bob Metcalfe and Ethernet

Bob Metcalfe, father of Ethernet and founder of 3COM, told Scott Kirsner how young MIT engineers often come to him for advice. After they go through his six-story town house in Boston's Back Bay, many of them say something like "Wow! What a great house! I want to invent something like Ethernet." At this point Metcalfe has to sit them down and explain, "No, I don't have this house because I invented Ethernet. I have this house because I went to Cleveland and Schenectady and places like that. I sold Ethernet for a decade."

## Are You Listening to the Networks?

**You need to** listen to the networks. The best way to do that is by talking to people. Every time you use another person—an interviewer, a reseller, a focus group moderator—as a messenger, you are adding a filter. Get out and talk to people directly.

> **Know what customers are saying.** What do they tell their friends about your company? About your competitors? How satisfied are they with current solutions in the marketplace?

> **Use all possible approaches to hearing buzz.** Do you read what is being said about your company on different newsgroups, chat rooms, Web sites, and other on-line forums? Do you regularly talk with customers on an informal basis?

> **Track what the industry is saying.** It's important to listen, not only to customer buzz but also to industry buzz. Customer buzz tells you what users are talking about *today*. Industry buzz can give you insight into what customers will be talking about *tomorrow*.

## Are You Working with Network Hubs?

**Hubs are the** key to influencing the network, so finding and influencing hubs is crucial in building buzz.

> **Identify your network hubs.** Who are the network hubs in your category? Which are regular hubs and which are mega-hubs? Which are expert hubs and which are social hubs? What do you know about your regular hubs and how to reach them? Do you know who might be the "connectors," bridging the distance between clusters?

**Use all available techniques to find even more hubs.** Are you listening when such hubs identify themselves? Can you think of categories of people who might become network hubs for your product? People who by virtue of their position have many ties with people you would like to reach? Have you used surveys to identify potential hubs? Have you looked for hubs within your own company—an executive with the contacts and charisma to be a mega-hub, or potential champion/activists from engineering, marketing, or R&D?

**Track your hubs.** Do you keep good records of their names and addresses? Have you developed a profile for each—what type of hub this person is, what type of influence he or she has, useful connections, etc.? Is your database accessible to others in the organization so that they can draw on the information and update it?

**Give your hubs what they need.** Do you get out the word when there is something new? Do you provide hubs, especially expert hubs, with relevant facts? Are you putting the product in their hands?

**Be receptive and responsive to their feedback and input.** Is it easy for customers to talk to you? (It's in your best interest if everyone who has had a bad experience calls your 800 number instead

## Hubs: The HP 35 Calculator

David Packard, cofounder of Hewlett Packard, recalls how the HP 35 calculator was introduced back in 1972: "About a month before its release, Barney Oliver gave samples of the 35 to several leading engineers and Nobel physicists. The crowds they drew when casually showing off this 'toy' at meetings and conventions probably accounted for our being unable to meet the initial demands for the 35," Packard writes in his book, *The HP Way.* The fact that these engineers and scientists had some exclusive information in the palms of their hands was the moving force behind the buzz.

of becoming, in effect, a hub passing on negative buzz. Do you have an 800 number that is easy for customers to find? One large beer company had an 800 number—printed in black on the bottom of the six-pack carton. They received almost no calls until they moved the 800 number to a prominent position on the package handle—and then the phones started to ring.) Are the people at your company responsive to inquiries, acting as facilitators rather than gatekeepers? Do you adequately acknowledge referrals, rewarding customer loyalty without making the customer feel uncomfortable?

## Have You Considered All Possible Techniques for Building Buzz?

**Creating buzz is** an active process: You have to work at it. Have you thought of everything you can do to make it happen?

**Have you planned seeding efforts?** Does your plan include seeding with both mega-hubs and regular hubs (i.e., the grassroots level)?

## Inquiries: Littlearth and Oprah

"You never know where something's going to lead," says Ava DeMarco of Pittsburgh, cofounder of Littlearth, a producer of fashion accessories. In 1999 DeMarco and her partner Robert Brandegee were invited to *The Oprah Winfrey Show*, where they showed their recycled fashion products. When she traced back the origin of that invitation, DeMarco came up with the following chain: The researcher for the *Oprah* show learned about Littlearth from a book put together by the editors of *Entrepreneur* magazine, who in turn learned about DeMarco's company from an article in a local newspaper. "We ended up on *The Oprah Winfrey Show* due to some press that happened almost two years ago," she says.

**Can you limit access to your product,** so that scarcity builds interest at the outset?

**Can you use a sneak preview** to capture the imagination of a selected group of customers?

**What can you do that will surprise people?** People talk about the unexpected.

**Can you be outrageous?**

**Can you take your customers behind the scenes?** Can you show them how your product is made, who is making it, and why its producers are excited about it? (Even if you make a "boring" product, there must be something interesting in the way it's produced or in the way you came up with the idea.)

**Can your story include a hero?** Is there a human drama behind your product? Is there a charismatic leader in your company?

**Can you stage an event** that will feature your product and get people talking?

**Can you create a simple (paper) pass-it-on promotion?** Does your Web site have a pass-it-on mechanism? Is it easy to use? Is it presented in a friendly, polite way?

## Scarcity: *The Blair Witch Project*

"Any commodity will be valued to the extent that it is unavailable" is the basic concept of commodity theory devised by Timothy C. Brock of Ohio State University. *The Blair Witch Project*, a low-budget student film that became the surprise hit of the summer of 1999, was extremely successful the first week it opened on 27 screens. The following week its makers had the option to widen distribution to 2,000 screens. They chose instead to show it on only 1,100 screens. "Nothing is better than knowing that a film is sold out. Everyone wants to see it," Amir Malin of Artisan explained to *Variety*.

**Is your product visible?** Have you considered ways to use your staff and systems as part of the way that potential customers become aware of your product? (See FedEx and UPS.)

**Are your customers talking to one another?** (The more your customers interact, the more involved they will become with your product and the more they will have to tell others.) Do your customers share a common interest or bond? Can you find ways to help them socialize or exchange comments? Can your Web site allow them to talk to one another? Can you arrange face-to-face meetings, such as through special events?

**Is there something in your service that can make it more useful as more people use it?** Remember that customers will spread the word about your offering not because you have a cute way of asking them to, but because they perceive a benefit from doing so.

**Is your product being given as a gift?** Can you stimulate your customers to do this more often?

## Outrageous: Beauty and Birkenstocks

Outrageous stimuli get more buzz. A beautiful model who appears at a fashion show wearing beautiful dressy shoes is just another beautiful model. Let her wear the ugliest Birkenstocks and suddenly everyone will be talking about it. That's what designer Narciso Rodriguez did. He chose what importer Margot Fraser calls "the ugliest thing that we have" and put it into a fashion show with chiffon dresses. "It's so outrageous it's in every magazine," says Fraser, "and suddenly young women want to buy this." The same principle—outrageousness—helped build buzz behind *There's Something About Mary,* a politically incorrect comedy filled with scenes that are so shockingly unexpected you just have to share them with a friend (though probably not with your mother).

**Do you have a referral awards plan?** If so, do your customers like it and respond to it? Have you asked them for their feedback?

**Are you exploring all possible networks?** Even if you are busy listening to the networks where your product *is* generating buzz, are you also listening for the silence from networks where you aren't known?

## Are Your Ads Building Buzz?

**The techniques for** generating buzz don't necessarily end the need for conventional advertising. The challenge, though, is to advertise in a way that helps to build buzz, not dampen it.

**Do your ads help people articulate what is unique about your product?** If they can't explain what is new or special in, for example, a

## Events and Buzz: Macy's and the Latino Culture

For several years Macy's West has held in-store events celebrating Latino culture in the Los Angeles area. Fashion shows, cooking demonstrations, and celebrity appearances all have a Latin flair.

These events create two waves of buzz. The first occurs as people spread the word about the event itself: the day, the activities, and so on. The second wave follows the festival, as people share their impressions with their friends—for Macy's this has been good buzz, because guests have fun and are pleasantly surprised when the event goes beyond such clichés as piñatas and mariachi bands. A typical comment, according to Rochelle Newman of Enlace Communications, which organized the events for Macy's, might be that Macy's "understands the Latina shopper and isn't afraid to put on a fashion show with models who aren't Twiggies because that's not what Latinas look like or want to be like." Macy's found that its in-store traffic increased and sales at participating stores exceeded store goals by as much as 62 percent.

focus group, they won't be able to do it when talking with their friends.

**Can you use advertising to jump-start buzz for your product?**

**If you're using testimonials, are they credible?** Check with your customers: their opinion may not be the same as yours.

**Do your ads help your customers,** such as by giving them information that reinforces their reasons for buying?

**Can your ads themselves be made clever enough to create buzz?** Think of the white milk mustaches or the catchphrase "Where's the beef?"

## Visibility: FedEx and UPS

Services such as FedEx and UPS are good at using their delivery systems to build awareness of their product. Both have recognizable trucks marked with their distinctive colors and logos, and those trucks are seen everywhere, from inner cities to rural areas around the world. Both also have staffs who are visible and are good representatives of their company. The UPS deliveryperson's brown uniform is one of the best-known uniforms on the street today. And as Ted Sartoian, vice president at FedEx in its early days, says, "The driver, the courier at Federal Express, makes that company. The way they treat the customers, how they're on time and they hustle, they're never seen walking. They run."

## Jump-starting Buzz: Hotmail

Sometimes the right ad in the right place is all you need to get people talking. To get an initial group of users on each college campus, Hotmail advertised in campus newspapers. To start Silicon Valley talking, the company rented a single billboard, for five thousand dollars a month, on Highway 101, the Valley's major thoroughfare. "I can't tell you how many people would say, 'Oh, yeah, I saw your billboard,'" says Steve Douty, former VP of marketing at Hotmail.

**Is your advertising campaign giving buzz a chance to build?** Ads *can* kill buzz. People will talk more about what they discover themselves.

## Are Your Resellers Building Buzz?

**Some resellers can** play a major role in spreading the word about your product.

**Have you identified the channels that are most promising in terms of buzz?** These are the channels where there's real person-to-person interaction and where the salespeople are most trusted by their customers.

**Are you in direct contact with the front-line people in these channels?** Remember, excitement doesn't store well in warehouses, so build direct relationships not only with executives but with the people who talk to customers every day.

**Can you use shopping mall kiosks for demonstrating your product?** You'll get more traffic and therefore more exposure than if you demo inside a store.

**Have you seeded the channel?** And again, have you made sure that your seed products have reached the people who are actually talking with customers? Are people in the channel actually using your product? Do you give them inside information they can spread to clients?

**Can salespeople articulate what's new and special about your product?** Do you train them? Recognize them? Can they learn from your packaging what's special about your product?

**Do your on-line resellers spread the word?** Do they interact with customers? If so, are the people who interact with customers trusted by them? Do these channels offer customers a forum to interact with each other?

## Working with the Channel: Brooks Sports

Between 1983 and 1993, Brooks lost about $60 million as it was trying to compete with Nike in too many sporting categories. Prices eroded, and so did the quality of the shoes. The company decided to focus on serious runners. The first step in reviving the brand was to bring quality up again. Once that was taken care of, the question became how to spread the word about the new Brooks. The answer: identify retailers who enjoy high credibility among serious runners. Helen Rockey, the company's CEO, hit the road to meet them. "Creating validity in the specialty running store channel was crucial," she explains. Many of these retailers, serious runners themselves, liked the new products and started spreading the word to customers and friends. This tour was the beginning of a long-term campaign of working with these specialty stores, which eventually brought the company back to profitability.

## Multiple Initiatives: Yahoo! and BMW

To generate buzz you often need to use nontraditional marketing techniques, but it's hard to tell in advance which will work. Jim McDowell, VP of marketing at BMW, suggests that you start several simultaneous initiatives. "You have to be prepared to do ten initiatives with the hope that two of them will work really well, five of them will work just fine, and three of them could be minor disasters." Others confirm that it's hardly ever just one factor that determines whether people will talk about your product. What made so many people buzz about Yahoo!? "It wasn't one thing. It was a hundred things. Maybe five hundred things," says John Yost. "You have to be working all the levels at the same time," confirms Morgan Entrekin, who published *Cold Mountain*.

## How Can You Keep the Buzz Alive?

**Buzz is about** newness. It's hard enough to get buzz going, and harder still to maintain it. What can you do?

**Are you actively looking for new customers who haven't yet been exposed to your product?** Are there new market segments or new geographic areas you haven't yet reached? If your product is "old," has a new generation of potential users come along?

**Are you supplying the networks with a constant flow of innovations that people can talk about?** The biggest enemy of buzz is routine. To keep buzz going over a long period of time, even an excellent restaurant has to change its menu and decor. Are you adding enhancements that will be worth talking about? Are you letting people know what's new and improved?

*"Promise me you'll keep the buzz alive."*

**Are you keeping customers involved?** If your customers buy your product and never think about it again, you can't expect them to talk about it too much. However, if you involve them, engage them, make it interesting for them, they will talk. Involvement translates to action, which in turn translates to buzz.

# Glossary

**Adopter categories.** A classification of customers based on the relative speed at which they adopt new ideas or products. Everett Rogers distinguishes among five groups: innovators, early adopters, early majority, late majority, and laggards.

**Buzz.** The sum of all comments about a particular product or company at a certain point in time. This is a broad definition that views everything being communicated about a product as the buzz about it. In contrast, *Newsweek* defined buzz as "infectious chatter; genuine, street-level excitement about a hot new person, place or thing." This describes what I would refer to as *strong* buzz, which is an important subset of buzz.

**Clique.** Three or more nodes that are all connected among themselves (density is maximized).

**Clusters.** Areas in the networks where people are more densely connected to each other.

**Cognitive dissonance.** In the context of consumer behavior, a discomfort experienced by the buyer as a result of some postpurchase conflict. For example, hearing about a low rating of a product may cause cognitive dissonance among recent buyers.

**Comment.** In this book the word is used to describe the basic building block of buzz. An opinion about a product or service that is transferred from one customer to the other. As in, "*The Graduate* is a great movie."

**Connectors.** Sometimes also called "bridges." These are people who connect different clusters and cliques.

**Contagion process.** The interpersonal influence process that operates via both direct ties and comparison of status.

**Contagious products.** Products with some intrinsic attributes that make them spread faster. For example, products that become more useful as more people use them can become contagious.

**Cosmopolite.** In the context of the diffusion of innovations, a person who is oriented to the world outside the local system.

**Craze.** A stampede. Very high demand for a particular product. Typically associated with shortages.

**Critical mass.** The minimum percentage of participants necessary to sustain an activity.

**Degree.** In the context of social networks, degree is the number of other people that a person is directly connected to.

**Density of a network.** The number of actual ties out of all of those possible in a particular network.

**Diffusion of innovations.** The process by which an innovation is communicated through certain channels over time among members of a social system.

**Distribution channel.** The companies through which a product "flows" from manufacturer to the end user.

**Dyad.** A tie between two nodes in a network. The basic unit of analysis of social networks.

**Fad.** A fashion that takes off, peaks, and declines very quickly. Almost always associated with a lot of buzz.

**Heterophily.** The degree to which two people are different from each other.

**Homophily.** The tendency for people who are similar to like one another and therefore associate with one another.

**Hub.** A person who communicates (directly or indirectly) with more people than average about a certain product category.

**Hype.** A communication that sets high expectations that are not met.

**Industry buzz.** Buzz within industry circles. Different from buzz among customers because it is typically more intense and spreads more rapidly.

**Influential Americans.** A term used by Roper Starch to describe a group the company has been monitoring since the 1940s. An influential is defined as a person who is involved in certain public, political, or social activities, such as writing a letter to the editor, making a speech, serving on a committee, and so on.

**Invisible networks.** The term used in this book to describe social networks. The interpersonal information networks that connect customers to each other.

**Leapfrogging.** Actively creating a shortcut in the networks in order to accelerate natural contagion.

**Mega-hub.** A person who communicates to many people through mass media such as radio, TV, and the Internet.

**Network externalities.** The tendency of certain products and services to become more valuable as more users adopt them.

**Opinion leader.** See "hub."

**Rejection.** A possible outcome of buzz. Opposite of adoption. A distinction can be made between active rejection ("I don't want a PalmPilot") and passive rejection ("I like it, but not now").

**Saturation.** The condition that exists when virtually all the potential adopters of a certain product have adopted it.

**Shortcuts.** In the context of this book, connections between two distant nodes in the networks that link distant clusters or cliques. These shortcuts accelerate the speed at which information flows. Shortcuts happen by chance or as a result of leapfrogging.

**Six degrees of separation.** The common belief that any two randomly selected people on this planet can be linked through a maximum of six other people. Named after a play (and later a movie) by that name. See "small world phenomenon."

**Small world phenomenon.** The term used by researchers to describe the "six degrees" phenomenon. Sometimes referred to as the "small world problem," which essentially asks how many intermediate acquaintance ties are needed to link any two randomly selected people to each other.

**Social network.** A set of actors and the relations among them. Although this broad definition allows different types of actors (e.g., companies), this book focuses only on social networks that link individual people.

**Social network analysis.** Mathematical analysis that focuses on relationships between social entities (individuals, companies, countries, etc.).

**Social network threshold.** The proportion of adopters in an individual's personal network necessary for an individual to adopt.

**"Strength of weak ties."** The idea that weak ties are more likely to bring new information into a clique or cluster. Conceived by Mark Granovetter of Stanford University.

**Structural hole.** A separation between nonredundant contacts. In the context of this book, the gap between clusters or cliques that can be closed by human bridges. Conceived by Ron Burt of the University of Chicago.

**Two-step flow model.** A model that assumes that information flows from the media to network hubs and from them to "the rest of us."

**Visual buzz.** Comments that move visually (as opposed to verbally). For example, a new type of shoe creates visual buzz as people observe it.

**Viral marketing.** Marketing activities on the Internet that take advantage of or accelerate the contagion process. ICQ and Hotmail are examples for companies that grew through viral marketing.

**Word of mouth.** Any oral communication. In the context of consumer behavior, this term refers to oral communication about products with friends, family, and colleagues. Word of mouth is one of the ways in which buzz is transmitted.

# Notes

## Chapter 1: What Is Buzz?

p. 5. "After this experience . . .": A general comment about the statistics that follow: People don't like to admit that they are influenced by advertising, so they often overstate the importance of word of mouth, articles in newspapers, etc. Still, these numbers are so high that even if they are inflated, they certainly cannot be ignored.

p. 5. "Sixty-five percent of customers who bought a Palm organizer . . .": Interview with Ed Colligan, 4/23/98.

p. 5. "Forty-seven percent of the readers of *Surfing* magazine say . . .": The source of this number is *Surfing* magazine's 1998 Readership Survey Results.

p. 5. "Friends and relatives are the number-one source . . .": The source is a press release from the Travel Industry Association of America (1998).

p. 5. "Fifty-seven percent of customers of one car dealership . . .": Interview with Jim Callahan, 2/7/99.

p. 5. "Fifty-three percent of moviegoers rely to some extent . . .": This is based on data provided to me by Maritz Marketing Research, which conducted an AmeriPoll on word-of-mouth behavior in February 1995. The question in the Maritz study was "How much do you rely on others when selecting what movie to see?" Customers were asked to rate their answer on a scale of 1="not at all" to 5="to a great extent." I report here those who marked 3, 4, or 5. The same applies to other places where I cite this study, including the statistics that follow about selecting a new doctor.

p. 6. "Seventy percent of Americans rely on the advice of others": Based on data provided by Maritz.

p. 6. "Sixty-three percent of women surveyed for *Self* magazine . . .": The study was reported in 1998 in *Drug Store News:* Women take charge in choosing OTC and Rx medications." *Drug Store News* 20(9): CP31+.

p. 6. "The idea that a critical part . . .": Interview with Len Short, 1998.

p. 7. "Now, my definition of buzz . . .": In looking at all the person-to-person communication, my focus will be on customer-to-customer communications, but I also consider communication between a clerk at a toy store and a customer part of buzz. How about advertising? The line between buzz and advertising can be blurry—as in the case of good testimonial advertising—but as a general rule in this book, buzz will refer only to communication between *individuals.* The definition of buzz that I compare mine to appeared in Marin and Van Boven (1998).

p. 7. "People all around the world . . .": The image of comments leaping from brain to brain has its roots in memetics—an emerging discipline that perceives ideas as autonomous entities that spread like viruses. Douglas Hofstadter says that when he thinks of a meme he has the image of a "flickering pattern of sparks leaping from brain to brain, screaming 'Me, me!'" See Hofstadter (1985). In *The Anatomy of Buzz* I chose not to expand on memetics. Readers who are interested may want to refer to the growing literature on the topic. For example, Dawkins (1976), Brodie (1996), and Lynch (1996).

## Chapter 2: The Invisible Networks

p. 11. "Kamran Elahian is still proud . . .": Interview with Kamran Elahian, 6/11/98. This case is also based on an interview with John F. Rizzo (5/28/99), former VP of marketing at Momenta, and on several articles, including Larson (1998) and Cuneo (1992).

p. 12. "The PR campaign was . . .": Interviews with Andy Reinhardt, 8/17/99, and with Rafe Needleman, 8/16/99.

p. 12. "Why wasn't the buzz great? . . .": The advice to the Momenta team to stay humble is not simple when you think about the task at hand. "It wasn't because we just wanted to hype the product up," explained John Rizzo. The company was trying to meet very aggressive (and probably unrealistic) sales goals for the launch period. In pulling a project like Momenta off the ground, you must generate excitement to secure financing, encourage third-party developers to write software for your platform, recruit employees, and convince resellers to carry the new product. "Part of it was that we really believed in what we were doing," John Rizzo told me. But the excitement should have been contained. When the computer finally started shipping, people were less than thrilled. "We ended up creating a monster," Rizzo said. It takes tremendous discipline not to get carried away by your own enthusiasm. "I guess the biggest lesson here is to never believe your own hype," Kamran Elahian once said about the experience. (Quoted in *The Business Journal,* 4/21/97.)

p. 13. "The fact is that marketing budgets . . .": Interviews with Ed Colligan, 4/23/98, 3/18/99.

p. 14. "Customers can hardly hear you . . .": The estimate of how much information an average person in seventeenth-century England was exposed to is from Wurman (1989). The estimate of the number of ads we're exposed to is from Kotler and Armstrong (1991).

p. 14. "Customers are skeptical . . .": This is based on Porter Novelli's Credibility Survey (1996).

p. 16. "Ed Niehaus, president of NRW . . .": Interview with Ed Niehaus, 5/28/98. For a description of the Intel case, see Grove (1996).

p. 17. "The power shift is seen across industries . . .": Interview with Reid Rosefelt, 2/26/2000.

p. 18. "Several Internet start-ups are developing . . .": Interview with Bill Gurley, 7/27/99.

p. 18. "They also try to mimic word of mouth . . .": Interview with Nirav Tolia, 8/5/99.

p. 20. "Word of Mouth on Steroids . . .": Interview with Steve Douty, 1/15/99. Also see Bronson (1999). Regarding the fact that Hotmail didn't generate much revenue during its life as a start-up, I should also note that the people at Hotmail were successful in creating value for their shareholders. The company was sold to Microsoft for $400 million.

p. 21. "Bhatia and Smith started making the routine rounds . . .": Interview with Steve Jurvetson, 12/4/98.

p. 21. "The service was launched on July 4 . . .": See Jurvetson (1998).

p. 22. "Hotmail did almost no advertising . . .": Interview with Montrese Etienne, 2/23/99. Interview with Steve Douty, 1/15/99.

p. 23. "This is a useful perspective . . .": Interviews with Tom Valente, 2/21/99, 5/26/99. See also Valente (1995).

p. 26. "The second factor . . .": Word-of-mouth referral behavior may also differ from country to country. For a comparison of the phenomenon in Japan and the United States, see Money, Gilly, and Graham (1998). The section about the Hispanic market is based on interviews with Felipe Korzenny, 1/4/99, 1/13/99.

p. 26. "Age can play a role here, too . . .": The fashion data is based on a press release from *Mademoiselle* magazine announcing the results of a Roper Starch study done for the magazine (1996): "Word-of-Mouth Communication Most Powerful with '20 Somethings.'" The data on word of mouth about car purchases was provided by Maritz Marketing Research, which conducted an AmeriPoll on word-of-mouth behavior in February 1995.

p. 27. "The more connected your customers are . . .": Interview with Keith Fox, 10/8/98.

p. 27. "What this connectivity means to Cisco . . .": Fisher (1996).

## Chapter 3: Why We Talk

p. 29. "Buzz is powerful because it is in our genes . . .": The section about ravens is based on an interview with Bernd Heinrich, 5/8/98, and on Heinrich and Marzluff (1995). How did the researchers determine that the raven that detected the food was the same one that returned with the crowd? First, they saw a pattern in which a crowd of ravens arrived only after one or two ravens discovered the bait. Later they tested it further by tagging birds with radio transmitters and releasing them near the carcass. These ravens also flew away and came back with other birds.

p. 30. "This bonanza of food could . . .": Sharing food with family is very common in nature. By comparing the DNA of sample ravens, the researchers were able to determine that the birds were *not* all related to the one that discovered the food.

p. 30. "The most fundamental reason we talk . . .": For information on the role of word of mouth in the labor market, see Granovetter (1995).

p. 31. "Sharing information . . .": The quote is from Kaplan (1995), p. 35.

p. 31. "Another explanation for talking . . .": Dunbar (1996), p. 21.

p. 32. "I took a coffee break . . .": The quote from the CEO of dELia*s is from Munk (1997).

p. 33. "In other cases we use products to send messages . . .": The quote is from Fournier (1998).

p. 35. "Asking for advice can also reduce risk . . .": The data on word of mouth in selecting a physician was provided to me by Maritz Marketing Research.

p. 36. "Customers who are less experienced . . .": Interview with Michael Gale, 5/8/98.

p. 36. "Often we can benefit directly from talking . . .": This effect is related to "Metcalfe's Law," which states that the value of a network grows as the square of the number of its users. The story behind Metcalfe's Law is interesting: In the early days of e-mail, companies used to run experiments to test the usefulness of this innovation by letting just a handful of people use it. Obviously they missed the point. Bob Metcalfe, founder of 3Com and the inventor of Ethernet, put together a slide that illustrated that the benefits of a network become more significant as more people are connected. This concept was later named after him (this is based on a conversation I had with Metcalfe in March 1999). Bill Gates's quote in this paragraph is taken from a lecture he gave at Stanford University, 1/27/98.

p. 37. "Competitors often benefit from . . .": The information about the gas industry's reaction to Edison's innovation is based on Utterback (1994), p. 65. The information about FedEx is based on Sigafoos (1983), p. 105. The information about Kodak is based on Collins (1990), p. 51. Also see Leonard-Barton (1985) for a discussion of experts as negative opinion leaders.

p. 38. "Rumors are often based on . . .": The story appeared in *The Wall Street Journal*. See Stevens (1981).

p. 38. "What does this mean? . . .": Jeff Bezos's quote is taken from O'Malley (1998). Also see Leonard-Barton (1985).

p. 39. "Reports in the media about the loss of community . . .": For an excellent discussion of this issue, see Putnam (1995).

p. 39. "But that doesn't mean that we don't talk . . .": The Roper Starch study was reported in *The Public Pulse* 12(10–11): 2 in 1997. This section is also based on an interview with Diane Crispell, 11/5/98.

p. 40. "How Many People Do We Tell? . . .": This section is based on an interview with John Goodman, 6/10/99.

p. 41. "Moreover, the number of other . . .": Based on Priceline.com press release: "In 1999, People Talk More About Their Last Internet Shopping Trip Than Their Favorite Movie or Restaurant."

## Chapter 4: Network Hubs

p. 43. "And then there's the on-line world . . .": Based on an interview with Jim Thompson, 11/26/98. Thompson no longer runs "Jim's Health Care Pilot Page." He moved all of its content to a different site, which is maintained by another physician. Because he left his rural practice and moved to a different branch of medicine, he no longer has time to maintain the Web site.

p. 44. "Network hubs exist in every category . . .": Interview with David Unowsky, 2/10/99.

p. 47. "Social Hubs . . .": For an excellent profile of a social hub, see Gladwell (1999).

p. 49. "Ahead in adoption . . .": See Rogers (1995), p. 22. Rogers also points out that the exact degree of innovativeness depends on the system's norms. So in a very traditional village in Tibet, a network hub may actually oppose innovation. *The Anatomy of Buzz* assumes that the system views innovation as positive, a bias I believe exists in today's Western society.

p. 49. "Roper Starch Worldwide . . .": The information about Influential Americans is based on an interview with Diane Crispell, 11/5/98, and on Roper Starch Worldwide (1995). When this survey was initiated in the early 1940s, its goal was to learn who were the thought leaders in communities. An Influential American was defined as a person who was involved in certain political or social activities, such as writing a letter to the editor, making a speech, serving on a committee, and so on.

p. 49. "Network hubs are by definition connected . . .": About opinion leaders being cosmopolite, see Rogers (1995), p. 294.

p. 50. "Travelers . . .": See Robertson (1971), p. 95. For information on the hybrid corn study, see Rogers (1995), p. 33. The quote is from Roper Starch Worldwide (1995), p. 82.

p. 50. "Information-hungry . . .": Interview with Joe Gillespie, 5/19/98.

p. 51. "Vocal . . .": Roper Starch Worldwide (1995), p. 139.

p. 51. "Exposed to media . . .": The data about financial opinion leaders is from Stern and Gould (1988). For information on fashion, see Summers (1970). This idea applies to Western culture. In other cultures, Tom Valente has pointed out to me, these opinion leaders may be exposed to other external sources of information.

p. 51. "A common thread among . . .": In trying to identify network hubs, keep in mind that there are *several* measures of people's centrality in social networks. I have focused on a measurement researchers call "degree," which is simply the number of people a person is connected to. Some of the other measurements include "closeness," "betweenness," and "prestige."

p. 52. "Are All Network Hubs Early Adopters? . . .": The quote is from Sculley and Byrne (1988), p. 223. Also see Leonard-Barton (1985) for a discussion of experts as negative opinion leaders.

p. 53. "Is There a Correlation Between the Two? . . .": See, for example, Valente (1994), p. 36; Weimann (1994), p. 175.

p. 54. "Let's start with what network hubs *are* . . .": The definition of opinion leadership is from Rogers (1995), p. 354. Katz and Lazarsfeld's reservations about the term "leader" are from Katz and Lazarsfeld (1955), p. 138.

p. 55. "The Value Over Time of a Network Hub . . .": The data for this analysis is from *Car & Driver* 1997 Subscriber Profile. The *Car & Driver* document reported that subscribers recommended other types of cars (e.g., pickups and vans). To keep it simple, I refer in my calculation only to passenger cars. My assistant, Kerry Shaw, ran a previous version of this analysis by two car dealers, who helped refine the discussion. For a general discussion of the value of a customer over a lifetime, see Peppers and Rogers (1993) and Sewell (1990).

p. 56. "The History of Network Hubs . . .": For a comprehensive review of the research about opinion leaders, see Weimann (1994). In addition to coverage of the different theories about opinion leadership, Weimann's book includes chapters that analyze the concept as it applies to marketing, fashion, politics, family planning, science, agriculture, and health care.

p. 56. "In 1903 the French sociologist . . .": the quote about Tarde is from Rogers (1995), p. 281.

p. 57. "The pharmaceutical firm Pfizer . . .": See Valente (1995), p. 8. Also see Burt (1987) and Van den Bulte and Lilien (1998). In this latter paper the authors revisit the medical innovation study and argue that factors other than social contagion may have played a dominant role in the diffusion of tetracycline.

p. 57. "These early studies created . . .": Interview with Elihu Katz, 7/23/98.

### Chapter 5: It's a Small World. So What?

p. 59. "Principle 1: The Networks Are Invisible . . .": The formula to calculate the number of potential links in a network with N nodes is $N*(N-1)/2$.

p. 59. "Even in a close environment . . .": The study on informal networks in the workplace is by Krackhardt and Hanson (1993). The story about the "in" group on Echo appears in Horn (1998), p. 231. This section is also based on interviews with David Krackhardt, 6/15/99, and with Stacy Horn, 6/4/98.

p. 61. "As innocent as this principle may sound . . .": The information about PowerBar is based on an interview with Brian Maxwell, 11/19/98.

p. 61. "Maxwell's intuitive strategy . . .": The insurance agent study was reported by Evans (1963). The study with the tapes was done by Woodside and Davenport (1974).

p. 62. "The homophily principle has . . .": The Nintendo case is described by Sheff (1993). I also interviewed him, 4/22/98. The quote from Helen Rockey is from an interview my assistant, Kerry Shaw, conducted with her in April 1999.

p. 62. "Why do Hell's Angels travel in packs? . . .": This phenomenon can be seen everywhere. Have you ever wondered why churches, clubs, and professional organizations in your town are so homogeneous? It's Principle 3 again. These organizations recruit new members mainly through network ties. Most new members are similar to the members who recruited them. The few new members who are different from everyone else don't last long. "These atypical members are mutants in the membership pool of the organization," one study states. As these atypical members are attracted to *other* organizations (those organizations that have members who *are* like them), organizations become even more homogeneous over time. For more on this topic, see Popielarz and McPherson (1995).

p. 63. "Clusters and cliques are so common . . .": I first came across the prison story in an article by Dan Seligman (1998). When I met Russ Bernard, he referred me to an article that he coauthored where the case is slightly elaborated upon—Bernard and Killworth (1997).

p. 63. "Clusters can informally adopt . . .": The story of the Palms at Buck's was told to me by Steve Jurvetson.

p. 63. "Such clusters can be found everywhere . . .": The Korean villages study is from Rogers (1995), p. 304. For a comprehensive coverage of this study, see Rogers and Kincaid (1981).

p. 65. "The social psychologist Stanley Milgram . . .": This section is based on Milgram (1967).

p. 67. "When we look at a diagram . . .": For an in-depth look at structural holes, see Burt (1992). The definition quoted is from p. 18 in Burt's book.

p. 68. "It is important to identify the gaps . . .": Peter H. Reingen of Arizona State University is one of the few marketing scholars who has been writing about this topic. For a review of Burt's work as it applies to marketing, see Reingen (1994).

p. 68. "Imagine a woman from California . . .": Interview with Margot Fraser, 12/22/98.

p. 69. "Shortcuts that connect clusters . . .": The main argument is explained by Watts in *Nature*—Watts and Strogatz (1998). In the same issue of *Nature*, there is a good introduction by Collins and Chow (1998). See also Blakeslee (1998). Readers who are seriously interested in the small world phenomenon may want to refer to a recent book by Watts (1999).

p. 70. "Another example of people who . . .": The concept of venture capitalists as connectors was described by Rogers and Larsen (1984).

p. 71. "Barry Wellman and David B. Tindall . . .": From Wellman and Tindall (1993). The data about the R&D labs is from Allen (1977), p. 236.

p. 71. "In the same way that regional dialects . . .": See brief report: "U.S. Dialects Persist by Both Region and Race." *Science* 279 (27 February 1998): 1311.

p. 72. "In the late 1960s Mark Granovetter . . .": This section is based on an interview with Mark Granovetter, 6/11/99. See also Granovetter (1995). Notice that Granovetter never argues that strong ties are not important. Just that the bridges that connect different cliques and clusters are almost always weak ties.

p. 73. "It was the founders' landlady . . .": Zip2 is now an Internet technology company that partners with more than 140 newspapers in this country, including the *New York Times*. The company was acquired by AltaVista in 1999. Interview with Kimbal Musk, 1/7/98.

p. 74. "Since people tend to form networks . . .": One article that describes the concept of weak ties as it applies to marketing is by Brown and Reingen (1987).

p. 74. "It's easy to maintain weak ties on the Internet . . .": See Wellman and Gulia (1999). This section is also based on an interview with Valdis Krebs, 8/10/99.

p. 74. "This explosion in weak ties, however . . .": See Dunbar (1996).

p. 75. "It is difficult to determine how many . . .": See Dunbar pp. 76–77. As to the number of acquaintances, scholars are reluctant to come up with an exact number. The numbers I mention here are rough estimates mentioned in the literature.

p. 76. "Bill McGowan, the founder of MCI . . .": See Spurge (1998), p. 153. Interview with Seymour Merrin, 5/25/98.

p. 78. "Makers of hard drives . . .": See Christensen (1997).

## Chapter 6: How Buzz Spreads

p. 81. "One thing needs to be pointed out . . .": See Tarde (1903). See also Weimann (1994).

p. 82. "In the case of *Cold Mountain* . . .": This section is based on interviews with Leigh Feldman, 2/1/99; Elisabeth Schmitz, 5/1/99; and Morgan Entrekin, 1/29/99.

p. 83. "Mike Jordan, a professor . . .": This section is based on interviews with about a dozen readers of *Cold Mountain*, including Mike Jordan, 1/29/99, and Lynne Jenkins, 1/28/99.

p. 84. "While the two-step . . .": Interview with Jo Alice Canterbury, 5/24/99.

p. 85. "Some readers heard about . . .": Interview with Patricia Kelly, 4/30/99.

p. 88. "Such energy can be contagious . . .": Regarding the support from other book publishers: Of course, you can't always expect that. The fact that Grove/Atlantic is a midsize company that doesn't threaten the industry giants helped.

p. 88. "Entrekin is the first to . . .": The sales figures are as of May 1999. Source: Arnold (1999).

p. 89. "Mike Barnard first heard . . .": The point is that Kelly is not the type who praises every book on her list. That's how she maintains her credibility. Interviews with Mike Barnard, 5/17/99, and with Patricia Kelly, 4/30/99. The *Publishers Weekly* article is by Zeitchik (1999).

p. 90. "There is another important point . . .": Interview with Stewart Alsop, 6/3/98.

p. 93. "To return to *Cold Mountain* . . .": I should note that we are not only motivated by wanting to be like everyone else. We also want to be special. So it may be that after hearing all the buzz about *Cold Mountain*, you will object to reading the book. Some people feel the desire for individualism more strongly than others, and they will be influenced by a "crowding effect." For more on this effect, see Granovetter and Soong (1986).

p. 94. "At first a few innovators . . .": See Rogers (1995) and Moore (1991). This section is also based on an interview with Steve Hollander, 2/15/99.

p. 96. "The flow of information . . .": See Reingen and Kernan (1986).

p. 97. "Why is this important . . .": See McKenna (1985), p. 60.

p. 98. "Why are the two types of buzz different? . . .": The quote about clustering is from Michael Porter's article in the *Harvard Business Review* (1998).

## Chapter 7: Contagious Products

p. 103. "I'm not a car enthusiast . . .": Kern quote is from an e-mail interview with him, 2/5/99.

p. 105. " 'It wasn't some big company . . .' ": Interviews with Colligan, 4/23/98, 3/18/99. Andy Reinhardt's quote is from an interview with him, 8/17/99.

p. 105. "Colligan sounds apologetic . . .": Seybold's quote is from an interview with her, 5/28/98. It's amazing to me how many times Palm handheld users I talked to mentioned this simple fact: "The Palm does exactly what it's supposed to do."

p. 106. "That's how many new products spread . . .": The data about fashion is from the Yankelovich Monitor 1997 provided by Yankelovich's PR firm.

p. 108. "A product that took this idea to the next . . .": See *Brandweek*, 3/13/00, pp. 22–23.

p. 108. "Another product that has spread this way . . .": The section on Magnetic Poetry is based on an interview with Dave Kapell, 4/30/99.

p. 110. "Researchers theorize that . . .": See Hofstadter (1985), p. 50. In a fascinating article on viral sentences, Hofstadter discusses, among other things, the work of biologist Jacques Monod, who wrote in 1970 about the "spreading power" of ideas that may depend upon "preexisting structures in the mind."

p. 112. "Compatibility often is a matter . . .": See Rogers (1995), p. 40. Rogers mentions the French sociologist Gabriel Tarde in this regard, who in 1903 pointed out that innovations similar to ideas that have been already accepted are more likely to be adopted. Also, see p. 234 in Rogers.

p. 112. "Cameras were invented . . .": The section on Kodak is based on Collins (1990).

p. 113. "Technology products are not . . .": For information on *In Search of Excellence*, see Micklethwait and Wooldridge (1996) and, of course, Peters and Waterman (1982).

p. 114. "Another way to exceed expectations . . .": The pricing of the Mustang is from Iacocca and Novak (1984).

p. 117. "HBO expects to add . . .": The quote is from the *New York Times*, 4/10/00, p. C19.

## Chapter 8: Accelerating Natural Contagion

p. 118. "So trees have had to develop . . .": See pp. 13–14 in Dunbar.

p. 121. "Let's look at . . . FedEx . . .": The section on FedEx is based on an interview with Ted Sartoian, 1/12/99, and on Sigafoos (1983).

p. 123. "New products often spread . . .": The air conditioners experiment is described in Whyte (1954). This is a fascinating article by the same William H. Whyte, Jr., who wrote *The Organization Man* and *The Social Life of Small Urban Spaces*.

p. 124. "At a macro level, leapfrogging . . .": The section about White Castle hamburgers is based on Hogan (1997), pp. 74–78, and on an interview with David Hogan, 5/31/99.

p. 126. "Suppose you were introducing . . .": The information about Pictionary is based on an interview with Linda Pezzano, 10/24/98.

p. 126. "Companies that speed up buzz . . .": Interview with Keith Fox, 10/8/98. Interview with George Paolini, 6/4/98.

p. 128. "'Buzz Is Truth . . .'": The Tropical Fantasy case is described by Freedman (1991).

p. 130. "Hiring practices can also . . .": The information about Union Bank appeared in Colvin (1999).

p. 130. "Leapfrogging is not easy . . .": Interview with Jim Callahan, 2/7/99.

## Chapter 9: Working with Network Hubs

p. 133. "In the mid-1980s, Canadian physicians . . .": Interview with Jonathan Lomas, 7/5/99. See also Lomas et al. (1991) and Lomas et al. (1989).

p. 137. "It's also relatively easy to identify . . .": Interview with Karen Pennington, 11/9/98. The store relies mostly on customers who report what's being recommended.

p. 138. "And what if you're not part of the community? . . .": Interviews with Rochelle Newman, 1/19/99, 4/29/99.

p. 138. "The fact that they're vocal . . .": Interview with Jeff Tarter, 3/12/98. The quote from Kephart is from an interview with him, 3/23/98.

p. 139. "Another way to spot network hubs . . .": Interview with Diane Crispell, 11/5/98.

p. 140. "The pharmaceutical industry . . .": Interview with John W. Hawks, 3/5/99.

p. 141. "A project that tried to promote safe sex . . .": Kelly et al. (1991). For a summary, see Weimann (1994), pp. 226–28. Weimann also describes the experiment in Finland.

p. 142. "Self-designating method . . .": See Weimann (1994), p. 35.

p. 144. "Target Hubs First . . .": McKenna (1985), p. 67.

p. 144. "The same type of excitement . . .": Based on Interviews with Rafe Needleman, 8/16/99, and Ed Cooligan, 4/23/98, 3/18/99.

p. 145. "Joseph Mancuso, describing . . .": See Mancuso (1969).

p. 145. "Buzz needs ammunition . . .": The quote is from Warner (1994). The information about Jeep is also based on an interview with Gary Gray, 3/4/99.

p. 146. "Once you succeed in gaining the support . . .": Conversation with Ivan Juzang, 11/12/98.

p. 147. "Don't be concerned about boring . . .": Interview with Joe Gillespie, 5/19/98.

p. 147. "Don't Abuse the Relationships . . .": Interview with Heidi Roizen, 6/10/98.

p. 148. "Network hubs may be using your product . . .": Interview with Alyssa Berman, 7/99.

p. 148. "Luxottica Group uses . . .": Interview with Steve Hollander, 2/15/99.

p. 150. "The problem is that grassroots . . .": Interview with Jeff Tarter, 3/12/98.

p. 151. "Why Reach Hubs Early? . . .": Interviews with Tom Valente, 2/21/99, 5/26/99. See also Gladwell (2000).

## Chapter 10: Active Seeding

p. 154. ". . . when the makers of Trivial Pursuit . . .": This is based on an interview with Linda Pezzano, 10/24/98. The case is also described briefly in an excellent book about PR by Harris. See Harris (1991).

p. 155. "A good seeding campaign goes beyond . . .": Interview with Marleen McDaniel, 5/27/98.

p. 156. "The ideal seed customer . . .": The Chrysler campaign is mentioned by Walker (1995). See also *Newsweek*, 6/29/92, p. 41.

p. 156. "Seeding works only in categories . . .": If you use seeding for a product that people don't tend to discuss, the seed unit will just sit there, with the seed customers, but the word will never spread. A more appropriate way to promote products that don't generate much buzz is through mass sampling, which is essentially seeding on a grand scale—you give *each* customer a small sample of the product. Seeding, on the other hand, focuses on placing one to several units in many different networks. Tylenol samples have been very effective in getting people used to this drug. This refers to mail samples, and to massive sampling in hospitals. "They just oversampled like crazy," one pharmaceutical rep said, in explaining to me how Tylenol became so popular among doctors. It simply was always around.

p. 158. "Polaroid found ways to get people involved . . .": Interview with Arlene Henry, 10/98.

p. 158. "Tom Peters attributes . . .": This section is based on Peters (1987) and on an interview with Edward Burlingame, 1/8/99. Of course, it wasn't only the seeding that made *In Search of Excellence* so successful. As in all other cases mentioned throughout this book, many factors play a role in the success of a product. *In Search of Excellence* is a very interesting book that is fun to read. Its timing was perfect, too—right when Americans were starting to panic about competition from Japan. The authors' connections in corporate America helped as well. Most significant was the energy that they put into the writing and promotion. All these were factors that made the book successful. Seeding accelerated the process. Regarding Harper & Row's concern, Edward Burlingame adds: "Peters might be right about H&R's concern about their giving away 15,000 of the report, but I don't remember this."

p. 159. "In searching for beta testers . . .": Interview with Rob Bennet, 6/2/99. Also Rebello (1995).

p. 161. "One smaller company that . . .": Based on interview with Charlotte Stuyvenberg, 6/2/99. The company has been since acquired by Hasbro.

p. 162. "Technologies are not always willingly adopted . . .": Interview with Bill McKiernan, 5/12/98.

p. 163. "It's also important, of course . . .": The section on seeding IT managers is based on interviews with Ed Colligan, 4/23/98, 3/18/99. Of course, it's crucial to leave those influencers with the best possible impression of the technology. This sometimes takes special attention to details and an incredible dedication. When a 3COM employee noticed a mistake in the data on the Palm organizers the night before the conference, the team stayed up all night to load the correct data on thousands of units.

p. 165. "Both Simon & Schuster and Peck . . .": See Trachtenberg (1987).

p. 167. "Successful bands know . . .": Stephen Carpenter's quote is from *Guitar World*. Langer (1998).

## Chapter 11: The Elements of a Good Story

p. 170. "'The excitement in the theaters'": See Sheff (1993), pp. 4, 190. This section is also based on an interview with David Sheff, 4/22/98.

p. 171. "In his book *Influence* . . .": See Cialdini (1993), p. 237.

p. 172. "Part of the initial buzz around *The Blair Witch Project* . . .": The quote from Kevin Foxe was reported by Michael Eskenazi on Yahoo! News, 7/31/99.

p. 173. "The sense of mystery . . .": The Sony PlayStation section is based on an interview with Charlotte Stuyvenberg, 6/2/99.

p. 173. "Mystery is routinely drawn upon . . .": Interview with Chris Moore, 5/28/98.

p. 174. "Withholding too much . . .": The BMW example was pointed out to me by Susan Fournier of the Harvard Business School, who coauthored a case study about it. See Fournier and Dolan (1997). This section is also based on interviews with James McDowell, 6/21/99, and Jeff Salmon, 4/29/99.

p. 179. "Not every customer who . . .": The section is based on interviews with about ten early owners of BMW Z3. My assistant, Kerry Shaw, interviewed six BMW dealers around the country.

p. 179. "We humans are curious creatures . . .": The section about Natalie Imbruglia is based on an interview with Kevin Conroy, 5/4/99.

p. 180. "Present-day Hollywood . . .": Interview with Steve Rubin, 5/27/98.

p. 181. "The noise level in the networks . . .": The section about *Blazing Saddles* is based on Fuhrman (1989). I also had the opportunity to watch a recorded interview with the late Marty Weiser in which he described this publicity stunt.

p. 183. "An essential element in a good story . . .": See Weinraub (1998).

p. 184. "This was just one part . . .": For a good coverage of the Mustang launch, see Iacocca and Novak (1984) or Harris (1991).

p. 187. "'Put the pedal to the metal! . . .'": Of course, the "volunteer" may have been a BMW person, but this did not change the impact of the presentation.

## Chapter 12: Viral Marketing

p. 191. "George is also more *motivated* . . .": Interview with Cynthia Typaldos, 7/8/99.

p. 192. "Such promotions are very easy . . .": The quote is from an interview with Barry Berkov, 4/19/99. To understand why the response from these promotions is not overwhelming, let's look at an example. A good direct mail campaign to a cold list produces a 1- to 2-percent response rate. Let's say that your customers really like you, and their response will be ten times higher than that. This means that 20 percent of your customers will pass on the coupon. Out of this group of friends, again only 1 to 2 percent respond normally, but let's assume that this offer is so incredible and that your customers have so much influence on their friends that 10 percent of the people who received the coupon decided to order— 10 percent of 20 percent is 2 percent. It's a healthy response rate, but not overwhelming.

p. 192. "You can also use these paper tools . . .": Interview with George McMillan, 6/21/99.

p. 192. "Beyond the obvious advantages . . .": This was described by David Krackhardt from Carnegie Mellon University. See Krackhardt (1996). Scott Feld of Louisiana State University and David Krackhardt further point out that this effect depends on the extent to which people are tied to others with different numbers of ties from themselves. In other words, in an environment where everyone has the same number of ties, this effect will not take place.

p. 193. "Pass-it-on tools . . .": The section on Unilever is based on an interview with Jeff McElnea, 1/6/99, and on a short article in *Promo* magazine (1998). Share a Secret/USA. *Promo*, p. 34.

p. 194. "In 1991 MCI took this . . .": For a comprehensive review of the MCI campaign, see Shaver (1996).

p. 194. "Rather than focusing . . .": Interview with Len Short, 1998.

p. 195. "Arthur Hughes, vice president . . .": Interview with Arthur Hughes, 5/6/98.

p. 195. "The case of GolfWeb . . .": The number of page views is based on Sportsline press release, 1/30/98.

p. 195. "One reason it worked . . . for GolfWeb . . .": Interview with Cynthia Typaldos, 7/8/99. Interview with Steve Jurvetson, 12/4/98.

p. 196. "An interesting thing about ICQ . . .": The brochure anecdote was reported by Ami Ginsburg on Globes Arena (www.globes.co.il) on 2/18/98. The quote from Ted Leonsis appeared in Sandberg (1999).

p. 197. "Many companies that started selling on the Web . . .": Hof, Browder, and Elstrom (1997).

p. 198. "The point is that if almost every transaction stimulates . . .": Tristram (1999).

p. 199. ". . . If you can create a structure . . .": Jurvetson (1998).

p. 199. "How to create an on-line community . . .": For a good overview, see Hagel and Armstrong (1997).

p. 200. "Prompt Your Customer . . .": Interview with Hillary Graves, 8/10/99.

p. 200. "This is how everyone finds out about Blue Mountain . . .": E-mail from Jared Schutz to my assistant, Kerry Shaw, 7/1/99.

p. 202. "These promotions typically work best . . .": Interviews with Felipe Korzenny, 1/4/99, 1/13/99.

p. 202. "Tell-a-friend campaigns are not without problems . . .": E-mail from Scott Cook, 1/28/99.

p. 202. "Before you start . . .": Interview with Tanya Roberts, 2/24/98.

p. 203. "In some situations you can ask each customer . . .": Interview with Jim Callahan, 2/7/99.

### Chapter 13: Does Madison Avenue Still Matter?

p. 206. "Can Advertising *Stimulate* Buzz?": For more on this topic, see Robertson (1971).

p. 207. "Reach Hubs . . .": See for example 1997 *Car & Driver* Subscriber Profile.

p. 207. "Reassure Buyers . . .": See Valente (1995), p. 25. Robertson, Zielinski, and Ward (1984), p. 131.

p. 208. "Get the Facts Straight . . .": The source for the Alar story is Harris (1991), p. 187.

p. 209. "Advertising as Buzz . . .": The Taco Bell data was provided to me by TBWA Chiat/Day.

p. 210. "The 'Friendly' Tone . . .": See Dichter (1966).

p. 210. "One campaign that played . . .": See Landler (1997) and Cohen (1999).

p. 211 "Compare this to Budweiser's 'Whassup?!' . . .": See *Brill's Content*, May 2000, p. 30, and *People Weekly*, 4/24/00, p. 62.

p. 212. "Another company that . . .": Interviews with John Yost, 12/6/98, and with Paul Huber, 2/3/99.

p. 212. "Bringing real customers . . .": Wirthlin Worldwide (1999). "Buying Influence: Consider the Source, Wirthlin Worldwide": 1–8; www.wirthlin.com.

p. 212. "The people at GolfWeb found . . .": Interview with Cynthia Typaldos, 7/8/99.

p. 214. "One word that comes to mind is 'honesty' . . .": Interview with John Yost, 12/6/98.

p. 216. "Ask Your Customers to Articulate . . .": Interview with Jim Callahan, 2/7/99.

p. 216. "Start Measuring Buzz . . .": See Robertson (1971), p. 215. Interview with Tom Robertson, 5/27/98. About the film industry measuring word of mouth, see Rubin (1991), p. 211. This section is also based on an interview with Rubin (5/27/98).

## Chapter 14: Buzz in Distribution Channels

p. 220. "Even within each industry . . .": The quote from Helen Rockey is from an interview my assistant, Kerry Shaw, conducted with her in April 1999.

p. 220. "To create buzz about a product . . .": Interview with Seymour Merrin, 5/25/98.

p. 222. "There are also on-line resellers . . .": Interview with Jim Thompson, 11/26/98.

p. 223. "A key strategy for creating buzz . . .": Heidkamp (1991).

p. 223. "As always, execution counts . . .": Interview with Carl Lennertz, 5/19/99.

p. 224. "Another company that uses the channel . . .": The information about Kiehl's is based on Stout (1999) and Hawn (1996). If you haven't been to the company's store in the East Village, it's worth a visit. It's the best demonstration that buzz isn't about elegant showrooms or glitzy displays.

p. 225. "The introduction of Pokémon cards . . .": Interview with Charlotte Stuyvenberg, 6/2/99.

p. 226. "One of the first people in the publishing business . . .": The information about Jacqueline Susann is based on an interview with Edward Burlingame, 1/8/99, and on Seaman (1987), p. 310.

p. 227. "Mystery gets people talking . . .": Interview with Linda Pezzano, 10/24/98.

p. 228. "In Search of Validation . . .": The interview with Melanie Grimes was conducted by Meredith Alexander. The case is also based on my interview with Margot Fraser, 12/22/98.

## Chapter 15: Putting It Together

p. 231. "The idea for PowerBar . . .": The PowerBar case study is based on an interview with Brian Maxwell. My assistant, Kerry Shaw, interviewed several athletes who were early adopters of PowerBar.

p. 237. "With friction removed . . .": The first quote in this paragraph is from an article in *Forbes* by McDaniel (1997). The second quote is from my interview with her, 5/27/98.

p. 239. "A 1999 article in *Advertising Age* . . .": Gilbert (1999).

p. 240. "Yomega started in the mid-1980s . . .": The quote is from my interview with Joyce Amaral, 2/1/99. The estimated figures about the yo-yo industry are from Hochman (1999).

p. 240. "A large part of the buzz . . .": Interview with Alan Amaral, 8/10/99.

p. 241. "Sales began to take off . . .": Interview with Lucky J. Meisenheimer, 6/25/99. For a comprehensive history of yo-yos, see Meisenheimer (1999).

p. 242. "Yomega also took off in Israel . . .": Interview with Pini Gamzo, 2/26/99. As I demonstrated at the beginning of Chapter 10, buzz in Israel, as anywhere else, can get stuck in clusters. But in general, buzz in Israel seems to spread faster than in the United States, for example. One possible explanation is the high density of social networks in Israel. Related factors are geographical concentration and size. In the case of Yomega, the accelerated diffusion may have to do with the fact that families keep close ties even when members of the family move to another city. Many extended families meet every weekend, so cousins who go to different schools have a chance to create shortcuts among their schools' social networks.

p. 242. "What happened in Israel and Hawaii . . .": Interview with Beth Reynolds, 1/11/99.

### Chapter 16: Buzz Workshop

p. 250. "Personal Effort: Bob Metcalfe . . .": Based on Kirsner (1998). Also, personal communication with Metcalfe in March 1999.

p. 252. "Be receptive and responsive . . .": Interview with John Goodman, 6/10/99.

p. 252. "Hubs: The HP 35 Calculator . . .": From Packard (1995), p. 106.

p. 253. "Inquiries: Littlearth and Oprah . . .": Interview with Ava DeMarco, 2/25/99.

p. 254. "Scarcity: *The Blair Witch Project* . . .": Lyons (1999).

p. 255. "Outrageous: Beauty and Birkenstocks . . .": Interview with Margot Fraser, 12/22/98.

p. 256. "Events and Buzz: Macy's . . .": Interviews with Rochelle Newman, 1/19/99, 4/29/99.

p. 257. "Visibility: FedEx and UPS . . .": Interview with Ted Sartoian, 1/12/99.

p. 257. "Jump-starting Buzz . . .": Interview with Steve Douty, 1/15/99.

p. 259. "Working with the Channel . . .": Interview with Helen Rockey, 4/99. Gallagher (1999).

p. 259. "Multiple Initiatives . . .": Interviews with James McDowell, 6/21/99, and John Yost, 12/6/98.

### Notes About the Glossary

p. 263. "Adopter categories . . .": Rogers (1995), p. 22.

p. 264. "Contagion process . . .": Valente (1995), p. 15.

p. 264. "Cosmopolite . . .": Rogers (1995), p. 274.

p. 264. "Critical mass . . .": Valente (1995), p. 141.

p. 264. "Diffusion of innovations . . .": Rogers (1995), p. 5.

p. 265. "Social network threshold . . .": Valente, p. 141.

# Bibliography

Aaker, David A., and John G. Myers. *Advertising Management.* 3rd ed. Englewood Cliffs, N.J.: Prentice-Hall, 1987.

Allen, Thomas J. *Managing the Flow of Technology: Technology Transfer and the Dissemination of Technological Information within the R&D Organization.* Cambridge, Mass.: MIT Press, 1977.

Arnold, Martin. "A Success a Year Later." *New York Times,* May 27, 1999, B3.

Austin, Nancy K. "Buzz: In Search of the Most Elusive Force in All of Marketing." *Inc.,* May 1998, 44–50.

Bernard, H. Russell, and Peter Killworth. "The Search for Social Physics." *CONNECTIONS* 20, no. 1 (1997): 16–34.

Blakeslee, Sandra. "Mathematicians Prove That It's a Small World." *New York Times,* June 16, 1998, F3.

Brock, Timothy C., and Laura A. Brannon. "Liberalization of Commodity Theory." *Basic and Applied Social Psychology* 13, no. 1 (1992): 135–44.

Brodie, Richard. *Virus of the Mind: The New Science of the Meme.* Seattle, Wash.: Integral Press, 1996.

Bronson, Po. *The Nudist on the Late Shift.* New York: Random House, 1999.

Brown, Jacqueline Johnson, and Peter H. Reingen. "Social Ties and Word-of-Mouth Referral Behavior." *Journal of Consumer Research* 14, no. 3 (1987): 350–62.

Brunvand, Jan Harold. *Curses! Broiled Again!: The Hottest Urban Legends Going.* New York: W. W. Norton & Company, Inc., 1989.

Burt, Ronald S. "Social Contagion and Innovation: Cohesion Versus Structural Equivalence." *American Journal of Sociology* 92 (May 1987): 1287–1335.

————. *Structural Holes: The Social Structure of Competition.* Cambridge, Mass.: Harvard University Press, 1992.

————. "The Social Capital of Opinion Leaders." *The Annals of the American Academy of Political and Social Science,* 566 (1999): 37–54.

Cafferky, Michael E. *Let Your Customers Do the Talking: 301+ Word-of-Mouth Marketing Tactics Guaranteed to Boost Profits.* Chicago: Upstart Publishing Company, Inc., 1996.

Christensen, Clayton M. *The Innovator's Dilemma: When New Technologies Cause Great Firms to Fail.* Boston: Harvard Business School Press, 1997.

Cialdini, Robert B. *Influence: The Psychology of Persuasion.* Rev. ed. New York: William Morrow, 1993.

Cohen, Alan. "Reinventing a Brand." *Agency,* Winter 1999, 58–60.

Coleman, James Samuel, Elihu Katz, and Herbert Menzel. *Medical Innovation: A Diffusion Study.* Indianapolis, Ind.: Bobbs-Merrill Co., 1966.

Collins, Douglas. *The Story of Kodak.* New York: H. N. Abrams, 1990.

Collins, James J., and Carson C. Chow. "It's a Small World." *Nature* 393 (June 4, 1998): 409–10.

Colvin, Geoffrey. "The 50 Best Companies for Asians, Blacks, and Hispanics." *Fortune,* July 19, 1999, 52–58.

Cuneo, Alice Z. "From One Momenta to the Next—Poof!" *Advertising Age,* November 9, 1992, S-4.

Dawkins, Richard. *The Selfish Gene.* Oxford: Oxford University Press, 1976.

Dichter, Ernest. "How Word-of-Mouth Advertising Works." *Harvard Business Review,* November–December 1966, 147–66.

Dunbar, Robin I. M. *Grooming, Gossip, and the Evolution of Language.* Cambridge, Mass.: Harvard University Press, 1996.

Dyson, Esther. *Release 2.1: A Design for Living in the Digital Age.* New York: Broadway Books, 1998.

Evans, Franklin B. "Selling as a Dyadic Relationship—A New Approach." *American Behavioral Scientist* 6, no. 9 (1963): 76–79.

Farrell, Winslow. *How Hits Happen: Forecasting Predictability in a Chaotic Marketplace.* New York: HarperBusiness, 1998.

Fass, Craig, Mike Ginelli, and Brian Turtle. *Six Degrees of Kevin Bacon.* New York: Plume, 1996.

Fisher, Lawrence M. "Routing Makes Cisco Systems a Powerhouse of Computing." *New York Times,* November 11, 1996, D1.

Fitzpatrick, Robert L., and Joyce K. Reynolds. *False Profits: Seeking Financial and Spiritual Deliverance in Multi-Level Marketing and Pyramid Schemes.* Charlotte, N.C.: Herald Press, 1997.

Fournier, Susan. "Consumers and Their Brands: Developing Relationship Theory in Consumer Research." *Journal of Consumer Research* 24, no. 4 (1998): 343–73.

Fournier, Susan, and Robert J. Dolan. "Launching the BMW Z3 Roadster (N9-597-002)." Boston: Harvard Business School, 1997.

Freedman, Alex M. "Rumor Turns Fantasy into Bad Dream." *The Wall Street Journal,* May 10, 1991, B1.

Fuhrman, Candice. *Publicity Stunt!* San Francisco: Chronicle Books, 1989.

Gallagher, Leigh. "Runner's World." *Forbes,* February 22, 1999, 96.

Gilbert, Jennifer. "Women.com Eyes 6 Shops for Acc't." *Advertising Age,* March 1, 1999, 2.

Gladwell, Malcolm. "Six Degrees of Lois Weisberg." *The New Yorker,* January 11, 1999, 52–63.

———. *The Tipping Point: How Little Things Can Make a Big Difference.* Boston: Little, Brown and Company, 2000.

Godin, Seth. *Permission Marketing: Turning Strangers into Friends, and Friends into Customers.* New York: Simon & Schuster, 1999.

Granovetter, Mark. *Getting a Job: A Study of Contacts and Careers.* 2nd ed. Chicago: University of Chicago Press, 1995.

Granovetter, Mark, and Roland Soong. "Threshold Models of Interpersonal Effects in Consumer Demand." *Journal of Economic Behavior and Organization* 7 (1986): 83–99.

Grove, Andrew S. *Only the Paranoid Survive: How to Exploit the Crisis Points That Challenge Every Company and Career.* New York: Doubleday, 1996.

Hagel, John III, and Arthur G. Armstrong. *Net Gain: Expanding Markets Through Virtual Communities.* Boston: Harvard Business School Press, 1997.

Harris, Godfrey. *Don't Take Our Word for It!: Everything You Need to Know About Making Word-of-Mouth Advertising Work for You.* Los Angeles: The Americas Group, 1998.

Harris, Thomas L. *The Marketer's Guide to Public Relations: How Today's Top Companies Are Using the New PR to Gain a Competitive Edge.* New York: John Wiley & Sons, Inc., 1991.

———. *Value-added Public Relations: The Secret Weapon of Integrated Marketing.* Lincolnwood (Chicago), Ill.: NTC Business Books, 1998.

Hawn, Carleen. "A Company with Attitude." *Forbes,* October 7, 1996, 73–76.

Heidkamp, Maria. "Creating Word-of-Mouth for Literary and Midlist Fiction." *Publishers Weekly,* April 26, 1991, 34–35.

Heinrich, Bernd, and John Marzluff. "Why Ravens Share." *American Scientist* 83, no. 4 (1995): 342–49.

Hochman, Paul, "Yo-yos Are Back: This Time They Mean It." *Fortune,* May 24, 1999, 64.

Hof, Robert D., Seanna Browder, and Peter Elstrom. "Internet Communities." *BusinessWeek,* May 5, 1997, 64–85.

Hofstadter, Douglas R. *Metamagical Themas: Questing for the Essence of Mind and Pattern.* New York: Basic Books, 1985.

Hogan, David Gerard. *Sellling 'em by the Sack: White Castle and the Creation of American Food.* New York: New York University Press, 1997.

Horn, Stacy. *Cyberville: Clicks, Culture, and the Creation of an Online Town.* New York: Warner Books, 1998.

Iacobucci, Dawn, ed. *Networks in Marketing.* Thousand Oaks, Calif.: Sage, 1996.

Iacocca, Lee, and William Novak. *Iacocca: An Autobiography.* Toronto: Bantam Books, 1984.

Jurvetson, Steve, "Turning Customers Into a Sales Force," *Business 2.0*, November 1998, 102.

Kaplan, Jerry. *Startup: A Silicon Valley Adventure*. Boston: Houghton Mifflin, 1995.

Katz, Elihu, and Paul F. Lazarsfeld. *Personal Influence: The Part Played by People in the Flow of Mass Communications*. Glencoe, Ill.: The Free Press, 1955.

Kawasaki, Guy. *Selling the Dream: How to Promote Your Product, Company, or Ideas, and Make a Difference Using Everyday Evangelism*. New York: HarperBusiness, 1991.

Kelly, Jeffrey A., et al. "HIV Risk Behavior Reduction Following Intervention with Key Opinion Leaders of Population: an Experimental Analysis." *American Journal of Public Health* 81, no. 2 (1991): 168–71.

Kelly, Kevin. *New Rules for the New Economy: 10 Radical Strategies for a Connected World*. New York: Viking, 1998.

Kirsner, Scott. "The Legend of Bob Metcalfe." *Wired*, November 1998, 182.

Kotler, Philip, and Gary Armstrong. *Principles of Marketing*. 5th ed. Englewood Cliffs, N.J.: Prentice-Hall, 1991.

Krackhardt, David. "Structural Leverage in Marketing." In *Networks in Marketing*, edited by Dawn Iacobucci. Thousand Oaks, Calif.: Sage, 1996.

Krackhardt, David, and Jeffrey R. Hanson. "Informal Networks: The Company Behind the Chart." *Harvard Business Review*, July–August 1993, 104–11.

Landler, Mark. "Now, Worse Than Ever! Cynicism in Advertising!" *New York Times*, August 17, 1997, sec. 4, p. 1.

Langer, Andy. "Lost Highway." *Guitar World*, May 1998, 68.

Larson, Gina M. "Kamran Elahian Fears Nothing in the World of Entrepreneurship." *Entrepreneurial Edge* 1998, 46–50.

Lazarsfeld, Paul F., Bernard Berelson, and Hazel Gaudet. *The People's Choice: How the Voter Makes Up His Mind in a Presidential Campaign*. 2nd ed. New York: Columbia University Press, 1948.

Leonard-Barton, Dorothy. "Experts as Negative Opinion Leaders in the Diffusion of a Technological Innovation." *Journal of Consumer Research* 11 (March 1985): 914–26.

Levine, Rick, et al. *The Cluetrain Manifesto: The End of Business as Usual*. Cambridge, Mass.: Perseus Books, 1999.

Levinson, Jay Conrad. *Guerrilla Marketing: Secrets for Making Big Profits from Your Small Business*. Boston: Houghton Mifflin, 1984.

Lomas, Jonathan, et al. "Do Practice Guidelines Guide Practice? The Effect of a Consensus Statement on the Practice of Physicians." *The New England Journal of Medicine* 321, no. 19 (1989): 1306–11.

Lomas, Jonathan, et al. "Opinion Leaders vs. Audit and Feedback to Implement Practice Guidelines. Delivery After Previous Cesarean Section." *Journal of the American Medical Association* 265, no. 17 (1991): 2202–7.

Lynch, Aaron. *Thought Contagion: How Belief Spreads Through Society*. New York: BasicBooks, 1996.

Lyons, Charles. "Spooked by 'Witch.'" *Variety*, August 9, 1999, 7–8.

Marin, Rick, and Sarah Van Boven. "The Buzz Machine." *Newsweek*, July 27, 1998, 22–26.

Mancuso, Joseph R. "Why Not Create Opinion Leaders for New Product Introduction?" *Journal of Marketing* 33 (July 1969): 20–25.

McDaniel, Marleen. "A Safe Place Not to Browse." *Forbes ASAP*, December 1, 1997, 26.

McKenna, Regis. *Relationship Marketing: Successful Strategies for the Age of the Customer*. Reading, Mass.: Addison Wesley Publishing Company, Inc., 1991.

———. *The Regis Touch: Million-Dollar Advice from America's Top Marketing Consultant*. Reading, Mass.: Addison Wesley Publishing Company, Inc., 1985.

Meisenheimer, Lucky J. *Lucky's Collectors Guide to 20th Century Yo-yos. History and Values*. Orlando, Fla.: Lucky J.'s Swim & Surf, Inc., 1999.

Micklethwait, John, and Adrian Wooldridge. *The Witch Doctors: Making Sense of the Management Gurus*. New York: Times Books, 1996.

Milgram, Stanley. "The Small-World Problem." *Psychology Today*, May 1967, 60–67.

Misner, Ivan R. *The World's Best-Known Marketing Secret: Building Your Business with Word-of-Mouth Marketing*. Austin, Tex.: Bard & Stephen, 1994.

Mitchell, Russell. "A Marathon Man with Marketing Power." *BusinessWeek*, November 7, 1994.

Money, Bruce R., Mary C. Gilly, and John L. Graham. "Exploration of National Culture and Word-of-Mouth Referral Behavior in the Purchase of Industrial Services in the United States and Japan." *Journal of Marketing* 62 (October 1998): 76–87.

Moore, Geoffrey A. *Crossing the Chasm: Marketing and Selling Technology Products to Mainstream Customers*. New York: HarperBusiness, 1991.

Munk, Nina. "Girl Power!" *Fortune*, December 8, 1997, 132–40.

Norman, Donald A. *The Invisible Computer: Why Good Products Can Fail, the Personal Computer Is So Complex, and Information Appliances are the Solution*. Cambridge, Mass.: MIT Press, 1998.

Ogilvy, David. *Ogilvy on Advertising*. New York: Vintage Books, 1985.

O'Malley, Chris. "Jungle Fever on the Web." *Time*, December 7, 1998, 63.

Packard, David. *The HP Way: How Bill Hewlett and I Built Our Company*. New York: HarperBusiness, 1995.

Peppers, Don, and Martha Rogers. *The One to One Future: Building Relationships One Customer at a Time*. New York: Doubleday, 1993.

Peters, Tom. *Thriving on Chaos: Handbook for a Management Revolution*. New York: HarperPerennial, 1987.

Peters, Thomas J., and Robert H. Waterman, Jr. *In Search of Excellence: Lessons from America's Best-Run Companies*. New York: Harper & Row, 1982.

Piirto, Rebecca. *Beyond Mind Games: The Marketing Power of Psychographics*. Ithaca, N.Y.: American Demographics Books, 1991.

Poe, Richard. *Wave Three: The New Era in Network Marketing*. Rocklin, Calif.: Prima Publishing, 1995.

Popielarz, Pamela A., and J. Miller McPherson. "On the Edge or In Between: Niche

Position, Niche Overlap, and the Duration of Voluntary Association Memberships." *American Journal of Sociology* 101, no. 3 (1995): 698–720.

Porter, Michael E. "Clusters and the New Economics of Competition." *Harvard Business Review,* November–December 1998, 77–90.

Putnam, Robert D. "Bowling Alone: America's Declining Social Capital." *Journal of Democracy* 6, no. 1 (1995): 65–78.

Rebello, Kathy, and Mary Kuntz. "Feel the Buzz." *BusinessWeek,* August 28, 1995, 31.

Reingen, Peter H. "Structural Holes: The Social Structure of Competition [Book Review]." *Journal of Marketing* 58 (January 1994): 152–55.

Reingen, Peter H., and Jerome B. Kernan. "Analysis of Referral Networks in Marketing: Methods and Illustration." *Journal of Marketing Research* 23 (November 1986): 370–78.

Robertson, Thomas S. *Innovative Behavior and Communication.* New York: Holt, Rinehart and Winston, Inc., 1971.

Robertson, Thomas S., Joan Zielinski, and Scott Ward. *Consumer Behavior.* Glenview, Ill.: Scott, Foresman and Company, 1984.

Rogers, Everett M. *Diffusion of Innovations.* 4th ed. New York: Free Press, 1995.

Rogers, Everett M., and D. Lawrence Kincaid. *Communications Networks: Toward a New Paradigm for Research.* New York: Free Press, 1981.

Rogers, Everett M., and Judith K. Larsen. *Silicon Valley Fever.* New York: Basic Books, Inc., 1984.

Rogers, Everett M., and Thomas M. Steinfatt. *Intercultural Communication.* Prospect Heights, Ill.: Waveland Press Inc., 1999.

Roper Starch Worldwide. *Influential Americans: Trendsetters of the New Millennium.* 4th ed. New York: Roper Starch Worldwide, Cosponsored by *The Atlantic Monthly,* 1995.

Rubin, Steven Jay. *Reel Exposure: How to Publicize and Promote Today's Motion Pictures.* Shelter Island, N.Y.: Broadway Press, 1991.

Sandberg, Jared. "The Friendly Virus." *Newsweek,* April 12, 1999, 65–67.

Schelling, Thomas C. *Micromotives and Macrobehavior.* New York: W. W. Norton & Company, Inc., 1978.

Sculley, John, and John A. Byrne. *Odyssey: Pepsi to Apple . . . a Journey of Adventure, Ideas, and the Future.* New York: Harper & Row, Publishers, 1988.

Seaman, Barbara. *Lovely Me: The Life of Jacqueline Susann.* New York: William Morrow, 1987.

Seligman, Dan. "Me and Monica." *Forbes,* March 23, 1998, 76–77.

Sewell, Carl, and Paul B. Brown. *Customers for Life: How to Turn That Onetime Buyer into a Lifetime Customer.* New York: Doubleday, 1990.

Seybold, Patricia B., and Ronni T. Marshak. *Customers.com: How to Create a Profitable Business Strategy for the Internet and Beyond.* New York: Times Business, 1998.

Shaver, Dick. *The Next Step in Database Marketing.* New York: John Wiley & Sons, Inc., 1996.

Sheff, David. *Game Over: How Nintendo Zapped an American Industry, Captured Your Dollars, and Enslaved Your Children.* New York: Random House, 1993.

Sigafoos, Robert A. *Absolutely, Positively Overnight!: Wall Street's Darling Inside and Up Close*. Memphis, Tenn.: St. Luke's Press, 1983.

Singhal, Arvind, and Everett M. Rogers. *Entertainment-education: a Communication Strategy for Social Change*. Mahwah, N.J.: L. Erlbaum Associates, 1999.

Spurge, Lorraine. *Failure Is Not an Option: How MCI Invented Competition in Telecommunications*. Encino, Calif.: Spurge Ink!, 1998.

Stern, Barbara B., and Stephen J. Gould. "The Consumer as Financial Opinion Leader." *Journal of Retail Banking* 10, no. 2 (1988): 43–52.

Stevens, Charles W. "Kmart Has a Little Trouble Killing Those Phantom Snakes from Asia." *The Wall Street Journal*, October 20, 1981, 29.

Stout, Hilary. "Ad Budget: Zero. Buzz: Deafening." *The Wall Street Journal*, December 29, 1999, B1.

Summers, John O. "The Identity of Women's Clothing Fashion Opinion Leaders." *Journal of Marketing Research* 7 (May 1970): 178–85.

Tarde, Gabriel. *The Laws of Imitation* (translated from French). New York: H. Holt and Company, 1903.

Trachtenberg, Jeffrey A. "The Best Kind of Advertising." *Forbes*, April 20, 1987, 91–92.

Tristram, Claire. "Takin' It to the Street." *Marketing Computers*, February 1999, 22–28.

Underhill, Paco. *Why We Buy: The Science of Shopping*. New York: Simon & Schuster, 1999.

Utterback, James M. *Mastering the Dynamics of Innovation: How Companies Can Seize Opportunities in the Face of Technological Change*. Boston: Harvard Business School Press, 1994.

Valente, Thomas W. *Network Models of the Diffusion of Innovations*. Cresskill, N.J.: Hampton Press, Inc., 1995.

Valente, Thomas W., and Rebecca L. Davis. "Accelerating the Diffusion of Innovations Using Opinion Leaders." *The Annals of the American Academy of Political and Social Science*, 566 (1999): 55–67.

Van den Bulte, Christophe, and Gary L. Lilien. "Is Social Contagion All It's Cracked Up to Be in New Product Diffusion?: Medical Innovation Revisited." The Wharton School, Marketing Department Working Paper #98-014 (1998).

Walker, Chip. "Word-of-Mouth." *American Demographics* 17 (July 1995): 38–45.

Warner, Fara. "Jeep Down-Shifts to Climb in Steeper Off-Road Stakes." *Brandweek*, May 16, 1994, 28–30.

Wasserman, Stanley, and Katherine Faust. *Social Network Analysis: Methods and Applications*. Cambridge and New York: Cambridge University Press, 1994.

Watts, Duncan J. *Small Worlds: The Dynamics of Networks Between Order and Randomness*. Princeton, N.J.: Princeton University Press, 1999.

Watts, Duncan J., and Steven H. Strogatz. "Collective Dynamics of 'Small-World' Networks." *Nature* 393 (June 4, 1998): 440–42.

Weimann, Gabriel. *The Influentials: People Who Influence People*. Albany, N.Y.: State University of New York Press, 1994.

Weinraub, Bernard. "Who Drives the Box Office? Girls." *New York Times,* February 23, 1998, B1.

Wellman, Barry, ed. *Networks in the Global Village: Life in Contemporary Communities.* Boulder, Colo.: Westview Press, 1999.

Wellman, Barry, and Milena Gulia. "Net-Surfers Don't Ride Alone: Virtual Communities as Communities." In *Networks in the Global Village: Life in Contemporary Communities,* edited by Barry Wellman, 331–66. Boulder, Colo.: Westview Press, 1999.

Wellman, Barry, and David B. Tindall. "How Telephone Networks Connect Social Networks." In *Progress in Communication Science* 12 (1993): 63–94.

Whyte, William H., Jr. "The Web of Word-of-Mouth." *Fortune,* November 1954, 140.

Wilson, Jerry R. *Word-of-Mouth Marketing.* New York: John Wiley & Sons, Inc., 1991.

Woodside, Arch G., and J. William Davenport, Jr. "The Effect of Salesman Similarity and Expertise on Consumer Purchasing Behavior." *Journal of Marketing Research* 11 (May 1974): 198–202.

Wurman, Richard Saul. *Information Anxiety.* New York: Doubleday, 1989.

Zeitchik, Steven M. "PW's Rep of the Year. Patricia Kelly, Publishers Group West." *Publishers Weekly,* April 5, 1999, 41–45.

This bibliography was compiled using EndNote. Special thanks to my friends who created, promoted, and maintained this tool over the years.

# Photo and
# Illustration Credits

# Index

## About the Author

EMANUEL ROSEN for nine years was vice president of marketing for Niles Software, the makers of EndNote, before—like scores of other Silicon Valley success stories—selling his share in the company and retiring on the proceeds. He has spent the last two years researching and writing this book. He lives in Menlo Park, California. His e-mail address is emanuel@emanuel-rosen.com.